6-25-75

Wall Street

and the

Security Markets

This is a volume in the Arno Press collection

Wall Street

AND THE

Security Markets

Advisory Editor
Vincent P. Carosso

Associate Editor
Robert Sobel

*See last pages of this volume
for a complete list of titles*

THE NEW YORK BOND MARKET

MARKET

1920–1930

CHARLES CORTEZ ABBOTT

ARNO PRESS

A New York Times Company

New York – 1975

Reprint Edition 1975 by Arno Press Inc.

Copyright © 1937, by the President and
    Fellows of Harvard College
Reprinted by permission of
    Harvard University Press

Reprinted from a copy in The University
    of Illinois Library

WALL STREET AND THE SECURITY MARKETS
ISBN for complete set: 0-405-06944-8
See last pages of this volume for titles.

Manufactured in the United States of America

--------••⦿••--------

Library of Congress Cataloging in Publication Data

Abbott, Charles Cortez, 1906-
    The New York bond market, 1920-1930.

    (Wall Street and the security markets)
    Reprint of the ed. published by Harvard University
Press, Cambridge, Mass., which was issued as v. 59 of
Harvard economic studies.
    Bibliography: p.
    1. Bonds--New York (City). 2. Finance--New York
(City). 3. Banks and banking--New York (City).
I. Title. II. Series. III. Series: Harvard
economic studies ; v. 59.
HG4651.A25 1975   332.6'323   75-2618
ISBN 0-405-06945-6

HARVARD ECONOMIC STUDIES

VOLUME LIX

THE STUDIES IN THIS SERIES ARE PUBLISHED BY THE DEPARTMENT OF
ECONOMICS OF HARVARD UNIVERSITY, WHICH, HOWEVER, ASSUMES
NO RESPONSIBILITY FOR THE VIEWS EXPRESSED

LONDON : HUMPHREY MILFORD

OXFORD UNIVERSITY PRESS

THE NEW YORK BOND MARKET

MARKET

1920–1930

BY

CHARLES CORTEZ ABBOTT

ASSISTANT PROFESSOR OF BUSINESS ECONOMICS
HARVARD UNIVERSITY GRADUATE SCHOOL OF BUSINESS
ADMINISTRATION

CAMBRIDGE

HARVARD UNIVERSITY PRESS

1937

PRINTED AT THE HARVARD UNIVERSITY PRESS
CAMBRIDGE, MASS., U.S.A.

PREFACE

THE AID which the author has received from various sources in the preparation of this study has been of great assistance to him, and he welcomes this opportunity to express his gratitude and appreciation. He is much indebted to the National City Bank of New York and to the former National City Company for the way in which their facilities were placed at his disposal in the early stages of this study, and for the advice and suggestions given him by various members of their staffs. The collection and analysis of many of the statistics used has been made much simpler than it would otherwise have been through the courtesies accorded the author by the *Annalist*, the *Bond Buyer*, the Brookmire Economic Service, the *Commercial and Financial Chronicle*, the Harvard Economic Society, Moody's Investors' Service, the Standard Statistics Company, and, particularly, the *Wall Street Journal*. The help of Professor W. L. Crum has been of the greatest value, as has that of Professor C. J. Bullock, whose aid the author feels he can not overestimate. The form of this essay would have been very different without the generous interest and benevolent criticism of Professor Bullock, and such merits as it possesses would have been much smaller without the inspiration afforded by consultation with him. The author also wishes to thank those other persons who read portions of the manuscript during its preparation, whose suggestions he has found most helpful. Financial grants from the Committee on Research in the Social Sciences of Harvard University have assisted the author at times when he would have found further progress in this undertaking difficult, and have made the publication of this study possible. Finally, the author is under great obligation to his wife for her assistance in correction of the proofs, for the interest which she has taken in his work, and for her diligence in preventing intrusions upon the time which he has had for research.

CHARLES CORTEZ ABBOTT

Adams House
Cambridge, Massachusetts
March, 1937

CONTENTS

CHARTS

APPENDICES

THE NEW YORK BOND MARKET
1920–1930

CHAPTER I

INTRODUCTION

THIS study was originally undertaken in the statistical department of the National City Company as an analysis of what were then essentially contemporary happenings in the financial world. Its primary purpose was to throw some light upon those deep-lying economic forces which determine the success or failure of flotations of new security issues. Subsequently it was revised to serve as a doctoral dissertation, and its emphasis was somewhat changed. To its previous objects were added two new aims: it attempted to clarify the relationship of the banking system, as it then was, to the capital markets, and it attempted to test the monetary theory then current with reference to the statistical data available. Rewritten, this work as published is, in substance, a financial history of the post-war decade and an analysis of the banking policies of that time.

However narrow the line which separates current events from history, the episodes and policies herein chronicled have long since crossed that boundary. Since 1930 the foundations of the financial world have been rudely shaken; during the economic cataclysm which has fallen on the world many of the old landmarks have been replaced by new; and many of the assumptions upon which this study was constructed have lost much of their validity. The post-war problems of the Treasury have been succeeded by new ones of equal or greater difficulty; the implications of gold imports, of excess member bank reserves, of the magnitude of the government debt have greatly changed in recent years; Federal Reserve policy has gone through a whole cycle of development since 1919; the banking system and the capital markets, though superficially the same, now operate in a manner quite different from the methods of the twenties.

In the same period a similar change has overtaken monetary theory. Many of its premises, many of what in the post-war years were accepted as the purposes of a banking system, have been questioned and cast aside. New policies and new objects of policy have arisen, modifying or displacing the old; and even where the old policies have continued, their significance has been radically altered by the new environment in which they are employed. This shift in the theoretical approach to banking problems has been so great and so rapid since 1930, and at the same time so subtle, that few persons save those in close contact with the change fully appreciate its magnitude. But, notwithstanding the common failure to recognize the extent of this movement, relatively few of the financial tenets of 1920 or 1925 have maintained their positions in the realm of banking theory, still fewer have not been challenged.

Consequently the occurrences dealt with here must be looked upon primarily as matters of economic history, and the point of view used as one representative of a particular stage in the development of economic thought, somewhat different from that which might be employed today. Furthermore, many of the generalizations made in this study, many of the conclusions reached by it, give little direct aid in interpreting the current financial scene. They apply, in large measure, to a situation that has ceased to exist. Yet in the large view the financial problems of today are simply the children of those of yesterday; the most recent developments in theory and policy are based upon the triumphs and disappointments of the past. To understand well the world as it is we must consider the world as it was, and to know why we think as we do this year we must remember what we thought a year ago. It is in this sense that any study of economic history or the history of economic thought, if successful, achieves its real significance.

CHAPTER II

The Bond Market

THE course of the bond market in the post-war decade forms an integral part of the financial history of that eventful period. The variations in the market's activity, the changing volume of its transactions, and the fluctuations in the values it established constitute a series of events that were currently of great moment in the financial world and which were destined in the succeeding years to influence economic and political affairs in many ways.

The importance which attaches to occurrences in the bond market is engendered, of course, by the character of the bond market's position in the economic structure. In close contact, on the one hand, with the banking system and, on the other hand, with the productive mechanism, of intimate concern both to the individual investor and to the body politic, the bond market concentrates within itself and brings into contact forces which extend into nearly every field of economic activity. It is in the bond market that financial institutions and private persons alike invest a great part of the surplus wealth of the nation; it is from the bond market that both private enterprises and public organizations draw much of the capital necessary for their activities. It is there that the value of a large part of the capital equipment of the country is determined, through the prices which the market puts upon the securities which financed such equipment, and it is through the market's actions that much current investment is directed into one or another of the myriad uses to which capital can be put. It has seemed necessary to begin this study by considering in brief fashion the position of the bond market as a social and economic institution, and by designating in summary fashion certain of the links which connect it with other parts of the economic fabric.

The essential feature of any market is the exchange of goods or services; in a money economy such goods and services are exchanged for money. But the mere fact of exchange does not create a market, for more is contained in the concept than an isolated purchase or sale. The idea of a market implies that there are numerous buyers and sellers, and that they — or at least their bids and offers — come together in some more or less formalized way and that a number of exchanges are completed.

Usually, for the sake of convenience and expediency, such bids and offers meet, and the exchanges are executed, in a stated place, a market place. Thus the term market possesses a geographical connotation. The connotation, however, extends far beyond the limits of the actual trading site, since the bids and offers concentrated there, as well as the many considerations upon which they are based, come from a far larger area. However, this area which produces the price-determining influences gathered in a trading center, is not a distinct entity. Its boundaries are generally ill-defined and impermanent, partly because the factors which influence prices are continually changing, partly because the distances from which the forces of supply and demand can be drawn into a market are not constant but depend upon a variety of circumstances. Moreover, within any one such market area there is often not one but a number of focal points where price-determining influences are massed and where exchanges take place. Although such focal points are geographically separate, they nevertheless are related, since the transactions in each are, to some degree, controlled by the same forces.

Since, in the case of almost any commodity, there exist other commodities which can, within limits, be used in place of it, the market for a particular commodity — that is, the bids and offers made for it and the prices at which it is sold — is often influenced by the factors that directly affect such related goods. The price of wheat is not determined irrespective of the current prices of other grains, nor are the rates for transportation by truck established without regard for the corresponding railroad rates. Although every commodity has its own peculiarities "market-wise," when commodities exist which can be substituted for a particular article or service, the markets of such substitute goods are all connected.

Also it must be recognized that the haggling of buyers and sellers at a given time and place is not, ordinarily, a unique phenomenon, isolated in time. The idea of a market implies, and the existence of a market presupposes, that trading has taken place in the past and that it will presumably take place in the future. Usually the traders are familiar with the prices, volumes, and other characteristics of the exchanges of the immediate past; usually they have formed opinions as to the probable course of future sales; and their actions are much influenced by their knowledge of the past and their guesses as to the future. In highly organized markets trading is so frequent as to be almost continuous, and gives rise to a steady flow of prices, volumes, bids, and offers. Such continuity in many instances is provided by the activity of traders, men who hope to make a profit from continual buying and selling, as contrasted with men who, in security markets, buy for investment or who, in commodity markets, purchase for consumption purposes, although it is not always possible to distinguish clearly the two types of transactions. In some trading centers, such as the security markets, this continuity, this ability always "to do a deal" at *some* price, is of the greatest importance. From certain points of view, indeed, it is an essential feature of a market, since when a purchase or sale can not be effected at any price the trading mechanism has, temporarily at least, broken down, and in the technical phrase there is, for the moment, "no market."

Finally, of the greatest importance in the activity of a market and in a comprehension of its behavior is the psychological element. Probably no exact statement of its significance or of its many manifestations is possible. But there is no doubt that it must always be reckoned with, and that at certain times it becomes the principal determinant of a market's actions. It is, of course, obvious that any exchange is predicated on a

desire of the seller to sell, and on a desire on the part of the
buyer to buy. Otherwise no exchange is possible. It is further
generally assumed — perhaps too readily — that such desires
spring from so-called rational motives, such as a wish for profit
or a need for the consumption of the particular commodity,
and that these desires will, within a reasonable probability, be
satisfied by purchases and sales. Yet no one at all familiar
with the workings of any market would admit that such a
statement adequately describes the importance of psychological factors. The recent history of the security markets in this
country has made it only too evident that there are times when
buyers rush into a market and bid up prices far above levels
which it seems likely — in view of past experience and current
knowledge — will be long maintained; and conversely, that
there are times when sellers, suddenly overwhelmingly anxious
to sell, sacrifice their holdings at prices far below those of the
immediate past and far below those which, it seems altogether
probable, will prevail in the future. Such movements are often
described as the result of irrational and unpredictable mob
psychology, in contrast to the calculating and reasoned action
of the rational man. But such a description, even if accurate,
affords no real explanation or evaluation of psychological
factors.

   In the terminology of various markets — including the
security markets — certain phrases circulate, such as "artificial
value," "depressed situation," "buyers' market," "collectors'
value," which attempt to do justice to particular situations and
values. Apparently the supposition upon which such phrases
are based is that these situations and values are but distantly
related to the actualities of the situation, to the "real" quantity
and character of the demand and supply of the commodity in
question, and exist only, or chiefly, in men's minds. Yet the
distinction between such situations and a presupposed "normal" becomes the more elusive the greater the efforts that are
made to establish it, and in the last analysis seems little more
than a matter of definition. In the present stage of economic
and psychological knowledge it does not seem possible to

do more than to admit the existence and importance of psychological elements in the behavior of markets, and to concede that they must be numbered, at present at least, among the "imponderables."

The factors that have been discussed, the presence of buyers and sellers, the centralization of their bids and offers, their susceptibility to a variety of influences, the flow of transactions resulting from their activities, all combine to produce that intricate social institution known as a market. To this general description the New York bond market is no exception. Its transactions are, for the most part, completed expeditiously and in a restricted space. The bids and offers which come into it originate over a wide area and are, as in any highly organized market, concentrated in the hands of a few men, the brokers. It is sensible to a multitude of influences, such as the activity of business, the temper of the financial world, the movements of interest rates, the policy of the Treasury and the Federal Reserve System, and the actions of the stock market. It has numerous parts and divisions, its prices fluctuate, and it is subject to alternating periods of activity and quiescence.

The bond market also possesses characteristics which distinguish it from other markets. Such peculiarities are to be traced almost entirely to the nature and economic functions of bonds. The needs and actions which bring bonds into being, the sources and types of buying power which take them off the market, the relation of bonds to industry and banking, the significance which they have for the individual and for the economic mechanism as a whole are all elements in the structure and operation of the market.

Bonds are brought into being by the transference, upon stipulated terms usually drawn in the form of a contract, of financial resources from those persons or institutions which currently have a surplus to other persons or institutions currently in need of funds. They are evidence of money borrowed, that is to say, of "debt." In this respect the bonds of public borrowers, such as governments and municipalities, are similar to the bonds of private commercial borrowers, although in other respects they do not have the same economic significance. The private borrower ordinarily uses the proceeds of bond issues in some profit-seeking enterprise, whereas the public borrower usually does not.

The private borrower uses bonds as one of the means for collecting the large agglomerations of capital necessary for modern large scale production, and their issue is a method for raising capital additional to that which can be secured through stock issues or through short term loans. Since bonds are evidence of obligations incurred, they are to be distinguished from stocks, which represent a share of ownership, although the funds acquired through stock and bond issues are usually put to much the same uses. Since bonds, for the most part, are long term contracts the proceeds of their sale provide part of the permanent resources of a business unit and are generally used in the acquisition of fixed assets. In this respect bonds are quite different from the various types of short term loans, which are usually characterized by liquidity and quick repayment, and which are generally used to provide working capital and funds necessary in periods of seasonal stress.

Ordinarily, certain conditions are attached to the use of funds borrowed through the issue of bonds. It is commonly stipulated that interest shall be paid at a fixed rate at regular intervals over a long term, and that the loan shall be amortized in some particular way or repaid at some set date. In the event that these conditions are violated the borrower is usually made subject to certain penalties; in the case of specifically secured loans, for instance, the lender acquires special claims against stated assets of the borrower if the terms of the contract are broken. Consequently, the fact that bonds are issued in any particular instance postulates that the borrower either has, or will acquire through the use of the borrowed funds, sufficient income to pay the necessary interest, and that he will either be able to amortize the principal against the day when it falls due or maintain his ability to borrow in such a way that he will be able to refund the loan at maturity. However, since bonds are long term contracts, the ability of a borrower to fulfill his obligations is always contingent upon the future, which it is never possible to foresee entirely at the time the bonds are issued. When, through any combination of circumstances, the conditions upon which money was loaned and bonds issued are not met — when, for instance, interest or amortization payments are not made, or the principal is not repaid at maturity — bonds fail to perform their proper economic and social function. For if the lender does not receive the income he expected, or if part or all of his capital is lost, the particular situation and relationship which it was intended the issue of bonds should produce is not consummated, and in the failure of a bond issue to establish the relationships for which it was designed, the economic process — upon which modern society depends — is interrupted to greater or lesser degree.

Because of their fixed character, interest and amortization payments have a special significance in the economic structure. They are payments that must be made, if the penalties attendant upon their omission are to be avoided, and hence are not subject to the borrower's control in the way that many of his other expenses are. Consequently, if there occurs during the life of a commercial bond a fall in prices, output, or earnings which requires that costs and production schedules be changed if the issuer continue business at a profit, the rigidity that pertains to these "fixed charges" can make extremely difficult such readjustments as are necessary. This inflexibility of fixed charges is, in fact, in certain types of economic analysis, as in those dealing with industry's cost structure, and in certain situations, as in those arising during a corporate reorganization, the characteristic of bonds which is of prime significance.

To banks, which as a category are perhaps the most important class of bond purchasers, to other types of financial institutions, and even to business concerns at such times as they have free funds which they can not profitably employ in their own occupations, bonds afford an extremely important method of investment. As repositories of surplus funds, not immediately needed in current transactions and from which an income is desired, they combine the advantages of relative security, liquidity, and yield to a degree that is not equalled by most other forms of investment.

To the individual investor, as to the institutional purchaser, the security, liquidity, and income of bonds are important. However, the motives which lead him to purchase bonds are not entirely analogous to the motives actuating institutions. He seeks, particularly, security for his savings, for the funds which he has set aside to provide for the future; and the uses to which he plans to put these funds, or the income from them, differ from the uses of banks or of business concerns. It perhaps hardly need be pointed out that the bonds the individual acquires are not bought, as are commodities, to be consumed, but are purchased for the incomes, for what the economists call "utilities," which they will yield him in the future. Thus his demand for bonds is similar to his demand for any durable commodity, and is derived from the satisfactions that will be obtained from future interest payments.

The nature and functions of bonds, which have been briefly discussed, give to the supply of them, as it comes into the market, and to the demand for them, a number of characteristic features. Since they are durable goods, which continue in existence for considerable periods of time, old bonds, formerly issued, continually return to the market in greater or lesser volume, and the stocks of bonds on hand, "the floating supply," is composed at any given time of both old and new issues. But bonds do not deteriorate — as do many commodities — merely with the passage of time, and old issues are not, merely because of their age, discriminated against in the market.[1] In this respect the supply of bonds can be con-

---

[1] There are, of course, some commodities, such as stocks or certain kinds of real estate, which do not depreciate with age and which compete on an even footing in the market with new supplies. Some commodities, such as wines and antique furniture, even appreciate with the passage of time. But most commodities do deteriorate with age, and in the case of these goods, when a "used" market exists, there is usually a price differential clearly traceable to a difference in age.

Of course insofar as the security upon which bonds are based, such as buildings or equipment, suffers with the passage of time, and proper reserves for depreciation and obsolescence are not set aside, bonds may, in one sense, be considered as falling in value with increasing age. Those instances in which

sidered as homogeneous, though in other ways it can not. For instance, in the analysis of the market the various types of new flotations, such as new capital and refunding issues, or those offered by public and private institutions, must often be distinguished. Likewise it is often important to determine, so far as possible, the various causes that at any given time bring old issues back into the market, since, for instance, "distress selling" and sales intended to release funds for use in the stock market do not have the same significance. However, the motives that actuate sales by any individual or group of individuals are so numerous and so difficult to discover that it is seldom possible to ascertain them with any accuracy.

Finally it may be noted that the supply of bonds is divided into groups which are not identical in character. A bond on the legal list is not the same as one not on it, and a purchaser seeking a "first grade" investment will not, ordinarily, be willing to buy a "third grade" bond. Certain types of purchasers, of course, such as trustees and savings banks, are, in most states, compelled by law to buy only the better grades of securities. The various groups of bonds, however, are not absolutely fixed and rigid in character. Over a period of time a bond may move from one classification to another, from a second class rating to a first — whereas it is impossible for a grade of cotton or of wheat ever to move from one classification to another.

Although each group of bonds caters to a type of investment demand slightly different from that of any of the others, yet between closely allied groups there is always a considerable amount of competition for the funds currently offered for investment. Moreover, within any one particular group there is usually a number of different issues, approximately equal as regards security, liquidity, and yield, any one of which can satisfy the needs of an individual investor. A buyer is thus offered a wider choice in the bond market than he is in other markets when, for technical reasons, he is restricted to a special

---

sudden new inventions, changes in fashions or habits, and shifts in population destroy the security upon which bonds are based form still another special instance in which the passage of time, in a sense, reduces the value of bonds.

commodity or to a special grade of one commodity. Consequently, within one group, and even between groups, a substantial degree of competition exists among the sellers of the various bonds. In the sale of bonds of a particular issue an even greater degree of competition is likely to prevail, with the exception of those instances in which a single seller or group of sellers controls the supply, as in the flotation of a new issue or a pool operation; and such competition is commonly entirely on the basis of price, since, when bonds of the same issue are identical in maturity and other features, a buyer will ordinarily have no preferences of a non-financial character but will buy from whichever seller offers the bonds at the lowest price.

The demand for bonds does not arise from the immediate material wants of man, as is the case with consumptive goods. They are not bought to be consumed, but for the income, the "utilities," which they will yield during their lifetime. The funds which are used to purchase them, which constitute the "demand" for them, are free funds, in the sense that they are not needed immediately for the purchase of consumption goods, the furtherance of commercial transactions, or for other purposes. But these free funds are of two sorts, of very different import, although the two can not always be differentiated distinctly. On the one hand there are the savings of society, the resources set aside and not used in current consumption. Such funds comprise the ultimate demand for bonds, in the sense that they alone permanently "absorb" bonds and take them off of the market. On the other hand there are those surplus funds, temporarily invested in bonds, which from time to time come into or leave the market in large or small volume, and which, at any given time, are of the greatest importance. In a general way, the quantity of such funds offered at a particular time depends upon the degree of business activity and the ease of credit conditions that currently exists. Although provided by various lenders, the principal source of such funds is the banking system. In the long run the volume of savings constitutes the real demand for bonds, but in the short run these other funds are, perhaps, of greater significance. Their import will be dealt with in greater detail when the mechanism of the market is considered.

The bond market has so far been primarily looked upon as a particular example of markets in general, as an individual species belonging to a large genus, and distinct from other markets principally by virtue of the peculiarities of the commodity with which it is concerned. As such an example, the bond market has been viewed as an institution or mechanism which, through the facility it gives to the performance of certain economic acts, aids in the satisfaction of social needs. If this evaluation is accepted, the bond market clearly can not be regarded as something strange, abnormal, and foreign to the natural actions of man. From this point of view, bonds, and the market in which they are traded, are merely devices, or instruments, which give a two-fold assistance to man in his twin activities, the production of goods and the provision for future needs. Like the service of the hoe and the plow to the farmer, they provide the business man with the means of furthering production. Like the hay stored by the farmer in his barn, they represent to the individual investor provision made for the future. Although surrounded by the intricate and at times confusing trappings of the financial world, their place and function in the economic fabric is basically similar to that of the simple tools of the workman. And, like the equipment and hay mow of the farmer, their position in the productive mechanism can be taken from them and their worth destroyed by a great variety of forces, social, economic, and political. In the same way that a burnt hay crop, stolen tools, and equipment destroyed mean a break in the economic process and a loss of capital, so does interest defaulted and repayment withheld, whether occasioned by a business depression or a political enactment, signify an interruption of the productive mechanism and a destruction of a portion of the framework which separates civilized society from the penury of barbarism.

Some attention must now be paid to more technical aspects of the bond market and to factors which are of special significance in its workings. Probably the most important elements in any market are those forces which so act upon the bids and offers, the supply and demand, as to exercise a dominant influence over the prices at which transactions are completed. The supply of bonds, as has been noted, is created by borrowers who wish to employ capital in some of its infinite number of uses, and the demand for bonds is ultimately derived from the savings of society. But such forces do not alone determine the prices of bonds. The degree of probability that interest payments will be maintained and capital returned at maturity, the degree of "risk," as indicated by the earnings of commercial borrowers and the incomes of public borrowers, also greatly affects bond prices. Earnings and incomes are, of course, regulated by a wide variety of factors, such as the level of prices, of business activity, and of taxes. But in addition to these forces which determine the security of particular bonds, bond prices are intimately connected with movements in short term interest rates.

The tendency for short and long term rates to move in harmony is well known, and it is generally recognized that the prices of long and short term capital are closely related, although the precise nature of this relationship is not understood. Short term rates appear to be more sensitive than long rates, but it is not known what the normal or typical difference between various kinds of short and long rates is, nor how large and prolonged a movement of short rates is necessary in order that long rates be affected. Neither is it clear whether movement of short rates is the immediate factor which brings a change in long rates, or whether movements of both are motivated by a common cause. Although the inverse movements of short rates and bond prices has, at times, been considered as being almost automatic,[2] it has also been suggested that "It seems at least as reasonable to suppose that the declining interest rates for short term money and the advancing prices

[2] "In a period of rising interest rates . . . the market price of bonds will tend to decline in direct proportion to the element of pure interest involved in the return on the securities . . . irrespective of their credit position" (Lawrence Chamberlain and G. W. Edwards, *Principles of Bond Investment*, 1927, p. 580).

of bonds . . . are both effects of a common cause." [3] In view of this disagreement, and in the light of what knowledge we have of economic forces, it may be hazarded that both views are, in part, correct. There are obvious connections in the financial world which tend to harmonize movements of short and long term rates, but there are also movements of interest rates which can not be explained by these relationships and which must be accounted for by admitting that other factors exist which affect one or the other or both types of rates, sometimes in such a way as to produce similar, and sometimes dissimilar, results.

Movements of short and long term rates tend to harmonize, to keep "in line," because, within limits, short and long term securities afford, to the borrower, alternative methods of acquiring capital, and to the lender, alternative methods of investment. When long term rates are unduly high, compared with short term rates, borrowers will tend to use the cheaper, short term facilities, and lenders will tend to put more money into the long term market, and the spread between the two kinds of rates will, consequently, be narrowed. The changes which banks make in the proportions of their long and short term investments, as one or the other becomes more profitable,[4] are, perhaps, the most important influence that harmonizes movements of short and long rates, although not the only one.[5]

[3] R. N. Owens and C. O. Hardy, *Interest Rates and Stock Speculation* (1930), p. 173.

[4] The investment of bank funds is determined not only by the relative profit of various types of investment but by the security of the different investments, the degree of liquidity of the bank's assets, the bank's reserve position, and by a number of other factors. Also, banks are often deterred from shifting funds from long term investments to short term, as the latter become more profitable, because the capital loss involved in the sale of securities at a time of high interest rates will more than offset the profit made from the higher rates of the short term investments.

[5] The activities of those persons who purchase securities with borrowed money also tend to keep short and long rates in harmony. When short rates are below long rates there is a profit to be made by buying, and carrying, securities with borrowed money, just as, when short rates are above long rates, it is unprofitable to use short term loans to carry securities. The purchases and sales of securities occasioned by such profits and losses tend to keep the spread

But such shifting of funds from long term investments to short term, or vice versa, as one or the other becomes unusually profitable, only explains why the two types of rates move together. It can not account for the independent movement of one kind of rate, nor indicate how a discrepancy great enough to make a transference of funds profitable originates. After a movement of one rate has taken place and an abnormal difference between the two has been created, transference of funds will affect both rates and will narrow the discrepancy, but the original movement can be explained only as the result of other forces.

Many factors, of course, affect interest rates. The activity of business, the psychological temper of the people, gold movements, the policies of Treasuries and central banks, the presence or absence of excess reserves in the banking system, and other elements, all influence interest rates, the volume of funds that can be borrowed, and that intangible something speciously known as "credit conditions." Of these elements perhaps the most important in the modern world is the presence or absence of excess reserves in the banking system, since this is the factor which most often directly determines the willingness and ability of banks to lend. Although each of these forces acts upon short and long rates in different ways and different degrees, the mechanism — noted above — which serves to keep movements of short and long rates in harmony tends to prevent these various forces from producing diverse movements of the different types of rates.

In any market current prices much affect the volume of new supplies offered, and since in the bond market long term rates are the price of the commodity offered there, long term rates

---

between short and long rates within certain limits. Likewise, the different uses to which the working capital of business firms is put in times of advancing and receding business activity act to keep long and short rates together. In slack periods, when short rates tend to be low, working capital is released from active employment; such funds are then often invested in readily marketable bonds and prices of such securities tend to be increased and long rates to move downward in sympathy with the low level of short rates. The opposite, of course, happens in periods of increasing activity, and the two types of rates move upward.

and credit conditions influence to a large degree the flow of new issues coming into the market. When interest rates are high, new flotations tend to slacken, and when interest rates are low, new issues ordinarily increase. Technical peculiarities of the bond market, however, accentuate the influence which the price of capital has upon new offerings.

Aside from government bonds and the borrowings of investment trusts and holding companies, the demand for capital depends, in a general way, upon the growth of population, the material resources of the country, the progress of invention, changes in folk-habits, and such other factors as control the material wants of the nation. However, since capital can often be raised in other ways than by issuing bonds — as, for instance, by issuing stocks or by borrowing from banks — and since much capital expenditure can, within wide limits, be postponed, the amount of capital sought at a given time through bond issues is ordinarily affected to a very high degree by the relative cheapness or dearness of borrowing. In fact, in the short run borrowing appears to be more a function of the current price of capital and the condition of the market than it is of the material needs of the population.[6]

This influence which the price of capital exercises over the flotation of new issues is further increased by the fact that the business of issuing securities is done on a very narrow margin.[7] Consequently, success in the flotation of an issue depends very largely upon the timing of the offering, upon its being brought out during one of those temporary rises of the

[6] Whitney, in her investigation of interest rates in the post-war period, comes to much the same conclusion. In the stock and bond markets she finds that "demand is the controlling factor" — i.e., that low interest rates tended to increase the amount of borrowing rather than to reduce the volume of funds offered for long term investment (Caroline Whitney, *Experiments in Credit Control*, 1934, pp. 166–173).

[7] The margin upon which issue houses work varies both with the type of issue and with the current conditions in the market. The less speculative the security and the broader the market for it the narrower is the margin between the buying and selling price of the investment banker, and in a rising market all margins tend to be narrower than in a falling one. The interest rate the issue houses are forced to pay for the funds they use to carry a new flotation during its distribution of course affects the margin. When short rates are high, margins must be higher than they are in a period of low short term rates.

market that continually recur as the market fluctuates.[8] Thus
the flow of new offerings is much more sensitive to price changes
and market movements than is the flow of new units in other
markets, and a slight rise in prices brings out in a rush the
flotations that have been waiting for favorable conditions, and
a slight fall checks them sharply.

A considerable degree of irregularity thus characterizes the
flow of new issues, and this irregularity is heightened by the
fact that new issues do not constitute the total supply on hand,
nor even a constant part of it.[9] As has been noted, bonds are
durable goods, and old issues continually return to the market,
in greater or lesser amount, and in no fixed relationship to the
volume of new issues currently offered. This double source
of supply for the stocks of bonds on hand means that any
development which makes for strength or weakness in the
market may or may not have its effect concentrated on the
flow of new issues. When new flotations constitute the principal part of stocks on hand any buoyant, or depressing, development influences the flow of offerings in greater degree than
when such offerings form only a small part of the current floating supply.

As has been noted, the supply of bonds, which is much influenced by the price of borrowing, comes into the market in
an irregular flow. These bonds are taken from the market —
indeed, ultimately can only be taken from the market — by
being purchased by the savings of society. Like the supply of
bonds, the supply of savings fluctuates — how much, it is impossible to say. But it seems probable that the fluctuations of
the supply of savings are not at all times equal to the fluctua-

---

[8] The successful flotation of a new offering is often thought to depend, in
many cases, upon its being issued within so short a time as one or two days.

[9] The relation of new issues to the supply in the market at any one time
is not so indeterminate as might be supposed. Every sale of a bond creates a
potential purchase, insofar as the funds received are not spent in consumption,
hoarded, or put into another form of investment. Even when the funds received
are left on deposit in a bank there is a possibility of a purchase of bonds by the
bank, since such funds strengthen its reserve and tend to place it in a position
where it may increase its security holdings, although not, of course, to an extent
equivalent to the amount of funds received.

tions of the supply of bonds. It is often assumed that savings accrue at a relatively stable rate, at one considerably more stable than the rate at which bonds are offered in the market, especially since it seems very likely that the return on savings — the price of borrowing — influences the volume of saving much less than it does the volume of bonds offered.[10] Although the interest rate doubtless does influence the volume of saving, its influence is often diluted or counteracted by that of other forces, and it seems probable that the supply of savings does not vary so rapidly or to so great an extent as does either the price of capital or the supply of bonds.

The relation between the supply of saving and the supply of bonds is further complicated by the "free funds," previously mentioned, which come into the market now in greater and now in lesser degree and augment the demand for bonds represented by the supply of savings. For the most part such funds come, directly or indirectly, from the banking system, although they come into the market in various ways. But whether they are invested for the banks' own accounts, or are lent to issue houses to enable them to carry new flotations, or are lent to the public in the form of security loans, they swell the volume of funds seeking investment. However, the willingness and ability of banks to increase their security loans and investments depends far more upon the relative scarcity or abundance of their surplus reserves, and upon the relative ease or tightness of credit, than it does upon current return on capital. Stringent credit conditions, in fact, often operate so as to contract security loans and investments of banks, in spite of the high current yield of securities; and the high price obtainable for loans often will not induce an increase in the supply of loanable funds to the degree that high prices tend to increase the supply of commodities in other markets.

In summary, the foregoing discussion indicates that at any given time the demands for capital placed in the bond market

---

[10] Dewing states: ". . . the quantity of capital offered is not . . . a direct function of the price of capital" (A. S. Dewing, *The Financial Policy of Corporations*, 1926, p. 1167).

are more influenced by the current price of capital than they
are by the needs of industry for long term loans. However,
the price of long term capital does not seem to influence greatly
the supply of such capital in the short run, since the volume
of savings does not change directly and commensurately with
changes in interest rates, and since the banks, the principal
source of such other funds as go into the bond market, do not
base their investment policy solely or even chiefly upon the return obtainable from long term investments and the relative
movements of long and short term interest rates. The policies
of banks are mainly determined by other factors, by the state
of business activity, the liquidity of banking resources, the
amount of excess reserves, gold movements, the policies of
central banks and Treasuries, and by a host of other considerations. And it is factors of this type which, through their influence on banking policy, at any given time largely determine
the volume of funds — aside from the increments of new savings — which shall be invested in the bond market, and which,
through the effect such funds have on the market, to a considerable degree control both bond prices and the flow of new issues.

The free funds, the surplus reserves of the banking system,
which have such important consequences for the bond market,
were accumulated in various ways during the period of this
study.[11] Gold imports, considerable and unexpected reductions
in the accommodation which industry asked in the form of commercial loans, returns of large quantities of money from circulation — such as occurred in 1920 and 1921 — purchases of
government securities and acceptances by the Federal Reserve
Banks, all served to increase such funds. Conversely, gold exports, large and sudden increases in demands from industry
for bank loans, increases in money in circulation, and sales of
securities by the Reserve Banks, all tended to force liquidation
of member banks' security loans and portfolios. Of course, these
several factors did not at all times work in the same direction;

---

[11] It should be noted that many of the forces and relationships of importance
in the financial world in the interval 1920–1930 have, since that time, come to
possess a different significance, and many of the generalizations made in regard
to them here are no longer valid.

often certain of them acting in one direction were offset by others operating in the other; and at various times there were other offsetting influences present in the financial world which served to reduce or counteract the effects which these factors, left to themselves, presumably would have produced upon the credit structure.

Open market operations of the Federal Reserve System functioned differently than did the other forces mentioned, since they could be, and were, initiated consciously by the Reserve authorities, and, through the changes they occasioned in the surplus funds of member banks and the amount of such funds placed in the bond market, served to counteract or intensify inflationary or deflationary tendencies already existing through the operation of other factors. Purchases of government bonds by the Federal Reserve System of course stimulated the bond market to a greater extent than did purchases of acceptances, since they not only directly affected the bond market but had a secondary result as well, in that the funds so expended ordinarily came into the hands of member banks and permitted them either to decrease their indebtedness with the Reserve Banks, or to increase their earning assets (including security loans and investments), or to do both. Purchases of acceptances had only the single result of supplying member banks with funds.

The influence which Federal Reserve purchases of governments and which purchases of bonds by member banks had upon the bond market was very great. In the years 1922, 1924, and 1927, in the latter part of 1929, and in 1930 the Reserve Banks bought significant quantities of government bonds.[12] Other types of banks [13] also substantially increased their security portfolios in 1922, 1924, 1927, and 1930.[14] The effect which such purchases had on bond prices, on the volume of trading, and on the number and volume of new issues was direct and immediate. Bond prices rose sharply in the latter part of 1921 and the first part of 1922, from 1924 through 1927,

[12] Chart XI, p. 60.
[13] Member banks and savings banks are both included in this statement.
[14] Chart VIII, p. 38.

and in 1930.[15] Likewise the volume of bond trading on the
Stock Exchange reached very considerable peaks in 1922, 1924,
the latter part of 1926 and the early part of 1927, and in 1929.[16]
The volume of new flotations increased rapidly in the latter
part of 1921 and in 1922, in the latter part of 1924 and the
early part of 1925, in 1927, and in 1930.[17] The number of new
issues also rose sharply in 1924 and 1927.[18] Although it is,
perhaps, not entirely true to say that security purchases by
the Federal Reserve Banks directly caused these developments
in the bond market, it nevertheless appears to be very significant that in the years when the Reserve Banks bought large
quantities of securities other types of banks also purchased
substantial amounts, and that it was almost precisely at such
times that the bond market was most active and buoyant.

In the long run the forces which are of significance in the
bond market and which determine its movements are of course
very different from those — some of which have just been discussed — that are important in the short run. In the long run
all those elements are of moment which bear upon the proper
performance of the economic function of bonds and of the
bond market. All those factors which are related to the transference of resources from those who have a surplus to those
who are in need of additional means, and those which affect
the maintenance of the obligations incurred by such transference, must be taken into account; and all the forces which
distribute resources among various uses and which are connected with the trading mechanism and the freedom of the
market must be reckoned with. Intricate and complex as is
the short run analysis, the long run analysis of the bond market
is even more difficult.

Primarily, of course, the long run analysis is concerned with
the problem of long run, or "normal," value. To the economist this concept implies an even, steady functioning of the eco-

---

[15] Chart I, p. 28.   [16] Chart II, p. 29.   [17] Chart V, p. 32.
[18] Chart IV, p. 31. Statistics for the number of new issues are not available
before 1923, so that it is not possible to determine whether the rise in the
volume of issues in 1922 was reflected by a rise in the number of new issues.
The number of new issues did not share in the advance of 1930.

nomic process and the sale of goods in quantities and at prices that are in the nature of equilibria, in the sense that when they are disturbed they tend to be reëstablished. In the case of commodities such a concept means that all the costs of producing commodities are recouped, and that neither excess profits are made nor losses suffered — in short, that all price-determining forces are in balance. Although the elements that must be considered in the case of the bond market are not the same as in the case of commodity markets, long run analysis of it likewise involves the concept of balanced forces and the steady performance of the market's process, though it is perhaps even more doubtful whether such a balance is ever approximated in the bond market than it is in commodity markets.

If a statement is ventured as to what the principal forces are which in the long run affect bond prices and what the relationship of these forces would be were they in equilibrium, it may be said that such a situation could not exist unless over a period of time the material needs of the population, which stimulate borrowing for both productive and unproductive purposes, were in such condition, relative to the stage of technology and the other factors that control the output of goods, that the need for such amounts and kinds of capital as could properly be raised in the form of bond issues could be accommodated by the saving habits of the people at a rate of interest and amortization not too great to be supported at the level of prices and output existing during the life of the bonds. This is an extremely complex statement, and probably not an entirely comprehensive one. Psychological factors, for instance, and the existence of a society in which property is secure, are included only indirectly. But certainly none of the elements mentioned can be neglected in any consideration of the forces which determine the prices of bonds over a period of time.

In this study the bond market is viewed primarily from the short run point of view. The analysis is based upon such magnitudes and factors as the volume and number of new issues, movements of long and short term interest rates and stock yields, changes in commodity prices, business activity, and the international balance of payments, and the policies of the Treasury and the Federal Reserve System. Only in the last chapter is some slight attempt made to appraise the market from the long run point of view, and to estimate — however imperfectly — certain forces present in the 1920–1930 period which were significant for the concept of equilibrium, such as the relationship of new debt to the volume of saving, and the relationship of the interest burden created to the ability of industry to support it.

CHAPTER III

MARKET MOVEMENTS, 1920–1930

IN THIS study statistical series of price movements, the volume of trading, and the number and volume of new issues are used to describe the course of the market. It would have been desirable to follow other aspects of the market if adequate statistics had been available, but in the absence of such data it is believed that these series provide as complete a record of the market's movements as can be obtained. Although many factors, such as Federal Reserve policies and business activity, influenced market movements and must be considered in an interpretation of them, such elements can not properly be included in a record of the market's actions.

The indices of bond prices used are the average yields of Moody's Aaa and Baa bonds, shown in Chart I.[1] The two indices were employed in order to include both first and second grade bonds in the study. Price movements, of course, are one of the most important elements in any market; but bond prices are much influenced by forces in a sense external to the bond market proper, such as short term interest rates and banking policies, and consequently bond prices do not always reflect precisely all of the changes in market conditions. Stable prices may conceal for a considerable time significant changes in the strength of the market, and the long, slow rise in bond prices that continued from 1923 through 1927 gave little evidence of some important developments that took place in the market during that period. An account of market conditions can not be complete unless the evidence afforded by price movements is combined with that of other indices.

The best index of the activity of the market that could be procured was the volume of bonds traded on the New York Stock Exchange. This series, however, is not entirely satis-

---

[1] The figures from which this chart is drawn are given in Appendix A.

factory, since there is no reason to suppose that it accurately reflects the activity of the over-the-counter market, and probably the volume of trading on the over-the-counter market was larger during this period than that done on the Exchange.

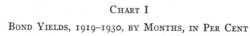

CHART I

BOND YIELDS, 1919–1930, BY MONTHS, IN PER CENT

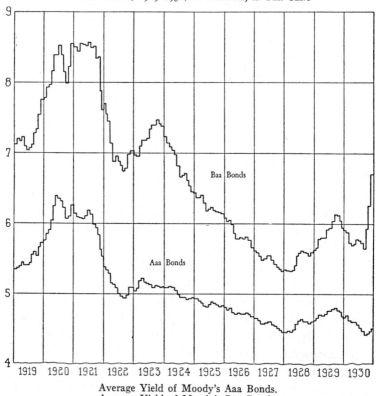

Average Yield of Moody's Aaa Bonds.
Average Yield of Moody's Baa Bonds.

The monthly volumes of bonds traded on the Exchange, and a twelve-month moving-average of them, are shown in Chart II.[2] The curve representing the actual volume of trading fluctuates so widely that it is difficult to draw conclusions from it. The smoothness of the twelve-month moving-average curve is in some ways misleading, but its high and low points appear

[2] The figures from which this chart is drawn are given in Appendix B.

to be significant; the downward trend of this curve probably
reflects a decline in the trading done on the Exchange rather
than a decrease in the total amount of bonds traded.

The number of new issues offered in the New York market
was compiled on a monthly and on a quarterly basis from

CHART II

BONDS TRADED ON THE NEW YORK STOCK EXCHANGE, 1920–1930, BY MONTHS

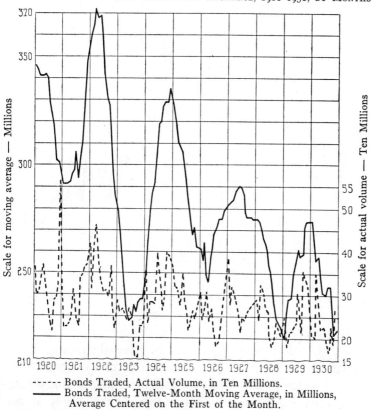

------ Bonds Traded, Actual Volume, in Ten Millions.
———— Bonds Traded, Twelve-Month Moving Average, in Millions,
    Average Centered on the First of the Month.

1923 through 1932. Figures prior to 1923 could not be secured,
and in order that the basis for studying seasonal and other
types of fluctuation in this series should not be distinctly
smaller than in other series used, the compilation was continued through 1932. It is believed that substantially all of
the financing done in the New York market is covered by the

compilation, since it includes all domestic and foreign long and short term financing, except Canadian provincial issues and short term United States Treasury Bills. In Chart III the number of new issues is shown on a monthly basis, both the actual number of new flotations each month, and the series corrected

CHART III

NUMBER OF BOND ISSUES, 1923–1932, BY MONTHS

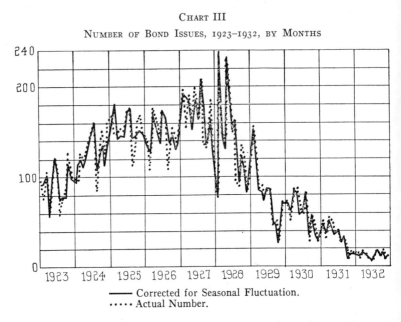

―― Corrected for Seasonal Fluctuation.
••••• Actual Number.

for seasonal fluctuation. In Chart IV are given the number of new issues each quarter and the series corrected for seasonal fluctuation.[3] The curves of Chart IV show somewhat more clearly than do those of Chart III the general character of the changes that took place in the number of new offerings.

The number of new issues by itself does not, of course, adequately represent the situation relative to the supply of new issues coming into the market. The volume of new issues is in many ways more significant. But the number of issues is particularly useful as an index of market conditions, since it is not influenced, as is the volume of issues, by unusually large flota-

---

[3] The figures from which these charts are drawn are given in Appendix C. The character of the seasonal fluctuation in this series is considered in detail in Appendix Q.

CHART IV

NUMBER OF BOND ISSUES, 1923–1932, BY QUARTERS

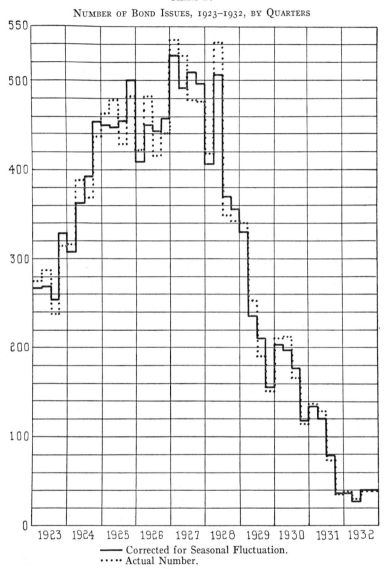

—— Corrected for Seasonal Fluctuation.
••••• Actual Number.

tions. Indices of the number and the volume of new issues together give a more comprehensive description of market conditions than does either one by itself.

The statistical series of the volume of bond issues are based on the tabulation of security issues published in the *Commercial and Financial Chronicle,* and on a compilation of federal government issues of more than one year's maturity taken from the annual reports of the Secretary of the Treasury. The *Chronicle's* tabulation includes domestic and foreign corporate

CHART V

VOLUME OF BOND ISSUES, 1919–1931, BY QUARTERS, IN MILLIONS

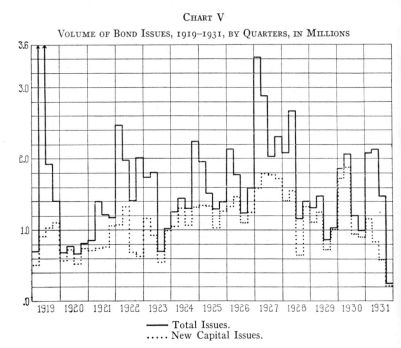

——— Total Issues.
..... New Capital Issues.

issues, foreign government issues, Federal Farm Loan issues, and municipal issues of the United States, its possessions, and Canada.[4] It is believed that these two compilations include every issue which materially affects the market.[5]

In Chart V are shown two curves, "new capital" issues and "total" issues. The differences between these two represents "refunding" issues. The curves have been computed in quarterly totals for the years 1919 through 1931. The new capital

[4] The stock issues included in the *Commercial and Financial Chronicle's* tabulation were, of course, omitted from the calculations.

[5] When the *Chronicle's* tabulation was first published in 1921 — the tabulation itself includes figures for the years 1919 and 1920 — the *Chronicle* described it, in part, as follows: "Our purpose in the tabulation we begin today is to cover

computation is taken directly from that classification in the *Chronicle's* figures. The refunding computation includes the refunding classification of the *Chronicle* and the issues of the federal government. The curve of total issues is the summation of these two series.[6]

The curve of new capital issues affords a good index of capital requirements as expressed in the form of bond issues, although this classification includes some issues, offered by holding companies and investment trusts, which do not represent "original" demands for new capital. But such an allowance should not be large for the aggregate of bond issues, however important it may be in the case of particular companies.

---

the entire country. . . . We do not confine ourselves to the offerings in this city, or even to those brought out on the Atlantic Seaboard. . . . In order to indicate in a general way the plan we are pursuing in our compilations, we would say that we make every effort to limit our statements to such securities offered in the United States as actually pass beyond the issuing corporation's control for a monetary consideration. In pursuance of this practice our statements are rigidly restricted to the following: (1) Issues which the offering bankers stated they had purchased or underwritten. (2) Issues which, while it was not claimed were directly purchased or underwritten, were offered by banking houses to give practical assurance of a definite commitment on their part. (3) Subscription privileges extended to shareholders where the right to subscribe to additional stock was of such value as to make the taking of the stock a practical certainty. (4) Offerings by a corporation of its own securities direct, where assurance was to be had that the securities had been sold." Offerings of the following nature were excluded: "(1) Offerings by brokers where it was uncertain if the issue was underwritten or only being sold on a commission basis and the amount disposed of was not known. (2) Offerings by corporations of their own securities direct, where it could not be ascertained whether or not the same had been sold. Stated in brief, our totals embrace merely definite and tangible flotations — those that actually found a market and passed into the hands of investors and bankers, or were taken by the owners of the enterprise" ("Current New Capital Flotations," *Chronicle*, CXII, 1216–1218, March 26, 1921). To this may be added the statement made by an editor of the *Chronicle* to Mr. G. C. Means: "Bond investment houses all over the country report to us all their offerings, sending us complete details so as to get a notice in our paper, and in addition we have virtually all the newspapers of the country searched for information regarding bond and stock offerings of every kind. We have a very extended clipping service of our own, subscribing for hundreds of newspapers, and in addition get clippings from numerous clipping agencies. In the circumstances we do not see how we could fail to learn of any offerings of securities" (G. C. Means, "The Growth in the Relative Importance of the Large Corporation in American Economic Life," *American Economic Review*, XXI, 29, n. 42, March 1931).

[6] The figures from which this chart is drawn are given in Appendix D.

The curve of new capital issues, however, does not represent the supply of new funds that the bond market had to find to accommodate the capital needs given expression there. It takes no account of outstanding issues concurrently called or matured, whose proceeds were presumably for the most part reinvested and reduced the demand for new funds. An attempt to estimate the requirements not offset by such reinvestments was made by computing from various sources [7] the bonds called and matured in each quarter of the years 1920 through 1930. The quarterly totals of such bonds were then subtracted from the corresponding totals of bonds issued, to find the "net" amount of accommodation required of the bond market.[8] Chart VI shows the total amounts of bonds issued, less these deductions, with the residue of new funds asked of the savers of the country in each quarter.[9]

Chart VI, as would be expected, shows that such "net" offerings were considerably smaller than the total, but that the trends of the two series were the same. The chart also shows that the "net" series was much more irregular than that for the total volume of issues, and that in five quarters — each one of which was one of the "low" third quarters, when offerings were always light — more bonds matured or were called than were offered. Consequently, at such times the "net" offering figures became negative amounts, and the supply of available investment capital was temporarily increased by the surplus of obligations paid off. It is believed that the sources from which these deductions were compiled are substantially accu-

[7] The figures for called and matured foreign bonds and for corporate domestic bonds were compiled from computations in the *Wall Street Journal*; the figures for called and matured municipal bonds were taken from computations of the *Bond Buyer*; decreases in the government's interest bearing debt were compiled from the monthly Statements of the Public Debt of the United States.

[8] The sum arrived at by deducting the volume of bonds called and matured from the total volume issued represents the "net" amount of new money required by the bond market in a given period only on the assumption that funds received by the holders of called and matured bonds are reinvested — directly or indirectly — in new issues of bonds. While this assumption is certainly not universally true, yet it is perhaps approximately valid. Certainly the total volume of new issues can not be taken as equivalent to the demand for new, additional investment funds (in the form of bonds) in a given period.

[9] The figures from which this chart is drawn are given in Appendix E.

1875242

rate, but for municipal bonds quarterly computations were not possible, as annual decreases in the amounts outstanding were the only figures available. In this case the entire annual deduction was prorated evenly over the four quarters. For this

CHART VI

VOLUME OF "NET" BOND ISSUES, 1920–1930, BY QUARTERS, IN MILLIONS

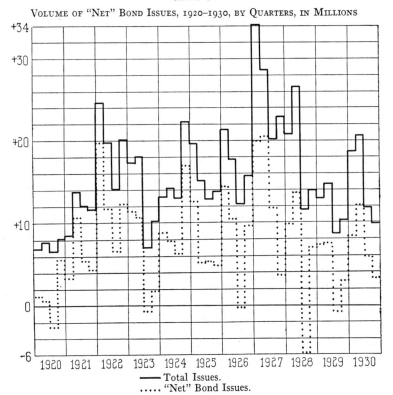

——— Total Issues.
..... "Net" Bond Issues.

reason, as well as on account of errors and omissions in the sources from which the figures were compiled, the quarterly deduction figures and the "net" offerings series are only approximately accurate.

It is evident that in the three series representing the total volume of offerings, the volume of new capital offerings, and the volume of "net" offerings, a strong seasonal element is present. This fluctuation is most strongly marked in total offerings, least apparent in "net" offerings. An attempt was

made to eliminate this fluctuation by treating the three series
with seasonal indices constructed by the link relative method.
The three series thus adjusted are shown in Chart VII.[10]
Satisfactory indices, which appear to give consistent results,

CHART VII

VOLUME OF BOND ISSUES, 1920–1930, CORRECTED FOR SEASONAL FLUCTUATION,
BY QUARTERS, IN MILLIONS

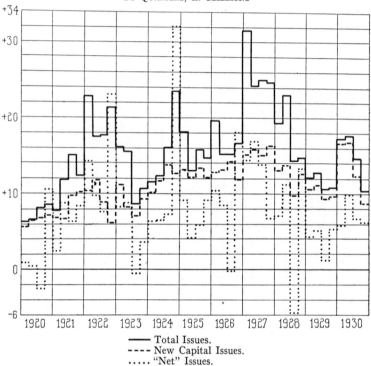

——— Total Issues.
- - - - New Capital Issues.
· · · · · "Net" Issues.

were readily effected for the series of total offerings and for
new capital offerings; a satisfactory index for "net" offerings
was more difficult to obtain.[11] The configuration of the adjusted
curves of Chart VII does not differ much from that of the
unadjusted curves of Charts V and VI. The trends and the
turning points of the two sets of curves are almost the same;
the adjusted curves are slightly smoother than the unadjusted,
and their turning points somewhat more distinct.

[10] The figures from which this chart is drawn are given in Appendix F.
[11] The seasonal fluctuation in these series is considered in detail in Appendix Q.

A very rough attempt was made to discover to what degree the funds necessary to absorb new bond issues each year were supplied by various types of bond buyers — by banks, including all member banks and savings banks, by life insurance companies operating in the state of New York,[12] and by others, a classification that represents, in a general way, the "public," including in this category trusts, all institutions (other than banks and life insurance companies), private bankers, and brokerage houses. In this attempt annual totals of the "net" volume of new bond issues — that is, total issues less all issues called and matured — were compared with year-to-year changes in the bond holdings of banks and life insurance companies. The annual totals of "net" issues were thought of as representing in a rough way the volume of new investment funds needed to purchase bonds floated during the year; the increase in bond holdings of banks and insurance companies was considered as indicating the extent to which such funds were supplied directly by banks and insurance companies. The differences between the bond purchases of these financial institutions and the annual totals of "net" issues were taken as showing the amounts of funds furnished by others, by the general public.

The results of this attempt are given in Chart VIII.[13] The area below the heavy black line in each column is the annual total of "net" offerings. The solid black area represents the increase or, as in 1920 and 1929, the decrease in bond holdings of banks at the end of the year, as compared with the beginning of the year.[14] The horizontally shaded area represents

[12] Almost all the large American life insurance companies operate in the state of New York.

[13] The figures from which this chart is drawn are given in Appendix G.

[14] The figures for bond holdings of member banks are as of the last call date each year. They are compiled from the Abstract of Condition Reports of State Bank and Trust Company Members and of All Member Banks, as published through 1925 by the Federal Reserve Board, and thereafter from the Member Bank Call Reports, also published by the Federal Reserve Board. The figures used are those under the B/S headings "U. S. Gov't Securities" and "Other Bonds, Stocks and Securities." No attempt has been made to estimate or eliminate the stocks and the mortgages carried under this heading.

The bond holdings of savings banks are as of June 30 each year. The

increases in bond holdings of insurance companies at the
end of the year.[15]   The diagonally shaded area represents the

ANNUAL TOTALS OF THE "NET" VOLUME OF BOND ISSUES, 1920–1930, COMPARED
WITH YEAR-TO-YEAR CHANGES IN BOND HOLDINGS OF VARIOUS TYPES OF
BUYERS, IN MILLIONS

Others than Institutions.

Life Insurance Companies.

Banks.

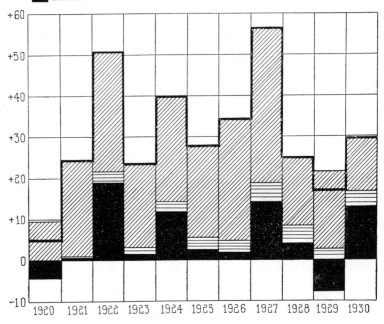

difference between the year's total of "net" offerings and the
summation of the other two areas which represent the bond

---

figures are compiled from the Annual Reports of the Comptroller of the Currency. No adjustment whereby these figures could be put on a year-end basis
was possible.

Since for the sake of simplicity in representation all banks are here grouped
together, it should be noted that there is not always uniformity among the purchasing policies of different types of banks. (See App. G.) In 1921 country
banks reduced their bond holdings, when other types of banks were increasing
their portfolios, and city banks sold bonds in 1923, 1925, and 1926 when other
types of banks were buying.

[15] The figures for bond holdings of life insurance companies were compiled
from the security listings in the Annual Reports of the Superintendent of Insurance, State of New York. Stock holdings have been eliminated.

purchases of banks and insurance companies; that is, it represents that part of the funds necessary to absorb the total of "net" offerings which was not furnished by these institutions but by others, by the public. In the years 1920 and 1929, when there were sales of bonds by banks, the diagonally shaded area extends above the heavy line that represents the total amount of "net" offerings, since it is evident that, in these years, purchasers of bonds other than banks bought more than the total volume of "net" issues.[16]

Only very general conclusions can be formed from this chart, not only because of the uncertainties contained in the figures from which it is drawn, but also because the bond holdings of banks vary greatly during any given year, and their holdings at year-ends are not necessarily significant. However, the chart seems to indicate definitely that the bond purchases of life insurance companies are the smallest of the three types of demand considered; that the purchases of banks fluctuate greatly from year to year; and that ordinarily the general public, as here defined, provides the larger part of the funds necessary to absorb new issues. It also seems evident that the banks bought bonds heavily in 1922, 1924, 1927, and 1930, and that in 1920 and 1929 they sold heavily. The fact that the peak years for bank purchases — 1922, 1924, 1927, and 1930 — are the same as the peak years for "net" bond issues also appears to be significant.

This summary of the market's movements, particularly that part of it relating to bond prices and the number and volume of new issues, seems to show that the bond market passed through a single cyclical movement of great length and amplitude during these eleven years. Dropping back from the levels reached in 1919, both prices and the volume of new issues fell to very low levels in 1920. The movement was then reversed; new offerings advanced — though not without considerable fluctuation — and long rates fell, till 1927. This year was the high point in the post-war bond market. Thereafter the volume of issues — if government flotations are over-

[16] Purchasers of bonds other than banks bought all the "net" offerings of bonds, plus the bonds sold by banks.

looked — declined, and long rates rose, through 1930 and beyond the limits of this study.

The fluctuations that interrupted this movement are very marked, particularly the decline of 1923. The low point in this year might, perhaps, be thought to divide this eleven-year period into two cycles. But the low levels of 1920 were hardly broken through in this decline, and both the decline itself and the subsequent recovery were so rapid that it seems more accurate to consider this merely an intermediate movement in a longer cycle.

The fluctuations of these curves also indicate that there were, during this eleven-year cycle, a number of more or less distinct periods, when the market was strong or weak and moved up or down. Such periods, of course, are not clearly separated from one another; they are, in fact, closely related, and merge into one another; and it is often extremely difficult to designate turning points in the market's movements. However, it is clear that at certain times the character of the market was quite different from what it was at other times, and that in certain periods interpretation of the market's movements must be based upon forces and influences quite different from those important in other periods.

As the post-war boom of 1919 collapsed and the depression of 1920 developed, the volume of new issues and the volume of trading dropped to very low levels, and long term interest rates rose as bond prices declined. Capital needs, however, which had been suppressed during the war, quickly checked the decline in the volume of new issues. The low point for the seasonally corrected volume of new issues was reached in the first quarter of 1920, and thereafter, as restrictions on the capital markets were removed, new flotations increased rapidly and with few set-backs until 1922,[17] although the low point of the business depression was reached in 1921. Bond prices checked their fall in the middle of 1920, and the prices of first

---

[17] This advance was participated in by total issues, new capital issues, and "net" issues. The curve for "net" offerings fluctuated more widely than did the other series, as is always the case, but nevertheless showed a distinct upward tendency.

grades started up, although second grades did not have a sustained advance till the third quarter of 1921. The volume of trading began to increase at the beginning of 1921, and reached a distinct peak in the early part of 1922.

It is difficult to determine at what point the rise of 1920 and 1921 slackened and turned into the decline that culminated in the third quarter of 1923. The volume of bond offerings reached the high point of its advance in the first half of 1922.[18] The indices for total offerings and for "net" offerings remained at a high level till the middle of 1923; these indices, however, include government issues; and the high level which they maintained at this time was caused by the very large flotations of governments currently brought out to refund the short term debt inherited from the war. Without such government flotations these indices would have receded in the third quarter of 1922, as did the index for new capital issues, which does not include government offerings. Bond prices also started to fall in the second half of 1922, as did the volume of trading, so that it seems to be more accurate to choose the middle of 1922, rather than some later date, as marking the beginning of the decline.

In any case the recession that began in 1922 ended in the third quarter of 1923. At this time the indices for the volume of issues, the number of issues, the volume of trading, and prices of second grade bonds [19] all reversed their movement and started up. This advance, which was rapid and well-marked, lasted till the end of 1924, although bond prices continued to rise and long rates to fall without much interruption until 1927.

The years 1925 and 1926 seem to have formed a period of considerable stability. During this time the indices for the volume and number of new issues fluctuated within a narrow range, somewhat below their previous highs. The index for "net" offerings was the least stable and in the third quarter of

---

[18] The indices for total and for "net" offerings reached their high points in the first quarter of 1922; the index for new capital reached its high point in the second quarter of that year.

[19] Prices of first grade bonds had begun to improve somewhat earlier.

1926 dropped to a very low level. The stability of these years is most apparent when they are compared with the immediately preceding and succeeding periods.

The year 1927 was the apex of this eleven-year movement in the bond market. In this year bond prices reached the highest levels that they attained during the period; the volume of new issues was enormous; their number was very large, and the index of trading rose to one of the four peaks which it achieved during this time. The indices of the volumes of total and of new capital offerings remained at very high levels throughout the full twelve months, and although the index of "net" offerings dropped sharply in the third and fourth quarters, the total demand for new funds, which it represents, was greater in this year than in any other considered. The boom in stocks, which culminated in 1929, had, of course, already begun, and a general buoyancy marked all the security markets. After 1927, as the increase in stock prices and speculation became the dominant feature of the capital markets, a general recession in the bond market set in.

This decline did not affect all the indices of the bond market simultaneously. The index of total offerings, for instance, remained at a high level throughout the first half of 1928, whereas the index of "net" issues fell before the end of 1927. Nor was the recession steady and continuous; it was interrupted in 1930, when all the indices of the bond market rallied strongly. Nevertheless, subsequent to 1927 the chief feature of the bond market was the decline in prices, activity, and new offerings; and in spite of the objections that may be found to treating this interval as a unit, this consideration seems to justify grouping these years together. By the end of 1930 all the indices used to describe the condition of the market were far below their 1927 levels, save only that of first grade bonds, and that index was falling rapidly.

CHAPTER IV

1919

AT THE beginning of 1919 the United States faced a variety of problems, political and economic, domestic and international. In part inherited from the war, in part concurrent with the return of peace, these problems were closely interrelated, especially in their financial aspects, and constituted an extremely complex whole. Moreover, since the difficulties and questions confronting the country were not then, perhaps are not even now entirely evident, their solutions seemed all the more remote. Little was certain at the time, nothing obvious, save the very complexity of the situation, and the fact that the United States was to play a new and most important part in the impending realignment of the economic forces of the world. As the then Secretary of the Treasury said, it was essentially a period of "readjustment." Such a period must always seem confused to those who have to face its problems, yet as we look back on the early post-war years, the structural lines, the prominent features of the situation stand out.

Traceable directly to the war, and touching every field of finance, was the inflation that permeated the monetary and banking structure of the country in January 1919. Closely related to the expanded financial situation was the condition of industry. Business, like finance, was on a war basis, and a return to a peace footing as quickly as possible was imperative. Nor was this necessity for "demobilization" confined to finance and industry. The men in the army and many members of the innumerable civil organizations that had sprung up during the war were intent on getting home, and, if possible, back to their old jobs. The government, though desirous of furthering such movements, and of restoring more stable conditions in the country, found its most immediate task the funding of the floating debt, which had grown alarmingly since the Armistice.

This in itself raised still another problem, in that the necessity for a further government loan implied the retention, at least in part, of the already irksome restrictions placed upon the security markets during the war. Such, then, were some of the more pressing issues raised by the cessation of hostilities.

In a sense offsetting these problems, and tending to make their solution easier, were other factors, which, though they raised further questions on their own account, none the less facilitated a return to what President Harding was to call "normalcy." During the war the United States had accumulated a far greater part of the world's gold supply than she ever had before, and this increase in her holdings had broadened the base of her credit structure and made its inflation less top-heavy than it would otherwise have been. Moreover, the Federal Reserve System, though its operations had been greatly extended, found itself at the end of the war in a position probably stronger than that of any other central bank, with a reserve ratio of about 50 per cent. In the succeeding months it was able to maintain this ratio and to avoid a policy either of inflation or of deflation. In addition to these favorable elements, the business recession that had followed the Armistice was already yielding in the spring of 1919 to the spectacular increase in industrial activity that culminated in 1920.

The United States possessed a further advantage. Among the leading combatants she had been furthest removed from the scene of hostilities, she had participated in them the shortest time, and consequently had suffered a relatively smaller dislocation of her productive, distributive, and financial mechanisms. Nevertheless, the war had altered her financial situation in one fundamental respect. The traditional position of the United States as a debtor country had been completely reversed, and she had been transformed into a creditor nation on an unprecedented scale.

Although these various circumstances facilitated in many ways the return of the United States to a peace footing, they raised new problems, both for the immediate and for the more distant future. Immediately, Europe had a pressing need of food, supplies, and capital of all kinds, which could only be supplied by the United States during the interval necessary for the European economic mechanism to return to its normal functions. Such requirements found expression in the great and steady increase in American exports during 1919. From a longer point of view, it seemed likely that the United States would henceforth be required to supply not only all of her own capital needs but a large part of the needs of the rest of the world as well.

The financial world in January 1919 was dominated by the consideration that although the war was over, the war financing was not; and that until this had been completed, the claims of peace financing could hardly be allowed. On December 20, 1918, almost as soon as he came into office, Secretary Glass had issued a proclamation designed to hold the War Loan Organization together till the last war loan was floated. Throughout the spring of 1919, and in fact until November of that year, the policy of the Federal Reserve System was carefully molded to fit the needs of the Treasury. An incipient speculative movement, however, was already under way. The forces which, in Governor Strong's terms, made for "business as usual" were becoming restive under the restrictions which had been imposed on the financial world by the exigencies of the war. Pressure from these forces, a feeling that the usefulness of many such restraints had passed, tended toward their removal.

The result was the disappearance of those special bodies of control that the war had imposed on the financial mechanism. On December 31, 1918, the Capital Issues Committee suspended active operations, and on August 30, 1919, it was formally dissolved by the President. The War Finance Corporation, though it continued operations on its old commitments, suffered a thorough reorganization of its personnel after the Armistice, and it was currently supposed that its last large financial operation was the flotation of 200 millions of bonds in March to aid the railroads. On January 24, 1919, the Money Committee of the Stock Exchange, yielding to speculative influences, formally ended its activities, and the confining influence it had exercised on the security markets since the preceding August was thereby removed, despite the desire of the Treasury and of the committee itself that it should continue in operation till the war financing of the government was completed. By June 1 the war-time restrictions of foreign exchange transactions had practically all been removed, and after June 25 the government ceased to require statistical reports of the exchange traders. In spite of such relaxation of war regulations, however, the prospect of a further great government bond issue, the necessity that the operation be successful, substantially controlled the bond market, the activity of the Federal Reserve System, and the policy of the Treasury in the spring of 1919.

The financial world had known since the Armistice that a further government loan would be necessary. On November 27, 1918, Secretary McAdoo had addressed to the banks and trust companies of the country one of those open letters which the Treasury had used during the war to make known its financial needs and plans. In this letter he pointed out that, although the surplus of the Fourth Liberty Loan was practically exhausted, nevertheless the extraordinary expenses of the government would continue and might even increase in the next few months. He indicated, moreover, that the Treasury did not feel it was desirable to borrow further against tax receipts while in doubt as to what tax legislation Congress would pass; nor did the Treasury wish to institute a system for the continuous sale of government bonds. Consequently he announced that the government planned a final bond issue, to be sold by popular campaign, in the spring of 1919. In the meantime, he explained, loan certificates would be issued at fortnightly intervals against the proceeds of this loan. This policy was put into effect at once. The first of these issues was dated December 5, 1918, and thereafter they were offered every other Thursday till the end of April.

The expenditure of the government continued through December and January at the rate of almost two billions a month, and on January 31 there were outstanding nearly five billions of Treasury certificates, of which over three-fifths had been issued in anticipation of the forthcoming government loan. The amount was so great that there was doubt whether it could be raised by ordinary processes, and current financial opinion split sharply on the question as to whether this loan could be sold in the manner of previous issues, by an appeal to patriotism and a popular campaign, or whether changed conditions required that it be a "business proposition." The Treasury adhered to the former view, that a final "Victory Loan" could be successfully sold. But the Treasury officials also believed that in order to give the country as much time as possible to recover from the effects of the Fourth Liberty Loan, to permit the continuance of the year's "progress of readjustments to the utmost limit," and to prepare the ground as thoroughly as possible for this loan floated under the new conditions of peace, it was essential that its offering be postponed as long as possible, probably till some time after March 4, when Congress had adjourned.

For the Treasury to issue this Victory Loan at some indefinite time in the future when Congress was not in session, it was necessary for Congress to grant the Treasury greater power over the terms of the loan that it had given in connection with the others. To secure such wider discretion Secretary Glass began consultations with the House Committee of Ways and Means and with the Finance Committee of the Senate in January. On March 3 Congress passed the Victory Loan Act. If the Act did not give Secretary Glass quite the latitude that he had asked for, at least it expanded to a maximum of seven billions the limit to which government loans might be issued, it strengthened the market for government bonds by new tax exemptions for outstanding issues, and gave the Treasury power to determine the coupon rate of the issue, its terms, and, within wide limits, its maturity date and exemption provisions.

In consequence of this action, on March 12 the Treasury announced that the Victory Loan would be sold in the period April 21 to May 10, by means of a campaign similar to those of previous issues. On April 14 the total amount of the loan, four and one-half billions, was made public, together with the terms of the issue, and a promise was given that this should be the final government war loan. With the aid of the old War Loan Organization the issue was over-subscribed 16.6 per cent, and eventually bonds to the amount of $4,927,177,650 were issued in adjustment of allotments.

The successful flotation of the Victory Loan ended the government's direct demands on the bond market, though the accommodation it continued to require of the banking system lasted till the end of the year and influenced the market indirectly even longer. For the government, in spite of the Victory Loan, still had a considerable amount of unfunded Treasury certificates outstanding, and to refinance these at maturity the aid of the banking system was essential. Nevertheless, the Treasury's position after the flotation of the Victory Loan was greatly improved.

On July 25 Secretary Glass was able to address a very optimistic letter to the banks and trust companies in which he stated that the Treasury's expenditures, unless unforeseen contingencies arose, would not exceed its revenues during the year by more than the 1,032 millions of unpaid installments on the Victory Loan, and that consequently the government would be able to fulfill its promise that there would be no more government loans. He added, however, that the expenses of the government would be so heavy during the next few months that the Treasury would be forced to resume the fortnightly issues of loan certificates, which it had discontinued since the Victory Loan, and also that the Treasury would continue the issues of tax-anticipation certificates. The banks were asked to stand ready to take each month these new issues in amounts approximately equal to 1.6 per cent of their total resources. But this request contrasted favorably with that made eight months earlier by Secretary McAdoo for subscriptions of 5 per cent, and Secretary Glass even held out the hope that by the end of the year the monthly quotas might drop to 0.8 per cent.

Pursuant to this plan, loan certificates were offered on August 1 and 15, which, by August 31, increased the government debt to $26,596,701,648.01, the highest point it reached till 1934. In spite of this great drain on the country's financial resources, the applications for these two issues were so large that the banks were not asked to take any specific allotments in the offering made September 2. Thereafter, the improvement in the Treasury's condition continued so rapidly and the receipts from the issues of tax certificates continued so large that only one more issue of loan certificates, on December 1, was required during the year. Secretary Glass, writing his report in November, looked forward confidently to the complete retirement of this floating debt after the turn of the year, when he expected that the government would be able to finance itself, with the aid of tax certificates, entirely out of current receipts; and for a few months in the early part of 1920 the Treasury actually did find itself in this comfortable position.

The conclusion of the Victory Loan campaign, however, signified to all elements in the business and financial world, both to those which for want of a better term are called "normal" and to the speculative interests, that the government's war financing was over, and that henceforth they were free to follow their own inclinations and operate in the security markets and elsewhere unhampered. The results of this belief were not long delayed. The stock market celebrated the end of the Victory Loan campaign with the "biggest week," according to contemporary comment, that it had had since 1901, and advanced four points in May and five more in June and July.[1] The incipient increase of business activity of January and February had become a boom by midsummer; and in spite of the tendency of time money to mount, a tendency shared by other rates after September, stocks, business activity, prices, all swirled upward in "a year of speculation such as New York had never seen," in a veritable "competition of buyers."

This speculative rise of prices, however, did not extend to the bond market. Aside from a brief rally in May and June, bond prices declined continuously during the year. In December the yield on Moody's Aaa bonds was 5.73 per cent, as contrasted

---

[1] The index of stock prices used in this study, except when otherwise indicated, is the general stock market average of the Standard Statistics Company, given in Appendix N.

with 5.35 in January, and on Baa bonds, 7.77 as contrasted with
7.12. This steady fall of bond prices can not be wholly explained
by the rise in short rates, since, till October, time money alone
showed a tendency to mount. Nor can the operations of the
Federal Reserve and the Treasury in connection with the Victory Loan be held entirely responsible. If their operations were
designed to restrain the speculative elements, they were also designed to keep the bond market firm. Probably the principal
cause of this decline was the heavy demands put upon the
market for new capital. Not only was it required to absorb the
Victory Loan, but it also had to accommodate the large volume
of capital requirements which, suppressed during the war, had
inundated the market after the Armistice.

These new issues were brought out in progressively greater
volume throughout the year. From a total of about 700 millions
in the first quarter, the volume, excluding the Victory Loan,
jumped to almost a billion in the second quarter, largely on
account of a 200 million dollar issue of the War Finance Corporation. From that figure offerings mounted to approximately
1,300 and 1,400 millions in the third and fourth quarters respectively, foreign issues forming a substantial part of this increase.
Total offerings for the year, omitting the Victory Loan of almost
five billions, were almost four and one-half billions; including
the Victory Loan, total offerings reached a level not touched
again till 1927, when new issues slightly exceeded ten and one-
half billions.

This flood of flotations was accompanied by extraordinary
activity in the market. The magnitude of the turnover, commented on again and again in contemporary surveys, is roughly
indicated by the 3,770 millions of bonds traded on the New York
Stock Exchange in 1919, a figure almost double that of 1918,
and about six times the average of the period 1910 through
1914. The quantity of new issues and the revival of business
and speculation were important factors in this activity, but they
did not form the whole of it. The large turnover was in part
attributable also to the great redistribution of bonds that took
place at this time. Liberty Bonds had been sold under tremen-

dous pressure, principally to and through banks, and they had
to find permanent holders. Both government securities owned
by member banks and loans on such securities increased substantially throughout the spring, until the Victory campaign had
been completed. Thereafter these holdings and loans declined
rapidly, so that by the end of the year there had been a net decrease in government bonds held by member banks of about 435
millions, and in loans on government securities of about 200
millions.[2] Further, as American exports grew and means of
payment were sought by foreign countries, a very large volume
of American securities returned to this country from abroad.

The exports of the United States in 1919, it was estimated,
exceeded imports by something more than 4,000 million dollars,[3] although this credit balance was offset in part by other
items. Nevertheless, some 1,082 millions[4] were, apparently,
added to the balance owed the United States on its international
transactions, increasing the visible deficit to almost two and
one-half billions.[5] This surplus of exports was largely financed
by government credits of various kinds, and by the extension
of extraordinary facilities to exporters by the banking system.
Such a situation inevitably affected the bond market; directly,
through its tightening effect on money rates and the stimulus it
gave to the repatriation of American securities; indirectly,
through the future flotations of foreign bonds it implied, flotations which actually began on a small scale in the latter part of
the year.

Intimately connected with these financial developments was
the banking situation, which continued in its extended condition throughout the year.[6] The discounts of reporting member

[2] *Annual Report of the Federal Reserve Board,* 1919, p. 17.

[3] *Annual Report of the Secretary of the Treasury,* 1920, p. 75.

[4] *The Balance of International Payments of the United States in 1922* (Trade
Information Bulletin 144), pp. 20–21.

[5] *Annual Report of the Federal Reserve Board,* 1919, pp. 24–25. See also the
Annalist, XV, 115 (Jan. 19, 1920).

[6] It has been suggested that by January 1919 member banks were in a position to reduce substantially their borrowings from the Federal Reserve, but
failed to do so because of psychological factors holding over from the war
(W. W. Riefler, *Money Rates and Money Markets in the United States,* 1930,
Chap. VIII).

banks grew steadily month by month, from 1,731 millions in January to 2,115 millions in December. At the same time, the total earning assets of the Federal Reserve banks increased from 2,359 millions to 3,203, although their holdings of war paper declined both relatively and absolutely. The Federal Reserve System, moreover, as Governor Strong later testified in 1921, did not feel at liberty to take steps, other than "direct action," to contract credit till November, when the government's floating debt had been largely accommodated.[7] Before this time the money market had to be so regulated that the member banks, the principal media for the distribution of the Treasury certificates, did not take losses on their transactions, and the only rate changes possible were those necessary to make the rates for short time collateral loans secured by government obligations equivalent to the rates of the certificates themselves.

The volume of the bond market in 1919, its activity, and the difficulties it overcame, all give striking evidence of the transformation it had undergone since 1914. However, the greatest single change which the war brought was the increase in the number of actual and potential bond holders. Previous to the war, bonds were purchased almost exclusively by financial institutions and wealthy individuals; it was estimated in 1919 that not more than 300,000 persons owned bonds in 1914.[8] The Liberty Loan campaigns, which were directed at all classes in society and which were designed to appeal to the small saver, radically changed this situation. Liberty Bonds were issued in small denominations and were sold in small as well as in large blocks. Hundreds of thousands of persons who had never before bought securities purchased Liberty Bonds, and consequently were taught to buy investments. The development of this new outlet for bonds greatly increased the absorptive capacity of the American investment market; and the small saver, appealed to as a war measure, remained in the market after the return of peace. In 1919, for instance, it was estimated that the average purchase of the bond issues then being

---

[7] Benjamin Strong, *Interpretations of Federal Reserve Policy* (1930), pp. 129–134.   [8] *Annalist*, XIV, 327 (Sept. 15, 1919).

brought out was about $2,500, a figure much smaller than the typical purchase prior to the war.[9]

The advent of the small buyer in the security markets was of the greatest social and financial importance. The necessity, in the post-war period, that the United States finance not only her own capital needs but also a considerable part of the needs of the rest of the world made the discovery of new markets for investments imperative, and in part such markets were furnished by the new classes of bond buyers developed by the Liberty Loan campaigns. Moreover, the need for new markets was further augmented by the high income taxes, especially the super-tax, which the war brought. These taxes greatly altered the position of the old class of bond buyers, many of whom found they could no longer afford to purchase any securities except tax-exempt bonds or stocks of high yields. Thus the new types of buyers greatly affected the distribution of securities, and much of the change that took place during the twenties in the methods of issuing and merchandising securities can be attributed to their presence in the bond market. The interest of the new investors was not, however, confined to the bond market; it was presently attracted to the stock market as well, and the purchasing of stocks on a large scale by the general public was an important element in the boom that developed in the late twenties.

In addition to such sweeping alterations as the increase in volume, number, and purchasers of securities, the market of 1919 developed certain characteristics which distinguished it from the markets of the next decade. The total of offerings for each quarter of the year was greater than that for the preceding quarter — if the Victory Loan of the second quarter is disregarded — and no trace of the usual seasonal fluctuation of new issues, with the decline in the third quarter, can be observed. Moreover, it would appear that the amount of stocks offered in the market exceeded that of long term, new capital, corporate bonds offered in the second, third, and fourth quarters of 1919. This is not the usual relationship, and it occurred

[9] *National City Bank of New York Monthly Letter,* August 1919.

in only twenty quarterly periods from 1908 through 1930.[10]
Further, the relationships between short and long term rates
which Persons found to have existed from 1897 through 1925,
the period of his study, practically disappeared in 1918 and
1919.[11]

It is apparent, then, that the cataclysm of the war profoundly
altered every field of financial activity, the bond market not
least, and that many of the changes which then took place were
of a permanent character. However, the problems and difficulties of the return to peace, and the transitional character of
the period that directly followed the Armistice, are amply evidenced by those peculiarities which distinguished the bond
market of 1919 from those of the succeeding ten years. A
wider, a more complex array of stimuli affected it than affected
the markets of the twenties, and brought results more difficult
of analysis. It was dominated throughout the first half year by
the Victory Loan and influenced till November by the short
term credit requirements of the government. It was subject at
all times to reactions from the extended banking situation and
was under the necessity not only of completing and adjusting
the war financing of the government but also of accommodating
a considerable volume of new capital needs both at home and
abroad. Under such conditions, and disturbed by the uncertain
foreign situation and the constantly mounting uncovered balance of American exports, the bond market did not participate

[10] P. T. Ellsworth, "Some Aspects of Investment in the United States, 1907–
1930" (unpublished), pp. 102–103. Ellsworth's computation of bond offerings
includes only long term, new capital, corporate issues. In my computations,
which include issues other than corporate, as well as short term corporate
financing, and which classify refunding issues separately, stock issues did not
exceed bond issues except in the final quarter of 1928 and the first three quarters of 1929.

[11] Persons and Frickey found that in the period 1897 through 1925 changes
of 1 per cent in their adjusted index of short rates indicated, more often than
did changes of any other per cent, that bond prices were at, or near, a temporary high or low, and were presently to change the direction of their movement. This relationship between movements of short and long rates appears
to have been very close in the period before the war and in 1917, and fairly
close in the period 1921–1923, but seems practically to have disappeared in
1918 and 1919 (W. M. Persons and Edwin Frickey, "Money Rates and Security
Prices," *Review of Economic Statistics*, VIII, 29–46, January 1926).

in the feverish upswing of stocks and prices and business activity that marked 1919.

Nevertheless, during the year the United States made considerable progress toward financial rehabilitation. By December 1919 the government's war financing had finally been completed; most of the war restrictions on financial agencies and markets had been lifted; the more pressing financial needs, aside from European requirements, had been satisfied; and although the country was facing one of the sharpest deflations in history, it was free to consider the problem of how to conduct itself in its new role of a creditor nation and custodian of a third of the gold resources of the war-stricken world.

CHAPTER V

1920–1922

THE first phase of the post-war bond market has been considered as extending from January 1920 to the middle of 1922. The tremendous drop in the volume of new issues in the first quarter of 1920, from the levels of 1919, marked its beginning. The persistent tendency of new offerings to increase after this fall, their growth from the small volume of the beginning of 1920 to the large volume of 1922, give to this period a definite unity and constitute the principal characteristic of the market at this time. Although the volume of new issues continued large till well into 1923, the volume would have declined after the middle of 1922 if the Treasury had not then issued very considerable quantities of securities.

During this period the financial world was shaken, in 1920 and 1921, by one of the sharpest recessions in business activity and commodity prices that it had ever known; but by 1922 the corner had been turned, and prices and industrial activity were increasing. This recession had substantial repercussions upon the Federal Reserve System, which was faced for the first time with the problem of formulating suitable policies for times of peace. To this problem, of course, were added all the difficulties of the post-war reconstruction. The repercussions also extended to the member banks, and the amount of credit [1] which the member banks and which the Federal Reserve Banks extended varied greatly from year to year, both in quantity and in the proportions invested in different types of assets. The position of the banking system was further complicated by the enormous uncovered balance of American exports which existed when the war ended and which was increased still more in 1920, although it was reduced in 1921 and 1922 by gold im-

[1] In this study the term "credit" signifies in the case of both member banks and Federal Reserve Banks asset items, unless otherwise specified.

Chart IX

INDICES OF BUSINESS ACTIVITY AND WHOLESALE COMMODITY PRICES, 1919–1930,
BY MONTHS

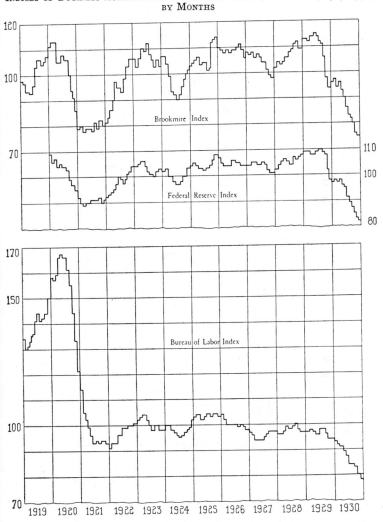

Federal Reserve Bank of New York Volume of Trade Index, I — Third Revision
of Sept. 28, 1931.
Business Index of the Brookmire Economic Service, Revised as of November 1930.
United States Bureau of Labor Revised Wholesale Commodity Price Index,
Relative 1926 = 100.

ports and the flotation of foreign dollar bonds. The needs of the Treasury also were a matter of considerable moment, both for the banking system and for the capital markets, for it was imperative that the very large floating debt which had accumulated during the war be reduced and refunded as rapidly as possible.

Of these various factors, the business recession, particularly as it affected the banking and credit situation, had the greatest import for the bond market. The depression and the subsequent recovery dominated the whole commercial and financial world, and some attention must be paid it before its effect upon the banks and the bond market can be considered.

The revival of business activity, which began after the Armistice and continued through 1919, carried past the turn of the year, and speculation reached its high mark in the first half of 1920. It is difficult to fix the exact point when the recession set in, for the decline began at different times in particular lines of activity. Different business indices [2] indicate various months as turning points within the limits of January and July,[3] and wholesale prices did not decline until June.[4] In any case, once the recession began it was precipitous, and continued uninterruptedly into 1921. The low levels reached by commodity prices and business activity in the first six months of that year, however, marked approximately the limit of the decline. After fluctuating in that range during the fall the indices slowly started to advance at the end of the year.[5]

The effect which the depression had upon the credit situation and upon the movement of interest rates is involved, partly because of the tremendous deflation which it brought in the earlier portion of these years, principally because the read-

---

[2] Chart IX, p. 57.

[3] Mitchell placed the high point in January (W. C. Mitchell, "A Review," Chap. XII in *Recent Economic Changes*, 1929, p. 892). Governor Strong testified that the reaction first developed in the Japanese silk market in March and April (Strong, *Interpretations*, pp. 68–77).

[4] Chart IX, p. 57.

[5] The Harvard Economic Society business index and the United States Bureau of Labor commodity price index did not reach the bottom of their declines till January 1922.

justments required by the new, post-war world were still continuing, and because, as one eminent commentator has remarked, "Federal Reserve policy prior to 1921 had to be conceived with large regard for Treasury requirements."[6] The depression itself is to be distinguished from the pre-war de-

CHART X

SHORT TERM INTEREST RATES, 1919–1930, BY MONTHS, IN PER CENT

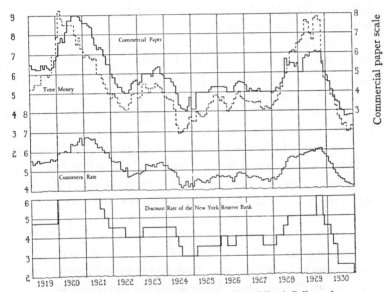

Average Daily Rates for Time Money, 90 Day, Mixed Collateral.
Average Daily Rates for Prime 90 Day Commercial Paper.
Weighted Average of Rates Charged Customers by Banks in New York City.
Discount Rate of the Federal Reserve Bank of New York.

pressions principally by the presence of a more flexible banking system in this country and by the fact that the United States was now a creditor instead of a debtor nation.

As the year 1920 began, the rates for time money, commercial paper, and the "customers' rate"[7] were advancing,[8] and on January 23 the Federal Reserve Bank of New York jumped its rate on 60–90 day commercial, agricultural, and

[6] H. L. Reed, *Federal Reserve Policy, 1921–1930* (1930), p. 2.
[7] The "customers' rate" is the "Weighted Average of Rates Charged Customers by Banks in New York" (Appendix I).
[8] Chart X.

live-stock paper to 6 per cent.[9] These rising rates reflected the tight credit conditions that were caused, as the business boom reached its climax, by the large and continued demands of industry for accommodation and the growing volume of money in circulation. Commercial loans of reporting member banks in leading cities [10] increased steadily during 1920, till a peak was reached of about 9,700 millions in October; money in circulation also persistently increased and reached its peak of 5,698 millions in the same month.

These factors, together with the gold exports of the first eight months of the year — which lowered the stock of money gold from 2,930 millions in January to 2,868 millions in October — forced up the member banks' rediscounts at the Federal Reserve, although these were already very large. Bills discounted increased, in spite of the attempt of member banks to obtain cash and restrict their borrowings through very considerable liquidation of security loans and portfolios, from 2,136 millions in January 1920, when they were 66 per cent of total Reserve credit, to 2,780 millions in October, when they were 79 per cent. This pressure for rediscounts slowly forced up total Federal Reserve credit outstanding to a peak of 3,522 millions in October, in spite of a drop of some 267 millions in bills bought in the open market.[11] Under such circumstances interest rates naturally continued to climb till the end of the year.[12]

But in November 1920 conditions changed, for the member

[9] The rate for 60–90 day commercial, agricultural, and live-stock paper has been used till July 21, 1921, and thereafter the discount rate for "all types of paper." It was not till the beginning of 1921 that a single rate for all types of discounted paper was established.

[10] Statistics of reporting member banks in leading cities have been used in this study as indicative of the situation of commercial banks as a whole. However, for the sake of brevity, reporting member banks in leading cities have generally been referred to as "member banks" or "reporting member banks," and these terms indicate this specific classification, except when it is otherwise stated.

[11] Chart XI, p. 60.

[12] Time money started to fall in March 1920 and continued its decline throughout the year. Little significance, however, can be attached to this movement, for it was above 6 per cent throughout the year, and hence affected with a scarcity value and, as was noted at the time, was practically unobtainable (*Annalist*, XVII, 70, January 3, 1921).

banks and for the Federal Reserve Banks. Gold imports, which had begun in September, now became of significant volume. Money in circulation started to fall, as did commercial loans of member banks. Total Federal Reserve credit outstanding also began to decrease as the demand for rediscounting slackened, and the easier credit conditions were reflected the next month by a recession of short term rates.

This relaxation of credit conditions and decline in short rates continued, almost without interruption, till the middle of 1922. Gold flowed steadily into the country, and between October 1920 and July 1922 the stock of money gold was increased 961 millions. Money in circulation declined 1,274 millions in the same period, and the funds placed at the disposal of the banks from these two sources amounted to 2,235 millions. Under these circumstances rediscounts and total Reserve credit outstanding declined steadily in 1921, though rediscounts continued to account for about 75 per cent of total Reserve credit; and after the customers' rate turned down in March, all short term rates fell rapidly, time money rates dropping below the yield of Moody's Aaa bonds in September, as did commercial paper rates in November. The situation was further relaxed by the Federal Reserve purchases of nearly 400 millions of government securities in the first five months of 1922, which permitted rediscounts to drop to 425 millions in July, when they were only about 35 per cent of total Reserve credit outstanding. The 2,355 million decline in rediscounts since October 1920 was almost exactly balanced by the 2,574 millions of funds placed in the hands of member banks by gold imports, the decline in money in circulation, and the Federal Reserve purchases of governments. This twenty-month fall in interest rates and reduction in Federal Reserve and member-bank credit was finally checked in the autumn of 1922, as reviving business and increasing seasonal needs for accommodation engendered larger credit requirements.

The rise of short term interest rates in 1919 had been accompanied by a decline in bond prices. As the business recession developed in 1920 the fall was accelerated, and bond prices dropped sharply in the first six months of the year. In the second week of February Liberty 4½'s broke 90 for the first time,[13] carrying the whole list down with them, and in April the New York Central and Pennsylvania railroads were forced to do their financing on a 7 per cent basis. Further advances of Federal Reserve rates in May tightened credit conditions still more, and in June, when new Treasury certificates had to be brought out with 5¾ and 6 per cent rates, Libertys again broke sharply. The Belgian government was forced to borrow on a 7.95 basis, and the yield of Moody's Aaa bonds went to 6.38 per cent, the highest point reached in the period covered by this study. In July, although the yield of Moody's Baa bonds made a new high of 8.52 per cent, the general fall in the market was checked, and, encouraged by a number of Federal Reserve rate reductions and the repayment in October of the half-billion dollar Anglo-French war loan, the market rallied till November. It was during this rally that the greater part of the "8 per cent foreign bonds of 1920" were floated.

During 1920 the pressure which industry put upon the banks for accommodation and the general uncertainty of the times occasioned a fall of over 600 millions in banks' security loans and a decline of about the same amount in their investments. This liquidation was partially offset by the acquisition by savings banks of some 250 millions of bonds. But purchases of bonds by life insurance companies were small in this year, the Federal Reserve holdings of governments remained stable, and the sales of bonds by commercial banks — in excess of the bonds purchased by savings banks — placed over 360 millions of bonds in the market for the general public — as distinct from financial institutions — to absorb, in addition to the new offerings of that year. Such selling tended, of course, to weaken the market considerably and, together with the rise in short

---

[13] It is sometimes claimed that the decline of government bonds in 1920 was caused by the efforts of the Federal Reserve System at that time to force such securities out of the hands of member banks and into the hands of private investors. Inasmuch as practically all of the factors significant in the bond market were currently conducive to a decline in the prices of all types of bonds — which took place — such efforts can at most be considered only as a contributory factor in the fall of governments.

term interest rates, explains the declining bond prices of 1920.

This weak market, however, was one of great activity, and, in spite of its declining prices, one in which the volume of new issues grew almost steadily. The large quantity of bonds traded was commented on again and again in contemporary surveys; [14] the volume of bonds sold on the New York Stock Exchange in 1920 — 3,955 millions — was the largest on record; [15] and the December sales — 562 millions — were the largest in any month covered by this study. Probably much of this activity was a result of the inducement which the business decline and credit stringency gave to bond holders, especially banks, to turn their securities into cash.

Although the tight credit conditions and rising interest rates of 1920 brought, at the start of the year, a tremendous decrease in the volume of new issues — total issues fell from 1,406 millions in the last quarter of 1919 to 687 millions in the first quarter of 1920 — thereafter total, new capital, and "net" issues all advanced till the latter part of 1922. The advance was subject to fluctuation, particularly in the case of "net" issues, which became a negative amount in the third quarter of 1920; but the upward trend is more strongly marked in the seasonally adjusted curves than in the curves of the actual figures, and appears to be a well-defined movement. Municipal and foreign bonds led this increase.[16] Corporate issues did not participate in it extensively; long term corporate issues did increase considerably in these years, but short term corporate

[14] The principal sources of contemporary comment on the market used are the columns of bond news and the annual "Survey of the Year in the Financial District" in the *Annalist*, scattered surveys of the bond market in the *Commercial and Financial Chronicle*, and the monthly letters of the National City Bank. [15] *Annalist*, XXI, 93 (Jan. 8, 1923).

[16] The issue of foreign bonds in this country had been unknown before 1914, and their amounts had been limited during the war, but in 1919 they were sold in substantial quantities. Their issue was given encouragement by a statement of the Treasury, published on January 24, 1920. This statement pointed out that the war-time restrictions on bond issues had been lifted, that the United States had a large unfunded credit balance on international account, and admittted that, although the Treasury had not wished foreign loans to compete with its own financing during the war, such was no longer the case. "Latterly, the attitude of the Treasury has been favorable to the issue, under proper safeguards, in our markets of sound investment securities of foreign Governments . . . and it may be assumed that the Treasury does not object

issues — which amounted to almost half of all such issues in
the first six months of 1920 — decreased sharply. Refunding
issues, excluding government issues, also showed a strong tendency to grow, notwithstanding the high interest rates. Such
issues amounted to 339 millions in 1920, and increased to 617
millions in 1921 and to 881 millions in 1922.

The advance in bond prices in the third quarter of 1920 was
short-lived. Fundamental business conditions had not yet improved, commodity prices continued to fall, short term interest
rates were still high, the member banks were steadily with-
drawing support from the market as they liquidated their security loans and investments, the stock market went off sharply
as the presidential election exerted its customary unsettling
effect, and the rally could not be sustained. The decline in
November and December carried bond prices back to the
levels of the early part of the year, and they remained, with
little fluctuation, in that range till July 1921.

But in the middle of 1921 the situation changed. By the summer of that year the deflation, in most fields of financial activity,
was at, or near, the end. Credit conditions were substantially
easier than they had been six months earlier, and indices of
business activity and of commodity prices had checked their
decline. In July time money came down to 6 and commercial
paper to 6.25 per cent, approximately the yield of first grade
bonds and well below the yield of second grades. The Federal
Reserve Bank of New York dropped its discount rate from 6

---

to such issues" (*Annual Report of the Secretary of the Treasury*, 1920, pp. 79–
80).

    This pronouncement was the first public, official recognition of the change
which the war had brought in the relations of American and European capital
markets, and doubtless it stimulated to some extent the flotation of foreign
securities in New York. The sale of foreign securities in New York was, of
course, a new development in American finance, and possessed implications
which were to extend very far. It demonstrated that the war, in addition to
transforming the United States from a debtor to a creditor nation, had made
New York an international capital market, and that henceforth world events
were to be of great concern to it and its transactions of great importance to
the world. Directly and immediately, the flotation of foreign securities was
chiefly significant in that they afforded a means of reducing the uncovered
American export balance and of funding the short term international loans
which the commercial banks were carrying.

to 5½ per cent, and in the next month the Reserve Banks began their usual autumn purchases of acceptances. At the same time there began a slow advance in the security loans and investments of reporting member banks, as the banks sought employment for the funds released by the deflation and by the reduction in the uncovered balance of American exports.[17] Influenced by these factors the bond market turned up in July and was followed by the stock market in September. The advance continued, supported by increasing security loans and investments of the member banks,[18] and, in November, by Federal Reserve purchases of governments in the open market. By December foreign governments could do their financing on a 6½–7 per cent basis, as compared with 8 per cent some nine or ten months earlier, and first grade rails on a 6 as compared with a 7 per cent basis.

The Federal Reserve System continued in the first half of 1922 the policy of open market purchases which it had inaugurated in the fall of 1921, and its holdings grew from 226 millions in December 1921 to 603 millions in May 1922. Although the Federal Reserve portfolio of governments decreased during the rest of the year, this reduction of credit extended to the market was in good part offset by the System's purchases of bills, which grew from 93 millions in April to 259 millions in December. Accompanying these Federal Reserve purchases of acceptances was a considerable increase in the security loans and investments of member banks and a rapid fall in short

[17] The banks carried a substantial portion of the large uncovered credit balance with which the United States ended the war. It was estimated (*Annual Report of the Federal Reserve Board,* 1919, pp. 24–25; *Annalist,* XV, 115, Jan. 19, 1920) that at the end of 1919 this balance amounted to about two and one-half billion dollars. In 1920 the balance was apparently increased another billion (*The Balance of International Payments of the United States in 1922,* Trade Information Bulletin 144, pp. 20–21). In 1921 and 1922, however, gold was imported on a very large scale, considerable quantities of foreign bonds were floated, the net merchandise export balance declined, and there was a net debit balance of approximately 814 millions. Presumably this fund was largely used to reduce the credit balance and contributed to the banking funds seeking investment in the latter part of 1921 and in 1922.

[18] These purchases by commercial banks enabled commercial and savings banks together to show a very slight increase in their security portfolios during the year, in spite of bond sales by savings banks of 84 millions.

term interest rates. Between December 1921 and June 1922 member-bank security loans grew from 3,770 millions to 3,910 millions, and in the same period their investments increased from 3,420 millions to 4,220; although their investments continued to grow during the remainder of the year, it was at a less rapid rate. Short term interest rates, which had all been 5 per cent or above in December 1921, dropped below the yield of first grade bonds with the turn of the year, and by June were close to 4 per cent. This easiness of credit conditions is, in good part, to be attributed to the Federal Reserve open-market purchases, and to the further decrease in the uncovered American export balance that took place in this year.

Stimulated by such developments, bond prices rose with hardly a check till September 1922. This advance was accompanied by a very great and rapid increase in the activity of the market and by a steady rise in the volume of new issues. The twelve-month moving-average of bond trading touched the highest point reached during the period of this study in March 1922, and, although it declined abruptly thereafter, bond prices advanced rapidly, and the volume of new issues increased to the highest level since 1919. Although the indices of both total and "net" offerings, after reaching the peak of their advance in the first quarter of 1922, remained at high levels well into 1923, it seems apparent that without the support of the large quantities of government bonds floated in the last half of 1922 and 1923 [19] the indices would have declined in the last half of 1922, as did the index of new capital issues.[20] Since government issues are of a nature somewhat different from that of other types of issues,[21] and since various factors affecting the bond market also changed in the middle of 1922, it has seemed more accurate to consider that the first phase of these eleven years ended at this time rather than at some later date.

[19] Chart XII, p. 67.

[20] This index, which excludes refunding issues, of course excludes government issues, at this time.

[21] Government issues are floated for reasons distinctly different from those which bring industrial, or even municipal, issues into the market. The timing of the offering of governments is much less affected by market conditions than

The volume of new issues does not usually expand in a weak market of low or falling bond prices. Ordinarily in a weak

CHART XII

TOTAL, 1919–1931, BY QUARTERS
CLASSIFIED AS UNITED STATES GOVERNMENT ISSUES, FOREIGN GOVERNMENT
ISSUES, FEDERAL FARM LOAN ISSUES, WAR FINANCE CORPORATION
ISSUES, MUNICIPAL ISSUES, CORPORATE ISSUES

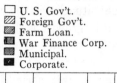
☐ U. S. Gov't.
▨ Foreign Gov't.
▧ Farm Loan.
▤ War Finance Corp.
▦ Municipal.
■ Corporate.

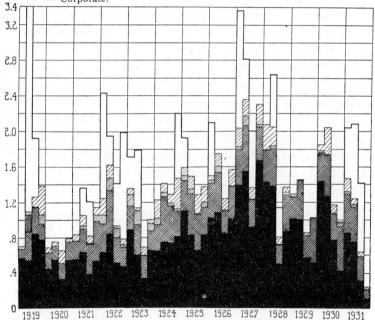

market offerings decrease, and increase in a strong market, when interest rates are low and prices buoyant.[22] However,

is the timing of other types of issues. Thus, since government issues are subject to influences different from those which affect other types, and come into the market in a different way, they must be considered in a separate category. Elimination of government issues from this study, however, would distort it more than does their retention; although in many quarters there were no government flotations, in other quarters they amounted to more than 50 per cent of the total.

[22] "The curve of bond issues, corrected for seasonal movements, was . . .

after its decline in the first quarter of 1920, the volume of new issues expanded in that year, in the face of the decline in prices during the first six months, and continued to grow till the latter part of 1922, in spite of the high interest rates that prevailed through the first half of 1921. This increase in 1920 and the first part of 1921 was contrary to the movement that would have been expected in view of the current situation in the money market. It has been suggested that this growth was mainly occasioned by the necessity of industry to fund commercial loans rolled up in the preceding boom period,[23] but the growth of corporate issues was not conspicuous in this period,[24] and the advance seems to have been mainly supported by municipals, foreigns, and Federal Farm Loan issues.

The operations of the Treasury did not play so prominent a part in the bond market in 1920, 1921, and 1922 as they did in 1919, but they were, nevertheless, important. During these years the government retired its unfunded floating debt and began refunding the 7,500 millions of short-dated floating debt inherited from the war; the cumulative sinking fund was put into operation; and the post-war reallocation of Liberty Bonds and their placement in the hands of permanent holders was largely completed.

At the beginning of 1920 there were hopes that the government's unfunded floating debt could be retired in the very near future. On January 12 the Secretary of the Treasury stated that the issues of loan certificates outstanding, all of which matured in January or February, would be paid either from

---

then compared with an inverted curve of bond yields. Close similarity in their fluctuations was observable. That is, rising yields were accompanied with declining issues, and vice versa" (Ellsworth, "Investments," p. 119).

[23] ". . . bond issues quite generally increase in periods of depression (1908, 1911, 1913–14, 1920–21, 1930) . . . in periods of depression interest rates are generally low. Inasmuch as there is usually an increase in the commercial debt of business firms at the peak of prosperity and just after the turn downward — debt which it is difficult to pay off during periods of low earning power — the easy money conditions of the depression period are utilized by many in this position to fund floating debt by the issue of bonds" (Ellsworth, "Investments," p. 116).

[24] Corporate issues were much smaller in 1920 than in 1919, and although they increased, absolutely, from the beginning of 1920 till the middle of 1922, their volume declined relative to the volume of total issues (Chart XIII, p. 69).

cash already on hand or from the proceeds of certificates presently to be issued, and that consequently a large refunding
operation would not be necessary. On February 16 he an-

CHART XIII

DIFFERENT CLASSES OF TOTAL VOLUME OF BOND ISSUES AS PERCENTAGES OF THE
TOTAL, 1919–1931, BY QUARTERS
CLASSIFIED AS UNITED STATES GOVERNMENT ISSUES, FOREIGN GOVERNMENT ISSUES,
FEDERAL FARM LOAN ISSUES, WAR FINANCE CORPORATION ISSUES,
MUNICIPAL ISSUES, CORPORATE ISSUES

☐ Farm Loan.
▨ U. S. Gov't.
▩ Foreign Gov't.
▧ Municipal.
▤ War Finance Corp.
▰ Corporate.

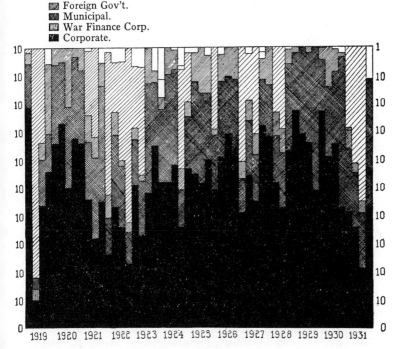

nounced: "With the maturity of loan certificates on February
16, 1920, the Treasury found itself in a position where it no
longer had any such certificates outstanding. All the issues remaining matured on income and profits tax installment dates
and the amounts of the various maturities in no case exceeded
the estimated amounts of income and profits taxes payable on
the maturity dates. . . ."[25] Thus for the moment the Treasury

[25] *Annual Report of the Secretary of the Treasury*, 1920, p. 13.

had no uncovered maturities, and with the disappearance of the loan certificates the unfunded floating debt was eliminated. As this floating debt had been largely carried by the banks, under, at times, a certain amount of pressure from the Treasury, its disappearance was of considerable significance.

But on February 28 the Transportation Act was passed, which returned the railroads to private hands and entailed considerable payments by the government; business went into a decline; money rates advanced; and the March 15 offering of tax certificates was only subscribed for to the amount of about 200 millions, in spite of its 4¾ per cent rate. These circumstances forced the Treasury to resort once more on April 1 to issues of loan certificates, and a number of such issues were put out during the year. These issues were all of maturities of less than a year, and hence are excluded from the computations of Charts V and VI; but since it was necessary for the banking system to take the larger part of them, they undoubtedly affected the bond market indirectly by their absorption of surplus funds.

By the spring of 1921 the Treasury was forced to issue another type of security, the Treasury note, of a few years maturity. In a letter to the chairman of the House Committee on Ways and Means dated April 30, 1921, Secretary Mellon outlined very thoroughly the situation that then confronted the Treasury.

The estimates of the receipts and expenditures for both 1921 and 1922 show clearly that while this government has definitely balanced its budget, the surplus of current receipts over current expenditures will not quite provide for what may be termed the fixed public debt redemptions . . . there will be practically no funds available in these years for the retirement of the floating debt represented by loan and tax certificates outstanding. . . . This means that the Treasury's earlier expectations as to the retirement of the floating debt have been upset by the continuance of unexpectedly heavy expenditures during the past twelve months, particularly on account of the Army and Navy and the railroads, and that the Government can not now expect to retire any material portion of the two and one-half billions of floating debt now outstanding during the fiscal years 1921 and 1922 out of current revenue. . . .

Within the next two years, or thereabouts, there will mature about seven and one-half billions of short-dated debt (including the outstanding floating debt). . . . In view of its early maturity, the Treasury must regard the short-dated debt as a whole, and within the next two years may expect to reduce it by perhaps one billion dollars. . . . The remainder of this short-dated debt, amounting to over six billion dollars, will have to be refunded. It will, therefore, be the Treasury's policy to vary its monthly offerings of Treasury certificates of indebtedness from time to time when market conditions are favorable with issues of short term notes in moderate amounts with maturities of three to five years, with a view to the gradual distribution of the short-dated debt through successive issues of notes in convenient maturities extending over the period from 1923 to 1928.[26]

The first two of these note issues were floated on June 15 and September 15 with great success. Five more issues of Treasury notes were sold in 1922, on February 1, March 15, June 15, August 1, and December 15. In October 1922 the Treasury found it expedient to offer the first issue of Treasury bonds since the Victory Loan,[27] and in connection with this issue the last of the unfunded loan certificates were retired, and the Treasury thereby eliminated the floating debt almost two years after it had hoped to do so.

On July 1, 1920, the cumulative sinking fund as provided for in the Victory Loan Act went into operation. The appropriation for the first year was some 256 millions, of which almost all was available in cash on July 1. With the aid of this sum the Treasury was able to reduce its interest-bearing debt some 850 millions in 1920, but in 1921 and 1922, as forecast in the letter of the Secretary of the Treasury of April 30, 1921, the interest-bearing debt of the government increased some 239 millions.

In addition to the refunding operations of the Treasury and

[26] *Annual Report of the Secretary of the Treasury*, 1921, pp. 3–4.
[27] ". . . the Secretary of the Treasury accordingly announced, on October 9, . . . a popular offering of 4½ per cent 25–30 year bonds dated October 16, 1922, maturing October 15, 1952. . . . The offering was for $500,000,000 or thereabouts. . . . Subscriptions on the primary offering amounted to $1,399,-851,900, of which $512,390,000 was allotted . . . (for cash). In addition to the subscriptions received on the cash offering, subscriptions aggregating $252,-060,900 were received on exchange . . . so that the total allotments on the offerings aggregate slightly over $764,000,000" (*Annual Report of the Secretary of the Treasury*, 1922, p. 5).

the institution of the sinking fund, the market for government
bonds in these years was disturbed by a number of other factors.
At the beginning of 1920, when the satisfactory progress of the
Treasury's financial program diminished the necessity for inducing member banks to buy government securities, the preferential rates of the Federal Reserve Banks on loans secured by
Libertys were abolished.[28] The revival of the loan certificates
in April 1920, however, apparently led to the reëstablishment
of these rates, for the *Annual Report of the Federal Reserve
Board* for the next year again announced that such preferential
rates had been abolished in the past twelve months.[29] The presence or absence of such rates naturally altered the value of governments in the eyes of the banks, and hence presumably
affected their price. Prices of government bonds were also
affected to some degree by the establishment of the sinking
fund, since it implied a reduction in the amount of these securities outstanding and consequently raised slightly the premium
on this type of bond in the minds of those who wished to reduce
their income taxes.[30] The very great decrease in the quantity
of government bonds held by banks — which shrank from over
three and a quarter billions in May 1919 to little over one and
a quarter billions in January 1921 — was also a factor of considerable moment in the market. Moreover, the large purchases
and sales of governments by the general public, and its lack of
discrimination market-wise, constituted an important, if somewhat uncertain, element in the market and prevented the establishment of a price structure based on the distinctions of yields
to maturity which persons more familiar with financial technique
would have constructed.[31] The policy of open-market purchases
upon which the Federal Reserve Banks embarked in the spring
of 1922 of course also affected the government bond market

[28] *Annual Report of the Federal Reserve Board*, 1920, p. 57.
[29] *Annual Report of the Federal Reserve Board*, 1921, p. 33.
[30] The desire to escape taxes, however, was somewhat reduced by the Revenue
Act of 1921, which lowered the super-tax and the very high rates paid by the
higher income brackets.
[31] In the spring of 1920 C. F. Childs, the specialist in government bonds,
wrote: "The market value of the several different loans is subject to the daily
vacillating sentiments of the present holders and prospective buyers. Every

at this time, and was of permanent significance, since it led directly to the formation of the "Open Market Committee" that played so important a part in the Federal Reserve operations in the succeeding decade.

When the years from 1920 through 1922 are regarded as a whole it is apparent that the varied course of business activity — with the culmination of the boom in the early part of 1920, the subsequent precipitate decline, the recovery that slowly set in late in 1921 and reached considerable proportions in 1922 — was the central factor in the financial world in these years. The bond market did not escape its influence. But the effect of the depression on this market was indirect in many ways, and its control over the movements of bond prices and volume of new issues was diluted by the influence of other forces. Unquestionably the great decline of commodity prices and the recession of activity unsettled conditions and disturbed confidence in the bond market, as elsewhere. Conversely, the stabilization of prices and the recovery of business produced the opposite result. But aside from psychological factors, not the less real because intangible, fluctuations of business activity mainly influenced the bond market through their effects on the banking system and the resulting changes in credit conditions and interest rates.

The rise of interest rates in the latter part of 1919 brought concurrently a fall of bond prices. This fall, however, did not check the flow of offerings appreciably till after the turn of the year. In the first quarter of 1920 the high yields required of new issues and the tremendous shock inflicted upon business

---

condition of local and foreign significance has a direct bearing on the market, which, however, is primarily governed by supply and demand. . . . However, as long as the vast number of public holders of these bonds (the government 4's and 4½'s) are unable to comprehend or to act with appreciable discrimination (so as to put these issues on equivalent yield bases, their prices differing only through maturity dates), but instead select for purchase or sale one issue instead of another, without reference to this technicality, it is not probable that any further factor except that of supply and demand will exercise any considerable market influence over prices until the greater portion of bonds are lodged in the hands of discriminating investors" ("United States Government Bonds," *Annals of the American Academy of Political and Social Science,* LXXXVIII, 46, March 1920).

activity and confidence by the deflation caused a precipitate fall in the volume of new issues. After this drop, however, new issues showed a decided tendency to increase, though the advance was interrupted in certain quarters. This increase can not be attributed to easier credit conditions, lower money rates, high bond prices, or improved confidence. Until the middle of 1921, when the deflation had substantially been completed and money rates had dropped to low levels, it took place independently of such factors. Perhaps the increase is to be explained in part by the need of business to refund bank loans contracted in the boom period; in part by the need of capital requirements, suppressed during the war, to gain expression, irrespective of what price had to be paid for new money; and, in the case of foreign countries, by the necessity to fund uncovered international balances. By the middle of 1921, however, business activity and commodity prices had been in large measure stabilized, and short term interest rates had dropped below the yields of second and even of first grade bonds. The stimulus given bond prices by these changed conditions was presently augmented in the fall of 1921 by the growth of security loans and investments of reporting member banks, and in the first half of 1922 by the open market purchases of the Federal Reserve Banks.

In addition to these factors arising from the current business depression and credit conditions, there were other forces of a different origin which played a considerable part in determining the course of the bond market. Progress was made in the reestablishment of what are, perhaps, to be called normal economic relations, both through the removal of the last of the war-time restrictions on the financial mechanism and through the formation of new financial agencies and practices. Many of the war debt settlements were completed, arrangements were made for facilitating international trade under the new, post-war conditions, and the reduction of the unfunded international credit balance of the United States was begun. Instrumental in this last was the flotation of foreign bonds in the United States, significant not only for the additions they made to the volume of offerings, but also for the relief they afforded the banking system by reducing commercial loans, and for the evidence they gave of the position of the United States as a creditor nation. In these years, also, the Treasury paid off or refunded a substantial part of the 7,500 millions of short-dated debt left from the war. Such operations were carried out with a minimum of repercussion in the money markets, but their very size placed the bond market under a certain strain, confused somewhat the movements of prices of government securities, and increased still further the very large turnover in the bond market, so characteristic of this time.

By the middle of 1922 the Treasury's refunding program had been thoroughly launched, the uncovered credit balance of the United States was falling, the easy credit conditions of the past year had brought a revival of business activity and prices, and the first phase of the post-war bond market appears to come to an end.

CHAPTER VI

1922–1924

ALTHOUGH in all respects the change is not clearly marked, a new phase of the post-war bond market appears to have begun in the middle of 1922. This stage lasted till the end of 1924, in spite of the substantial fluctuations in bond prices, in the volume of new issues, and in the activity of the market that occurred during this time. These thirty months constituted a transitional period that intervened between the earlier period of post-war readjustment and the comparative stability which was attained in 1925 and 1926.

During this interval both the bond market and general business activity experienced a rapid recession and an almost equally rapid recovery, which, although not so great as that of 1920 and 1921, was considerable. This recession took place while very large quantities of gold were being imported, and consequently excited a good deal of speculation and controversy at the time among financial observers. Much of the fluctuation in interest rates and in bond prices seems to have been caused by Federal Reserve policies and by the operations of its Open Market Committee, which was then becoming an important factor in the capital markets. During this whole phase short term interest rates were at a very low level — in 1924 they were lower than at any time in the period of this study except the final months of 1930 — and it was at this time that the five-year decline in long term rates began, which was of such importance in the capital markets during the latter part of the twenties. In these years the Treasury completed the refunding of the 7,500 million short-dated debt which had been outstanding at the beginning of 1921, flotations of foreign bonds increased to very substantial levels, and most of the domestic post-war readjustments seemed, at the time, finally to have been effected.

Although the advance of business activity and of wholesale prices which had begun in the early months of 1922 lasted through the summer of that year and well into 1923, and although the inflow of gold which had begun in 1920 continued, even if at a reduced rate, changes in other economic factors indicated that a new situation was developing in the bond market in the summer of 1922. In May the Federal Reserve Banks stopped their purchases of government securities, and during the latter part of the year their holdings declined; and notwithstanding the lowering of the New York discount rate from 4½ to 4 per cent in June, short rates in September began an advance that lasted almost to the end of 1923. In October this advance was reflected by an increase in long rates. Moreover, the rise of stock prices which had begun in the autumn of 1921 was checked in June and July, as credit conditions changed, and after a further short advance in the third quarter, the market broke badly in November. Finally, the volume of bonds traded on the Exchange, which had been very large in the spring of 1922, decreased rapidly in the latter part of the year.

In the spring of 1923 the continued advance of short term rates and the decline in the bond market began to exert an influence upon business activity and commodity prices. Wholesale prices reached their high point in March, and although business indices continued to rise till June, the Treasury later chose April,[1] the month in which the stock market broke severely, as marking the limit of the advance. After June 1923 business activity and wholesale prices moved downward for a year, till June 1924, when the indices were well below normal. At that time, however, their fall was checked, a rapid advance began, and by the end of 1924 they were close to the high levels of the early months of 1923.

Although gold came into the United States steadily during 1922, and although the Federal Reserve Bank of New York lowered its discount rate from 4½ to 4 per cent in June, in September commercial paper, time money, and the customers' rate all started up. Subject to some fluctuation, this advance con-

[1] *Annual Report of the Secretary of the Treasury*, 1923, p. 4.

tinued till the last quarter of 1923. The early part of this rise seems to have been caused in part by increasing seasonal demands for credit, in part by additional demands for credit brought by the concurrent industrial revival. Member-bank loans and investments, which had remained constant since January, began to increase in May 1922, and this advance lasted, with hardly an interruption, till May 1923, when they amounted to 16,490 millions and showed a net increase of 1,800 millions in twelve months. Almost all of the earlier part of this growth — that which took place between May 1922 and February 1923 — was caused by increases in bond investments and security loans,[2] so that it appears that the demand for commercial loans was supplemented by a strong demand for funds from the capital markets. The volume of new issues, especially of government issues, which were floated in conjunction with the Treasury's refunding program, was very large at this time, and in 1922 banks — grouping member banks and savings banks together — increased their portfolios 1,904 millions, the largest amount in any year under consideration.

Short rates continued to advance in 1923, however, after seasonal demands for credit had slackened, after the industrial revival had been checked, and after the growth in member-bank security loans and investments had come to an end in February. The explanation for this continued rise is apparently to be found in the changed volume of money in circulation and in Federal Reserve policy.

The gold imports of 1920, 1921, and the first part of 1922 had been used by the member banks to reduce their borrowings at the Reserve Banks. But in July 1922 the great decline in the amount of money in circulation that had begun in 1920 came to an end, and its volume began to increase. This rise was almost uninterrupted till December 1923, and lifted the figure for money in circulation some 620 millions. The stock of money gold in the same period increased only 415 millions. Conse-

---

[2] Between May 1922 and February 1923 total loans and investments of reporting member banks increased 1,540 millions; of this amount increases of their security loans and investments accounted for 1,400 millions.

quently the increases made in member banks' reserves at this time by gold imports were more than offset by the funds which the drain of money into circulation took from them.[3] The pressure which this drain put upon reporting member banks was accentuated by the concurrent decline in the Federal Reserve holdings of governments. Federal Reserve open-market purchases had some to an end in May 1922, and their holdings declined almost uninterruptedly thereafter till December 1923, dropping from 603 millions to 106 millions. Although this decline was offset, in part, by a rise in bills bought, the changes which these developments brought in the position of the member banks forced them to increase their rediscounts from 479 millions in May 1922, when they amounted to 40 per cent of total Federal Reserve credit, to 771 millions in December 1923, when they accounted for 61 per cent of outstanding Federal Reserve credit.

This tightening of credit conditions made particularly significant the increase from 4 to 4½ per cent in the discount rates of the Reserve Banks of New York, Boston, and San Francisco in February and March 1923. Although the Reserve Board declared that the previous inequality of rates in the Reserve cities had brought "an undue proportion of borrowing in the centers of low rates," and that "the effect of the rate advance of the three banks was to bring about a better regional distribution of credit . . . ,"[4] these increases had a distinctly restrictive in-

---

[3] The *Annual Report of the Federal Reserve Board* in 1923 described the use to which gold imports were put in the years 1920 through 1923 as follows: "In brief, the gold received during the period of liquidation in 1921 and 1922 enabled the member banks to recover a considerable degree of the independence of reserve bank support which they had lost in the preceding years, while the gold received since the middle of 1922 has enabled them to maintain their state of relative independence notwithstanding the great intervening growth of credit" (p. 19). The Board's Report in 1924 dealt with the subject in more detail: "In 1921 . . . balances arising out of $667,000,000 of net gold imports as well as the currency restored from domestic circulation were used to reduce indebtedness at the Reserve Banks. In 1922 . . . the larger part of the $238,-000,000 (imports) were used to meet currency demands, though a part remained as a basis for the growth in deposit liabilities . . . which occurred during the first half of the year. . . . In 1923 practically the entire amount of net gold imports of $294,000,000 was used by member banks in lieu of additional borrowing at the Reserve Banks to meet demands for currency . . ." (p. 8).

[4] *Annual Report of the Federal Reserve Board*, 1923, p. 4.

fluence and contributed substantially to the termination of the increase of business activity in the spring of 1923.

Moreover, in addition to selling governments and raising the discount rate, the Federal Reserve authorities in the spring of 1923 issued distinctly cautionary statements in their official publications. In March the Federal Reserve Bulletin [5] discussed the current financial situation, and pointed out that prices and production had advanced substantially in the past year; that basic production had increased 40 per cent, close to the possible maximum; and that the usual seasonal liquidation of loans in the first months of 1923 had been practically confined to security loans and had left rediscounts at a high level and member-bank credit close to the 1920 peak. Such a situation raised questions as to how further demands for credit could be met, except by recourse to the Reserve Banks, and whether additional credit, since the level of production was already high, would produce any effect save a further increase of prices. The *Bulletin* stated that "Expansion of reserve bank credit at a time when physical production is approaching the maximum, particularly if the growth of business extends to all districts, will bring the reserve banks into a closer relationship through their rediscount operations to the movements of production, trade, and prices than they have sustained for more than a year." [6] And the implication appeared to be that further credit restrictions were imminent. In the April and May bulletins the discussion of credit conditions followed the line that, although gold imports in the past fifteen months had allowed member banks to increase their loans very substantially without borrowing from the Reserve Banks, this increase of credit had started an internal drain of money into circulation at the very moment that gold imports appeared to be declining, and that maintenance of member-bank loans at the current level in the face of such a drain must almost certainly lead to further rediscounting. The implication was that such an increase in Federal Reserve credit would be reflected in higher prices rather than in increased production,

[5] *Federal Reserve Bulletin*, IX, 283–284 (March 1923).
[6] *Ibid.*, p. 284.

and that such an eventuality would lead to restrictive measures by the Reserve Banks. Articles of similar tenor appeared in the publications of the individual banks in the spring of 1923, and could only have been interpreted by the financial and industrial community as more or less direct warnings.[7]

It thus appears that the rise of short rates that began in September 1922 and continued till the last quarter of 1923 is to be attributed to influences of various kinds. The rise in the latter part of 1922 and the first month or two of 1923 was caused in part by the seasonal demands for credit, in part by the increased requirements of reviving industry, and in part by the support which the banks currently gave to the security markets, as well as by the increases in the volume of money in circulation, which more than offset the gold imports. The continued rise of short rates, however, is traceable to the restrictive policy of the Federal Reserve System — to its open market policy, to the warnings of its official publications, and to the increases in rediscount rates at the New York, Boston, and San Francisco Banks.[8]

[7] Reed inclines to the view that the rate increases in February and March 1923 were part of a mildly restrictive policy conceived by the Reserve Board in the latter part of 1922 and put into effect in the first part of 1923; and that this policy was undertaken to check the extraordinary increase in basic production, which had increased 69 per cent from the 1921 low, rather than to check any increase in prices, which had not had any such rise. He also points out that these were the first rate increases in the history of the Reserve System "which ignored considerations of the sufficiency of reserve ratios" (Reed, *Federal Reserve Policy,* pp. 33–42). This treatment does not seem to me to be entirely satisfactory in view of the considerations mentioned above.

[8] Federal Reserve policy in the latter part of 1922 and in 1923 was not currently considered as being particularly restrictive, principally because the effects of the System's operations were not then well understood. However, in the light of knowledge since acquired as to the effectiveness of Federal Reserve measures, mere perusal of the weekly Federal Reserve statements in the latter part of 1922 and in 1923 shows the System's policy to have been rigorous. At a time when increases in money in circulation were exceeding gold imports, and consequently tending to increase member-bank borrowing, the Reserve Banks took half a billion of cash from the money market by selling governments, and although part of this was returned through purchases of acceptances, the greater part of the acceptance purchases was a seasonal affair and did not affect the basic position of the member banks. As a result of this policy rediscounts increased upwards of 50 per cent in eighteen months. But not content with the changed position, the discount rate at New York, Boston, and San Francisco was raised in the early part of 1923, and the Reserve System's publications printed cautionary statements concerning the extended condition of credit.

Towards the end of 1923 the tight credit conditions that had developed in the previous eighteen months began to slacken. The first evidence was the recession of short term interest rates. Time money in October, commercial paper rates in November, and the customers' rate in December started a decline that lasted till the middle of 1924 and carried short rates to the lowest level in a decade,[9] and to the lowest point reached in the period of this study, except for the last few months of 1930. This decline in rates came concurrently with a relaxation of pressure for banking accommodation as the business recession gathered momentum. Total loans and investments of reporting member banks had ceased to grow as early as May 1923, and, although their commercial loans slowly increased after that date, such loans reached their maximum in October, the same month in which rediscounts were at their peak. In the last two months of the year commercial loans and rediscounts both declined.

The relaxation of credit conditions was carried further in December when the Federal Reserve Banks once more began to buy governments in the open market. These purchases continued till the end of 1924 and amounted to about 450 millions. The volume of acceptances and government securities held by the Reserve System increased from 348 millions in November 1923 to 912 millions in December 1924, a net increase of 564 millions. These open-market purchases of the Federal Reserve were accompanied by successive decreases in discount rates during 1924 that reduced the rate at New York from 4½ to 3 per cent. Moreover, some 244 millions of gold was imported into the country during the first six months of 1924. Since money in circulation ceased to increase this year, except in response to seasonal demands, this gold was used, for the most part, by member banks to strengthen their position.

As a result of these developments, rediscounts at the Federal Reserve dropped from 873 millions in October 1923 to 301 in December 1924, a net decline of 572 millions, and in the latter month constituted only 23 per cent of the total Reserve credit outstanding, compared with 72 per cent in the former month.

[9] *Annual Report of the Federal Reserve Board*, 1924, p. 2.

As credit conditions became easier, reporting member banks rapidly increased their total loans and investments. From 16,380 millions in October 1923 they amounted to 18,470 millions in December 1924. Of this net rise of 2,090 millions, 1,900 was accounted for by an increase of their investments and security loans.

In spite of the ease of credit conditions, short rates moved up again in the latter part of 1924. Time money began to advance in August, the customers' rate in September, and commercial paper rates in November. The increase was probably in response to seasonal demands for accommodation and the increased requirements of improving business. The rise, however, was not large, and was not reflected in the movement of long rates.

It is apparent that the relaxation of credit conditions in 1924 and the very low level to which short rates fell was in large part permitted, if not caused, by Federal Reserve policy. The funds put into the hands of member banks, in the period October 1923 to August 1924, and available for the reduction of member-bank indebtedness, from the three sources of gold imports, purchases of bills and securities by the Federal Reserve, and the return of money from circulation, were more than enough to pay off the total reporting member-bank indebtedness of 873 millions that existed in October 1923.[10] Such a supply of funds, of course, allowed credit to become unusually easy.

Numerous explanations have been advanced as to why the Federal Reserve allowed credit to become so plentiful and money so cheap in 1924. The unsatisfactory banking situation in the West and Northwest, the low prices of farm products, the need to finance cheaply American food exports to Europe in this year, the desire of the Federal Reserve to fortify its security portfolios have all been offered as partial explanations.[11] Certainly the desire of the Federal Reserve Board to facilitate monetary reconstruction in Europe and the return of England to the gold standard weighed heavily in the determination of

[10] Riefler, *Money Rates*, p. 184.
[11] See, for instance, Strong, *Interpretations*, pp. 255–261, and Reed, *Federal Reserve Policy*, pp. 64–77.

policy. But whatever the motives of the Federal Reserve in 1924, it is obvious that this was a critical year in the control of credit in this country, and that the extraordinary supply of funds currently in the hands of member banks, and the very low level to which interest rates fell, made it one of great significance for the bond market.

During these years the outstanding floating debt owed the United States on international account continued to be reduced. In 1922 the net debit balance of the United States amounted to 508 millions, in 1923 to 119 millions, and in 1924 to 212 millions.[12] A large part of the debit balances in 1922 and 1924 was accounted for by the considerable volume of foreign bonds which were floated in the buoyant markets currently existing. The weak market for second grade bonds that prevailed during the greater part of 1923 checked the foreign flotations sharply in that year, and it was the debit balance on current transactions, rather than that on capital transactions, which provided the United States with a debit balance at that time. This reduction in the floating debt of course relieved the position of the banks, since the burden had been largely carried by them, and released banking funds for other purposes.

The fluctuating course of business activity and commodity prices, the gold importations, the altered volume of money in circulation, Federal Reserve policy, the reduction in the international credit balance, the changes in the composition of member-bank assets and in short term interest rates all influenced the bond market to some degree during this period. Of these various factors the movements of short term rates had, perhaps, the most direct effect upon bond prices and the flow of new issues.

The increase in short term rates in the fall of 1922 was quickly reflected in the market. Bond prices, which had risen almost steadily since the middle of 1921, touched their peak in September 1922, when the yields for Moody's Aaa and Baa bonds were, respectively, 4.93 and 6.75 per cent. Libertys,

---

[12] *The Balance of International Payments of the United States in 1924* (Trade Information Bulletin 340), p. 26.

however, had reached their high the preceding July, and in October all bond prices began to fall as long rates rose in sympathy with the advance in short rates. This rise in long rates, and the increased price of borrowing it brought, quickly checked the flow of new issues. If government issues are disregarded, new offerings began a decline in the third quarter of 1922 which, although temporarily interrupted in the first quarter of 1923, did not cease until the third quarter of that year.[13]

Although the volume of bond trading on the Stock Exchange declined precipitately as prices fell in the latter half of 1922, the market was not weak. The city of Philadelphia 4's of '72 brought out in July on a 3.93 basis were one of the first issues since the war to be sold with less than a 4 per cent yield. Banks added very large quantities of bonds to their portfolios in 1922; it was currently estimated that during the year member banks bought one and one-half billions of securities;[14] and in 1922 member and savings banks together acquired a larger amount of securities than in any other year considered in this study. But bond prices declined steadily during the fall, and the Treasury 4¼'s brought out in October were quoted below par before the end of the month. The market for foreign bonds was unsettled in the summer by the Anglo-French altercations over German reparations, and in the autumn by the Graeco-Turkish crisis. The volume of new foreign issues, affected by these influences, as well as by the rising cost of financing, declined sharply in the last six months of the year. The total number of bond issues listed on the Stock Exchange, however, advanced sharply to 1,156 as compared with 1,115 in 1921, in the largest annual increase since the war.

As the improvement in business reached almost boom proportions in the first quarter of 1923 the volume of new issues advanced in a short-lived rally, though their number showed little tendency to increase. In January the leading industrial issues were the large Anaconda offerings — the 6 per cent first-mortgage loans for 100 millions and the 7 per cent convert-

---

[13] The movement is clearly marked in the index of new capital issues in Chart V, p. 32.   [14] *National City Bank Monthly Letter*, October 1922.

ible debenture issue for 50 millions; and although foreign loans, especially French and Belgian issues, broke badly that month as the French entered the Ruhr, they rallied again in February when it became apparent that war would not break out. The agreement reached in the same month by the American and English commissions on the terms of the war-debt repayments further steadied the foreign market, and also directly affected the market for United States government issues, since it was currently estimated that the repayments would absorb 150 to 175 millions of Libertys annually. Although bond prices continued to decline, the city of Philadelphia was able to place an issue on a 3.88 per cent basis early in February.

But credit conditions tightened steadily, and short rates continued to advance. In March time money and in April the customers' rate rose above the yield of Moody's Aaa bonds, and the stock market broke. Although first grade bonds checked their decline in April, when their yield had risen to 5.22 per cent, such was not the case with the Baa bonds, which fell till October. Even the completion of the Treasury's refunding program in June did not, apparently, produce any effect marketwise on long term rates or the flow of new issues, although the heavy over-subscription of the 25 million Austrian loan in July showed that it was possible, under proper conditions, to place substantial issues in the market.[15] But in August the commercial paper rate also went above the yield of first grade bonds, and the third quarter of the year brought a further decline in both the volume and the number of new issues, the index of "net" offerings dropping so low as to become a negative figure.

The last quarter of 1923, however, brought a striking change in the bond market. The business recession had, by this time, gathered momentum, and the pressure on the banks for accommodation was slackening. In September time money and in October commercial paper rates checked their advance and started down. They were followed in November by the yield of the Baa

---

[15] This was a new type of loan, secured by liens upon the customs revenue and the tobacco monopoly, and was guaranteed in varying proportions by almost every country in Europe. It was then considered one of the most constructive steps yet taken in the financial rehabilitation of Europe.

bonds, which had reached a high point of 7.46 per cent. In November the customers' rate reached the limit of its advance, and commercial paper rates dropped below the yield of first grade bonds, as did time money in December, though the customers' rate stayed above it till February 1924. The decline of long term rates that began in 1923 — in May for Aaa bonds and in November for Baa bonds — continued with hardly an interruption till well into 1928; it was practically unaffected during these five years by movements of short rates and formed one of the most striking features of the post-war bond market.

The effect of the cheaper cost of financing and the new strength of the market was quickly reflected in the volume and number of new offerings, which increased sharply in the last quarter of the year and began the advance that was to carry through 1924. The volume of bonds traded on the Stock Exchange also began to increase.

Stimulated by the progressively easier credit conditions of 1924 the bond market continued during that year, practically without interruption, the advance that had begun in 1923. The yields of both first and second grade bonds fell rapidly as prices rose; by the middle of the year yields of governments had fallen below the yield of first grade municipals for the first time since the war; and by December the return from all types of bonds was lower than it had been since 1916. Concurrently the market's activity greatly increased, and the index of trading reached one of the four peaks which it attained in the period of this study. Both the volume and number of new issues expanded substantially, and the steady and sustained advance in all three of the seasonally adjusted curves of the volume of new issues is particularly striking. In the last quarter of the year the "net" amount of new investment capital required was very large, double the quantity needed in any other quarter; such a relationship is most unusual, since the seasonal index of "net" capital offerings ordinarily declines from quarter to quarter during the year.

Oddly enough, so far as can be judged, business did not make particular use of this period of cheap money to refund outstanding obligations.[16] Refunding issues were slightly larger in 1924 than in 1920, 1921, and 1923, but were smaller than in 1922 and 1925.[17] But there can be no doubt that the low cost of financing played a considerable part in the large flotations of foreign government bonds in 1924. The year's total, 778 millions, and the total for the last quarter of the year, 357 millions, are record amounts. This 357 millions in the fourth quarter included the 110 million share of the United States in the German loan that initiated the Dawes plan. But in spite of their large volume, foreign government issues in 1924 amounted to only about 13 per cent of the total volume of issues. Although the yield of this foreign financing was, for the most part, distinctly higher than that of any but the most speculative domestic financing — the Japanese loan of February was sold on a 6.50 basis, the Swedish loan of November on a 5.50 basis, the German Dawes loan of the same month on one of 7.70, and the French loan of December required a 7.50 yield — the almost universal rule of 1920 of 8 per cent for foreign loans had by this time definitely disappeared. Moreover, the variations in the yield of foreign financing this year afforded evidence that the American public was beginning to discern differences in the credit standings of foreign countries. These foreign bond flotations, of course, relieved the pressure on the foreign exchanges and, together with the prevailing low interest rates, were largely responsible for the cessation of gold imports in the latter half of the year. In the last four months of 1924 there was even a net gold export for the first time since August 1920 .

The bond market was intimately affected in these years by the Treasury's treatment of the 7,500 millions of short-dated debt that had been outstanding in the spring of 1921. By the middle of 1923 this debt had been reduced by approximately 2,000 millions, and the remainder had been refunded.[18] This refund-

[16] This generalization is based upon the classification of refunding issues of the *Commercial and Financial Chronicle.*

[17] Governor Strong testified as part of his explanation of Federal Reserve policy in 1924 that business currently had great need to fund its short term debt and that the cheap money of 1924 gave it the first favorable opportunity for so doing in twelve years (Strong, *Interpretations*, pp. 255–261).

[18] *Annual Report of the Secretary of the Treasury*, 1923, pp. 19–20.

ing required the issue of very considerable quantities of obligations in 1922 and the first half of 1923. Most of these obligations had a maturity of five years or less, and fell due before
the maturity of the Third Liberty Loan in 1928. The maturities of these obligations were placed on quarterly tax-payment
dates in the period intervening before the maturity of the Third
Liberty Loan, at such intervals that the obligations might easily
be paid off or refinanced. By October 31, 1923, the short-
dated debt, exclusive of the Third Liberty Loan, had been reduced to 5,345 millions, and four-fifths of this amount was in
the form of Treasury notes.

It does not seem possible to determine precisely what effect
these operations of the Treasury produced on the bond market.
The reduction of the debt increased the supply of funds seeking
investment, probably by an almost equivalent amount, for presumably a negligible part of the funds so released were spent in
consumption.[19] Although the size of the Treasury's operations
would seem inevitably to have congested the market somewhat,
neither bond prices nor the flow of offerings showed any sudden
or striking change at the completion of the Treasury's refunding
program, probably because the government's issues were all of
a refunding nature and did not require any new investment capital. No doubt a large proportion of these issues were absorbed
by the banks when they were increasing their security portfolios
in 1922. There does not seem to be any direct evidence that
these issues postponed the flotation of other types of bonds.

In connection with these refunding operations there was
passed by Congress on March 2, 1923, an amendment to the
original act constituting the cumulative sinking fund which
allowed that fund to be used for the retirement of bonds and
notes issued subsequent to July 1920.[20] In its original form the

---

[19] Sprague and Burgess suggest that perhaps the reduction in the government
debt did not contribute commensurately to the supply of investment funds. Their
hypothesis is that, if taxes had been reduced and the funds so collected left in the
hands of the public, part of these funds would have been saved and invested,
particularly since tax reductions would have been of especial benefit to high-
income classes (O. M. W. Sprague and W. R. Burgess, "Money and Credit and
Their Effect on Business," Chap. X in *Recent Economic Changes*, II).

[20] *Annual Report of the Secretary of the Treasury*, 1923, pp. 49–50.

fund was not available for such obligations, and without such an amendment the fund could not have been used to retire the refunding obligations issued in 1922 and 1923.

There is one further peculiarity of this phase in the bond market that should be noted. From the beginning of 1920 to the end of 1922 the percentage of corporate issues to total issues declined very decidedly, from about 65 per cent to 25.[21] With the beginning of 1923, however, this tendency was reversed. From the low point of 1922 the percentage of corporate issues, though subject to considerable fluctuation, increased in a well-defined movement, till it amounted to about 70 per cent of total issues in 1928 and 1929. The proportion of corporate issues receded from this level in 1930 only slightly, in spite of the great drop in their absolute amount in that year. This long, cyclical movement affords an interesting comparison with the absolute growth in the amount of corporate issues, which appears to have begun in 1920.[22] Though the decline of total issues of 1923 is reflected in a reduction of corporate issues that year, the low point of such issues in the third quarter does not fall below the amount brought out in the first quarter of 1920, and the cyclical growth of corporate issues, subject to considerable fluctuation, appears to extend from 1920 to 1927, when its high point was reached. After 1927 the total volume of corporate issues declined rapidly, except for a brief revival in the first part of 1930.

This phase of the bond market, from the middle of 1922 to the end of 1924, was one of recession and subsequent advance for bond prices and the volume of issues, as well as for indices of business activity and commodity prices. The recession and advance of the bond market, however, did not exactly correspond with the recession and advance in business and commodity prices, nor did the turning points in the two sets of series exactly coincide. The recession and advance of business and commodity prices, which was much less severe than that of 1921, influenced the bond market indirectly through the changes it brought in credit conditions and interest rates. There were,

[21] Chart XIII, p. 69.   [22] Chart XII, p. 67.

however, other factors, such as gold movements, changes in the volume of money in circulation, and the policy of the Federal Reserve System which also greatly affected the abundancy or scarcity of credit, and which at times counteracted and at times supplemented the effects produced by business fluctuations.

The year 1924 was one of considerable significance, both in the administration of credit in the United States and in the bond market. It was one of the four years in the period covered by this study in which the Federal Reserve bought governments in large quantities. These purchases, together with other developments, permitted credit to become extremely easy and interest rates to fall to very low levels. This ease of credit conditions affected the bond market in various ways, but two appear to be of particular importance. First, the surplus funds which the member banks found in their possession allowed them to increase substantially their bond holdings, and these purchases, as well as the purchases of governments by the Federal Reserve, greatly strengthened the market. Second, the fall in long rates and the cheaper cost of borrowing, together with the support given the market by the banks, greatly stimulated new flotations, especially foreign issues.

The direct and immediate relationship between the movements of short rates, long rates, and the volume of offerings in this phase of the market is very striking. Movements of short rates, occasioned by the combined influence of gold movements, Federal Reserve policy, and variations in business activity are reflected, almost immediately, until the latter part of 1924, in the movements of long rates. The fall of long rates that began in 1923 and continued for almost five years will be considered in subsequent chapters. But these fluctuations in long rates, that is, in bond prices, and the concurrent changes they brought in the price of new financing, directly affected the volume of offerings, which increased as bond prices rose, and fell as they declined.

This phase in the bond market is also marked by the commencement in 1923 of the growth in the percentage of corporate issues to total issues. This growth continued practically to the end of the period covered by this study and is of considerable significance in the economic history of the United States after the war.

The wide and at times violent movements that had hitherto characterized the post-war bond market had, by the end of 1924, temporarily come to an end. Various factors combined to bring about such a situation. The most immediate of the problems inherited from the war had been disposed of, and attempts were being made to solve the remaining ones. The European economic structure appeared to be slowly readjusting itself to the new conditions; world markets and international financial relationships had been reëstablished; debt settlements had been signed; definite steps were being taken toward monetary reconstruction. The restoration of the world's industrial and financial fabric appeared well begun. In the United States the depression of 1920 and the recession of 1923 had, by the end of 1924, been succeeded by a substantial degree of prosperity. A large part of the international floating credit balance left from the war had been paid off or refunded. The Federal Reserve System had learned the importance of open-market policy and had developed a technique for its open-market operations. The Treasury had completed the refunding of the post-war short term debt and had made various arrangements, such as the institution of the sinking fund, that seemed capable of handling the national debt in the years to come without embarrassment to the government or inconvenience to security markets. Though fluctuations disturbed the bond market in the next two years, such fluctuations were of smaller amplitude than in the previous four years, and the market of 1925 and 1926 was characterized by a substantial degree of stability.

The *Annual Report of the Secretary of the Treasury* of 1924, written in the fall of that year, contained an excellent summary of the situation in which the country found itself, as it currently appeared.

While it has taken time for this situation [the depression of 1921 and the subsequent problems] to remedy itself, the adjustment has now been made, and both banking and business conditions are in a thoroughly sound position. Prices have been comparatively stable for two or three years, production has increased 20 or 25 per cent. Interest and discount rates, as a rule, have been reduced more than half. Discount rates of the Federal Reserve Bank of New York, for example, have been reduced from 7 to 3 per cent and rates on prime commercial paper from over 7½ per cent to 3½ per cent. Bank deposits have increased six or eight billion dollars from the low point of 1921, or over 20 per cent. At the same time reserves are unusually high, frozen loans have been almost completely liquidated, and the country's banking and credit structure was never in a stronger position and more able to support continued business and industrial expansion. The traffic handled by the railroads continues at almost record levels, and many roads are returning to a dividend-paying basis after years of financial difficulties and struggles to build up road and equipment to a basis of efficiency. The building and automotive industries are prosperous and in turn big factors in maintaining the country's general prosperity.[23]

[23] *Annual Report of the Secretary of the Treasury,* 1924, p. 3.

CHAPTER VII

1925–1926

In 1925 and 1926 bond prices, the volume, and the number of new issues were all more stable than in any other two-year period covered by this study. This situation reflected, perhaps it can even be said was caused by, the substantial degree of stability characteristic of banking and business conditions at this time. Of course these years were not ones of complete immobility and stagnation. There were fluctuations in the indices used to describe the bond market, in business activity, and in the volume and character of bank credit. The security loans of member banks increased more in 1925 than in any year of the post-war decade except 1927, and the stock-market boom of that year was currently described as one of the greatest bull markets of history. In 1925 and 1926 the spread between first and second grade bonds contracted extraordinarily, by more than 25 per cent, and at this time that important post-war change in business financing — the decline in short term commercial loans and the increase in long term, publicly-offered securities — first became apparent.[1] Yet in spite of such movements the bond market in 1925 and 1926 was characterized by a greater degree of stability, or at least by a slower rate of

---

[1] Hardy states that in 1925 an important change took place in the relationship between Federal Reserve credit and the total credit base, i.e., Federal Reserve credit, the monetary gold stock, and Treasury currency. "For the whole period from the end of 1921 to the end of 1925, the volume of Reserve credit remained practically stationary except for (a) seasonal changes due to fluctuations in the currency requirements of the country which have no significance as indicators of over- or under-expansion of credit, and (b) a sharp decline and an equally sharp recovery in connection with the depression and revival of 1924. The net change for the four years was only 36 million dollars, or 2½ per cent. . . . From the end of 1925 through 1929, instead of Federal Reserve credit alone, it was the total credit base, consisting of Federal Reserve credit plus monetary gold stock plus Treasury currency, which tended to remain constant. . . . In short, whereas from 1922 through 1925 the contribution of the Federal Reserve system to the credit resources of the world was approximately stable, in 1925–29 it was the *total* amount of support for currency and bank credit in the United States that was stable" (Hardy, *Credit Policies*, pp. 184–185).

movement, than in either the preceding or succeeding period. This relative steadiness was reached by certain statistical series in the latter part of 1924; others did not achieve it till the middle of 1925; still others retained their usual rapidity of movement during these years. Nevertheless, it seems accurate to consider that 1925 marked the beginning of a new phase in the bond market.

The advance in the latter part of 1924 had carried business indices above normal by December, and this improvement continued in the first few months of 1925. The various indices differ as to the month in which this rise was checked, but it is clear that in the second quarter of the year the advance ceased and, for a month or two, business activity even decreased slightly. In the second half of the year activity again increased, led by the real estate and stock markets, and by a boom in the building industry. The end of the year brought the peak of the movement, and in 1926 business indices slipped back slightly from their high point, although they remained very steady throughout the year. During this entire period all the indices were well above normal, and in Mitchell's analysis [2] business was considered as being at a high level till November 1926, when the recession that carried through 1927 began.

During the first quarter of 1925 wholesale prices, like business activity, continued the advance of the latter part of 1924. Although they receded slightly in April and May, this loss was regained in June and July, and prices were steady the rest of the year. In 1926 they moved slowly downward, falling below normal in July.

In the latter part of 1924 gold was exported for the first time since 1920. These exports continued throughout the first quarter of 1925, and amounted to about 160 millions, the stock of money gold dropping from 4,499 millions in December 1924 to 4,346 millions in March 1925. Concurrently, the Reserve Banks reduced their holdings of governments, which fell from 554 millions in December to 355 millions in April. These movements were not offset by any significant decline in the volume of

[2] Mitchell, "A Review," Chap. XII in *Recent Economic Changes*, vol. II.

money in circulation, which — except for seasonal changes — remained very steady in 1925 and 1926, and the depletion of member-bank reserves thus occasioned brought to an end the decline in rediscounts which had lasted through 1924. Although gold imports began again after the first three months of the year, rediscounts advanced steadily during 1925 and increased from 267 millions in January, when they amounted to 23 per cent of all Federal Reserve credit, to 688 millions in December, when they were 46 per cent of total Reserve credit. Notwithstanding the restrictive effect of these developments, the rise of short rates that had begun in the autumn of 1924 was checked in January and February, and short rates temporarily declined. On February 27, however, the discount rate at New York was raised from 3 to 3.50 per cent, and in March short rates advanced sharply. This advance, subject to fluctuation, continued till the last quarter of the year.

The most significant financial development in 1925, however, was the extraordinary growth in member-bank security loans. Total loans and investments of reporting member banks increased 940 millions during the year, although their investments decreased 210 millions.[3] Thus funds available for commercial and security loans increased 1,150 millions in 1925 — the sum of 940 and 210 millions. Since business indices rose in 1925, especially in the latter part of the year, and since their average was distinctly higher than in 1924, it might be expected that a large part of this 1,150 millions was used to finance trade and industry. But such was not the case.

Although the bond market advanced in 1925, its rise was almost insignificant compared with that of the stock market. The post-presidential boom of 1924 carried over, and the Standard Statistics Company average of stock prices advanced 18 points during the year.[4] Under such circumstances it is not surprising to find that security loans of reporting member banks increased 920 millions, absorbing about four-fifths of the 1,150

---

[3] Savings banks and country banks increased their investments in 1925; city banks' investments decreased. Banks as a whole increased their investments 275 millions. (See Appendix G.)

[4] Chart XIV, p. 118.

millions available for increases in both commercial and security loans. It is, of course, impossible to determine what proportion of this increase in security loans was used to support the stock market, and what to support the bond market. But it is apparent that security loans increased very rapidly at the same time that rediscounts were mounting and short term interest rates advancing. This increase in security loans of member banks carried the volume of such loans above the volume of their investments in June for the first time since 1922, and there they remained till March 1931.[5]

At the end of 1925 the stock of money gold was slightly less than it had been twelve months earlier, and the volume of money in circulation was slightly greater. Total loans and investments of reporting member banks were almost a billion dollars higher, and increases in their security loans accounted for nearly all of

[5] The Annual Report of the Federal Reserve Board described these developments as follows: "The increase of credit for commercial purposes, taking the year as a whole, was moderate in extent, and the growth in the volume of reserve bank credit during the year reflects largely an increase in the demand for loans on securities. During the first half of the year this demand was met by the use of funds released through the decline of loans for commercial purposes, while in the latter half of the year, when the volume of commercial borrowing increased in response to seasonal demands . . . the continued growth in the demand for security loans was reflected in a rapid growth in the volume of bank credit and a rising level of interest rates . . ." (*Annual Report of the Federal Reserve Board,* 1925, p. 4). "The large volume of business and financial activity carried loans and investments of member banks at the end of the year to over $31,000,000,000, a larger total than at any previous time. The increase for the year was about $2,173,000,000, nearly all of which represented an increase in member banks' loans, as the volume of their investments remained relatively constant during the year. That the growth in loans by member banks was largely in the form of loans on securities is indicated by figures for reporting member banks in leading cities which showed for the year 1925 an increase of nearly $1,200,-000,000 in total loans and of about $1,100,000,000 in loans on securities. Among the factors accounting for the rapid growth in member bank loans on securities have been the exceptionally heavy volume of domestic and foreign securities floated during the year and the rise in security values which have made necessary a larger volume of credit for financing transactions in securities" (*ibid.,* p. 21).

Riefler, when considering the extent to which the security flotations of 1924–1928 were carried by bank funds, points out: "The average annual growth in investment holdings of this group of banks (reporting member banks in leading cities) increased from $361,000,000 in the two years preceding March 1924, to $457,000,000 in the four succeeding years, while the average annual growth in security loans increased from $270,000,000 to $601,000,000" (*Money Rates,* p. 194).

the growth. Their commercial loans had expanded somewhat, but this advance was balanced by a decline in their investments. Rediscounts at the Reserve Banks had gone up about 400 millions, but the System's holdings of governments had declined, so that total Reserve Bank credit had increased only 219 millions during the year.

During 1926 the banking situation suffered very little change. Gold continued to flow slowly into the country, but the volume of money in circulation varied only with seasonal requirements. Total loans and investments of reporting member banks increased somewhat, and total Federal Reserve credit declined slightly, but the changes were insignificant and rediscounts were at exactly the same figure in December as they had been a year before.[6] Short term rates remained within a very narrow range in 1926, as they had in 1925. Although the discount rate at New York was raised in January to 4 per cent, short rates eased off distinctly in the first six months of the year. Commercial paper and time money fluctuated downward till they reached 4 per cent in May, and the customers' rate continued to fall till July, when it was 4.38 per cent. The New York discount rate dropped to 3.50 in April, but on August 13 it was brought back to 4.00, and all short rates turned up and rose till October. The advance was not large, however; time money alone reached 5 per cent; and in the last two months of the year short rates eased off again.

Debit balances on international transactions in these years

[6] Although Federal Reserve holdings of governments increased 40 millions between January and June, and then decreased 86 millions in the second half of the year, these changes were largely offset by a decrease in holdings of bills in the first six months of the year and an increase in the last six months, so that the volume of credit extended in these forms remained almost constant. The Reserve Board explained the purchases of governments in the spring and the succeeding sale in the fall as operations undertaken to support the decrease in the discount rate in April and the increase of the rate in August (*Annual Report of the Federal Reserve Board*, 1926, p. 3).

Hardy claims: "The outstanding facts in the credit history of that year (1926) are that the New York Bank rate was reduced and 65 million dollars of government securities were purchased in response to a sudden decline of 10 per cent in the average of stock prices, and that the rates were restored and the securities sold when the stock market had made back the lost ground" (*Credit Policies*, p. 123).

continued to reduce the outstanding credit balance of the United States. The net debit balance of 1925 was very small; the debit balance of 432 millions on capital transactions exceeded the credit balance on current transactions by only 3 millions. In 1926, however, the net debit balance was considerably larger. The credit balance on current transactions dropped to 13 millions, as the net credit balance of merchandise exports declined and gold exports stopped, and the debit balance on capital transactions grew to 522 millions, as foreign investments increased, so that the net debit balance amounted to 509 millions.[7]

The lack of sudden or violent changes in business and banking conditions in these years was reflected by the relatively even course which the bond market pursued at this time. The most striking development in the market was the gradual and almost uninterrupted fall in long term rates, which continued the decline that had begun in 1923, and which took place almost irrespective of the movements of short term rates.

The yield of Moody's Aaa bonds dropped from 4.95 per cent in December 1924 to 4.68 per cent in December 1926, and the yield of the Baa bonds declined from 6.46 to 5.68 per cent in the same period. Only once during these two years, in July and August 1925, was this fall checked for more than one month. Although this interruption coincided with an increase of short rates, the rise of long rates was so small, and ceased so abruptly, in spite of the continued advance of short rates, that it is not possible to be sure that the mounting short rates influenced the action of long rates. Moreover, there was at least one month in this period, March 1926, when bond prices weakened and long term rates temporarily rose, although short rates were falling at the time. This weakness of bond prices appears to have developed in sympathy with the contemporary sharp break in the stock market, and seems to have had no connection with short rate movements.

It should, perhaps, be noted that in spite of fluctuations short rates remained from the middle of 1924 to the end of 1927 in a

[7] *The Balance of International Payments of the United States in 1926* (Trade Information Bulletin 503), p. vi.

range distinctly narrower and distinctly lower than that of the preceding or succeeding years, and this behavior perhaps explains in part the absence of their usual influence on long rates. But even in the few and temporary instances when short rates were above the yield of the Aaa bonds — they were always below the yield of the Baa bonds — bond prices do not appear to have been much affected by the relationship.[8] Consequently it seems substantially accurate to say that in 1925 and 1926 — as during the whole period of the fall in long rates, from 1923 to the early part of 1928 — movements of short rates had very little effect upon the movements of long rates, and that the two types of rates pursued different courses.[9]

The five-year decline in long rates was accompanied by a very striking decrease in the spread between the yields of first and second grade bonds, a decline which lasted as long as did the fall in rates. From 2.30 per cent in August 1923 the spread shrank to 0.86 per cent in March 1928, but the greatest part of this drop took place in the years 1924, 1925, and 1926. In De-

---

[8] Ordinarily the connection between short and long rate movements is seen most readily when short rates advance above long rates, or when, having been above them, short rates fall below them. At such times there is usually substantial harmony of movement, and usually long rates rise abruptly when short rates go above them, or fall when short rates drop below them. But such a relationship is difficult, if not impossible, to find in 1925 and 1926. In November and December 1925 time money went to 4.87, slightly above the yield of the Aaa bonds, which advanced from 4.84 in November to 4.85 in December. The yield of the Baa bonds, however, continued to fall at this time. In September 1926 time money and the customers' rate both moved above the yield of the Aaa bonds; time money remained above through November, and the customers' rate through December. The effect of this changed relationship is difficult to determine exactly. In the preceding August the fall in the yields of both the Aaa and Baa bonds had been temporarily checked, and the decline in the yield of the Baa bonds was checked again in October. But during the other months in which time money and the customers' rate were above the yield of the Aaa bonds the fall in long rates was not interrupted.

[9] In regard to the behavior of interest rates in the post-war period Whitney states: "After 1923 a new situation developed. Bond yields ceased following the commercial paper rate in their minor cyclical movements although they did rise, but to a slight extent, in 1928 and 1929, when the commercial paper rate rose very steeply. . . . After the middle of 1931, bond yields rose with yields of stocks. . . . Evidently factors affecting the rate of interest on short term funds are transmitted to yields on long term loans . . . only at times when conditions are favorable to such a relationship" (*Experiments*, p. 150).

cember 1923 the spread amounted to 2.29 per cent; by December 1924 it had shrunk to 1.51; and in December 1926 it was only 1.00 per cent. The long-continued fall in bond yields and the narrowing spread between the yields of first and second grade securities seems to indicate that there was at this time a demand for fixed income securities greater than the available supply, and that investment funds, finding high grade securities less and less profitable, turned more and more to those of lower rating, disregarding to a progressively greater degree the larger risk attached to them.[10]

Thus movements of interest rates were marked by three principal characteristics at this time. First, from the middle of 1923 to the beginning of 1928 long rates fell almost steadily, apparently irrespective of the action of short rates, and there was not the usual harmony between movements of long and short rates. Second, short rates from the middle of 1924 to the end of 1927 fluctuated within a range lower and narrower than that of the immediately preceding or succeeding years. They appear, in fact, to have been so low and so stable as to have lost almost all of their usual influence upon long rates. Third, during the five-year decline in long term rates the yield of second grade bonds fell more rapidly than did that of first grades, and the spread between them was reduced by about two-thirds. Such behavior of interest rates appears to indicate definitely that from 1923 to 1928 credit conditions were unusually, if not abnormally, easy. This interpretation is supported by the rapid growth of banks' security loans in these years, especially in 1925 and 1927, since the increase of such loans reflects the presence of funds at the disposal of banks which commerce and industry currently do not wish or are not able to absorb.

The steadily rising bond prices of 1925 and 1926 brought a very considerable quantity of new issues into the market. Although the volume of total and of new capital issues remained

---

[10] It can hardly be argued that a difference of one per cent between the yield of first and second grade bonds adequately represents the difference in risk attached to the two types of securities, however difficult it may be to measure accurately such risks. From the end of 1926 to the end of 1928 the difference between the yields of Moody's Aaa and Baa bonds was one per cent or less.

somewhat below the peak reached at the end of 1924, such was
not the case with the number of new issues, which was consistently above the 1924 level. Both sets of indices, however, remained during these two years within a range narrower than that
of any similar period in the post-war decade. This stability is
particularly noticeable in the seasonally adjusted series for the
volume of total and of new capital issues. The index of the "net"
volume of issues, as usual, fluctuated widely, and in the
third quarter of 1926 dropped so low as to become a negative
figure. But the retirement of some 552 millions of government
debt in that quarter — an exceptionally large amount — was
the principal cause of this drop, and great significance can not be
attached to it. During this period the number of issues listed on
the Exchange increased from 1,262 to 1,367.

The steady fall in long term interest rates was accompanied,
as would be expected, by a large volume of refunding. If government issues are not considered, refunding issues in 1926 were
larger than in any other years covered by this study except 1927
and 1928. The large volume of government issues floated in
1922 in connection with the Treasury's refunding program of
course made the total of such issues for that year much larger
than that of 1926.

The strength and breadth of the market, commented upon
month after month in current surveys, induced the flotation of
large quantities of bonds, especially of foreign and municipal
issues. The German Rentenmark loan of 25 millions offered in
September 1925 on a 7.63 basis was heavily oversubscribed.
The Australian issue of 75 millions floated in New York the
same year was the first loan of a British possession ever brought
out elsewhere than in London, and by the end of 1925 municipal
bonds had been bid up to the highest prices in twenty years.[11]
In February 1926 New York City was able to sell an issue of
75 millions, the largest single piece of municipal financing
hitherto handled in New York, on a 3.75–4.15 basis.[12] The
severe break in the stock market in March hardly affected the

[11] S. C. Mosser, "Municipal Bonds in 1925," *Chronicle*, CXXII, 535 (January
30, 1926).   [12] *National City Bank Monthly Letter*, March 1926.

bond market, and in April the Dow-Jones average at 95.14 was a point above its previous high record of 1917. During the remainder of the year the average made new high records almost every month. The market for utility bonds was strengthened during the year when, under certain restrictions, they were placed on the "legal" lists of Massachusetts and New Jersey, although an attempt to have them placed on the New York "legal" list failed. The growth of corporate issues is well-marked in these years, both absolutely and relative to total offerings.

So far as the activity of the market can be judged from the volume of bonds traded on the Stock Exchange, the steady rise in prices was not accompanied by an increased turnover. From the high point reached in December 1924 the average fell almost steadily till May 1926, although in June it once more started up in an advance that was to continue till well into 1927.

It appears that by far the larger part of the purchasing power needed to absorb the "net" amount of offerings in 1925 and 1926 was supplied by the general public.[13] Insurance companies increased their security portfolios by about the same amount as in 1924, but their purchases were a very small percentage of the "net" offerings of these two years. Banks as a whole bought very few bonds in 1925 and 1926 — their purchases being much less than in 1924 or 1927. City banks actually decreased their security holdings in both years,[14] so that security purchases were confined to savings and country banks. The large growth of security loans in 1925, however, even though it is impossible to determine what part of it was used in the bond market and what in the stock market, makes it apparent that a substantial portion of the funds needed in the bond market was indirectly supplied by the banks.

Part of the money used by the public to buy these securities presumably came from the current reduction of the government debt. Although the Treasury floated long term issues in the first quarter of the year in both 1925 and 1926, such increases as these flotations caused in the government's long term debt were

[13] Chart VIII, p. 38. [14] Appendix G.

more than offset by reductions in the short term debt. By 1925 and 1926 the government had reached a point where it was reducing its total debt almost one billion dollars a year, and a large part of the funds released by these reductions presumably sought employment in other fields of investment.

The *Annual Report of the Secretary of the Treasury* for 1925 summarized the situation as follows:

Since 1919 . . . the Treasury has been paying its debts, and the retirement of the outstanding obligations has been greatly in excess of new issues, so that the net effect of the Treasury's operations during this period has been tending to bring about lower rather than higher money rates. Standing at $25,234,000,000 on June 30, 1919, the interest-bearing debt has been reduced to $20,211,000,000 on June 30, 1925. This represents an average annual payment of $837,000,000. . . . The effect of this policy of debt repayment on money is more apparent when it is considered that the principal reduction in the debt has taken place through the retirement of certificates of indebtedness and other short-term securities, which are largely held by banks and financial institutions. . . . For the period as a whole certificates of indebtedness were reduced by about $2,500,000,000 and notes by about $2,000,000,000. . . .[15]

Of very considerable importance to the bond market was the changing relationship of the banks to the security markets that began to be apparent in these years. It is now, of course, well known that during the twenties commercial paper and short term commercial loans of all types showed a decided tendency, if not to decrease, at least not to grow so rapidly as security loans and investments.[16] But in 1925 and 1926 this development was just becoming evident, and the *Annual Report of the Federal Reserve Board* for 1926 commented upon it at some length, pointing out that since 1922 there had been a distinct increase in the proportion of long term assets of member banks, and that

[15] *Annual Report of the Secretary of the Treasury,* 1925, pp. 44–46.
[16] See, for instance, Strong, *Interpretations,* seriatim; *Hearings before a Subcommittee of the Committee on Banking and Currency of the United States Senate, Seventy-first Congress, Third Session, Pursuant to Senate Resolution 71;* Whitney, *Experiments,* Chap. IV; L. B. Currie, *The Supply and Control of Money in the United States* (1934), Chaps. III, IV. The statistics of loans of national banks eligible to be rediscounted which Currie quotes (Table 2, p. 40) are especially significant.

security loans had risen more than any other type of loan or investment.[17]

This decrease of short term commercial loans is in large part to be attributed to the change in methods of financing business that took place after 1920, to the post-war tendency of business to issue stocks and bonds rather than to borrow from banks when in need of capital. The rapid growth in corporate bond issues after the war shows, perhaps more clearly than any other development, the extent to which industry came to rely upon the public security markets as a source of capital. Although there were a number of factors which combined to bring about this alteration in the financial habits of business and this shift from short term to long term borrowing, not the least of them was the ease of credit conditions which prevailed after 1923, and the inducement to sell securities which it provided.

The growing disposition of business to finance itself by borrowing from the public instead of from the banks affected the bond market in a number of ways. First, this change tended to increase the quantity of new bond issues. Second, through the flotation of these securities business concerns often acquired funds which they either could not constantly employ in their own operations, because of the seasonal fluctuation in their ac-

[17] "The growth in investments and loans on securities, which was characteristic of the two years preceding 1926, was in line with the general trend of the banking developments of recent years. Since the middle of 1915 loans and investments of all the banks in the country have increased by over $30,000,000,-000, and about one-third of this increase, or about $10,000,000,000, was in the banks' holdings of investments. These holdings constituted 30 per cent of total loans and investments in the middle of 1926, compared with 27 per cent 11 years earlier. At national banks, which constitute the larger part of the system's membership, there has also been a marked tendency in recent years to use an increasing proportion of their resources in long-term investments. This increased use of bank funds in longer term enterprises, which has continued for a number of years, has been particularly pronounced in the recent five-year period of growth of bank credit beginning in the spring of 1922. . . . During this period of nearly five years the proportion of loans and investments of member banks in leading cities that was in securities and in loans on securities increased from 49 to 57 per cent. The largest growth, both absolutely and relatively, was in security loans, which increased about 66 per cent during the period. All other loans, as reported by the member banks in leading cities, showed a much slower rate of growth during the five-year period than did security loans, the percentage of increase being 18 per cent, compared with 66 per cent for security loans" (*Annual Report of the Federal Reserve Board*, 1926, p. 8).

tivities, or which they could make use of only in the event their enterprises expanded. Consequently such funds were in many cases used to purchase securities, or were lent to brokers through the call-money market, or were left as time deposits with the banks; in each eventuality the bond market was affected. If securities were bought, the securities markets were immediately concerned. If call loans were made, the effect upon the capital markets was nearly as direct. Even if the funds were left as time deposits, the bond market was indirectly influenced, since such deposits tended to increase the loaning powers of the banks and the supply of funds seeking investment.

Furthermore, the greater independence of banking accommodation that these security issues gave to business reacted upon the banks themselves and changed their own relations with the security markets. The banks, as they found less and less opportunity to lend their funds for short term commercial purposes, more and more employed their resources in security loans and in the purchase of investments for their own account. The banks, in other words, came to be less concerned with the direct financing of industry and more intimately connected with the security markets at the same time that their control over the security markets was, in part, reduced by the increase of "outside" call money — that is, call money lent by others than banks. Although such changes in the relationship of banks, industry, and the security markets as have been here considered were taking place in the whole post-war period, the growth of security loans in 1925 made the new situation very apparent.

The period 1925 and 1926 was one in which the indices of business activity and commodity prices, gold movements, the volume of money in circulation, and the amounts of Federal Reserve and member-bank credit, were all substantially more stable than in the preceding or succeeding years. This stability was reflected in the bond market. The indices of new offerings, particularly when corrected for seasonal fluctuation, were remarkably steady. Bond prices were not subject to large or rapid changes, but continued the slow, continuous rise that began in 1923 and which continued till the early part of 1928. This rise of bond prices and the steadiness and strength of the market were, presumably, responsible for the steady flow of new offerings. Long term interest rates, as represented by bond yields, did not reflect the fluctuations in short rates, and it is difficult if not impossible to find that movements of short rates in these years had any great influence on the movements of long rates, and through them, any influence on the volume of offerings. This absence of the usual similarity of movement in long and short rates, as well as the steady decrease in the spread between the yields of first and second grade bonds, and the low level of short rates — compared to preceding and succeeding years — all seem to show that credit was unusually easy and abundant in these years. To this ease of credit conditions can be attributed the stability of the market, the rise of bond prices, and the only large change that took place in the form of bank credit in these years — the growth of security loans in 1925. Although this stability of business conditions and of short and long rates continued, in large measure, in 1927, there were changes in that year in other factors, particularly in Federal Reserve policy and in the volume of new offerings, that differentiate 1927 from the two preceding years.

CHAPTER VIII

1927

IN 1927 the bond market reached the climax of its movement in the post-war decade. Bond prices were higher [1] and new flotations larger than at any time during the period of this study, and all types of issues — new capital, "net" capital, and refunding, as well as corporate, municipal, and foreign [2] bonds — were brought out in record amounts. The volume of bond trading on the Stock Exchange reached the third of the four peaks it attained in the years 1920–1930; the long cyclical increase of corporate flotations that had begun in 1920 touched its high point, with a total of 5,546 millions for the year; and the refunding of the Second Liberty Loan was completed. The volume of total issues offered in the first quarter of 1927 exceeded that of any other similar period in the decade, as did the volume of "net" issues in the first two quarters, and the number of new issues, bolstered by the unprecedented total of 544 in the first quarter, amounted to 2,025 and was greater than in any other post-war year.

This boom in the bond market was accompanied by a slight business recession, which was particularly apparent in the building, automobile, and iron and steel industries. But the recession exerted no depressing effect either upon the bond market or upon the stock market, which advanced steadily from month to month as the boom that culminated in 1929 gathered momentum. This buoyancy in the security markets is presumably to be attributed, in large part, to the speculative fever

[1] The prices of Aaa bonds were slightly higher, for a month of two, in 1930, than they were in 1927; but the average for the year in 1927 was distinctly above that of 1930.

[2] Foreign government issues amounted to 777 millions in 1927 and were exceeded only in 1924, when they amounted to 778 millions (Appendix L). But the total volume of foreign bonds issued in the United States in 1927 — 1,593 millions — was greater than in any other year (*American Underwriting of Foreign Securities in 1929*, Trade Information Bulletin 688, p. 3).

which currently permeated the capital markets, to the great quantity of loanable funds which at this time were put at the disposal of the banks, and to the low level and narrow range of fluctuation which short term rates maintained. This low level was held — indeed, short term rates even declined slightly during the year — notwithstanding the heavy concurrent exports of gold, and such fluctuations as interest rates experienced were contrary to the customary seasonal movements.[3] This unusual behavior of interest rates seems to have possessed a particular significance, and one which can be fully comprehended only in view of all of the forces which operated in the financial world in 1927.

During 1927 business activity receded somewhat from the high levels of 1926, especially in the last six months of the year, and Mitchell described December as a month of "low" activity.[4] But the decline was neither large nor precipitous; its effect was, to some extent, offset by the reversal in June and July of the fall in wholesale commodity prices that had lasted since 1925; and the recession does not, actually, seem to have been a major factor in the situation that existed in 1927, save insofar as it influenced banking policy.

Of more importance than the fluctuations in business activity and commodity prices were the movements of gold and of money in circulation, which in 1927 were of greater significance, and at the same time more complex, than in the previous two years. Since the second quarter of 1925 gold had flowed into the United States almost without interruption. In 1926 gold imports amounted to 93 millions, but with the turn of the year the rate of inflow was suddenly increased. In the first four months of 1927, 118 millions of gold came into the country and the stock of money gold jumped from 4,492 millions in December to 4,610 millions in April, the highest figure it had

---

[3] The firmness of short term rates from March to July was contrary to the usual seasonal easing of rates, as was the decline in the late summer, when approaching crop movements tend to stiffen them; in the last quarter of the year short rates remained nearly constant, although they ordinarily rise to their high for the year between September and January.

[4] Mitchell, "A Review," Chap. XII in *Recent Economic Changes*, II.

ever reached. But in May imports ceased and exports began. These exports, which continued almost without interruption till the middle of 1928, had, by December 1927, reduced the stock of money gold 231 millions.

During the first three months of the year, while gold was being imported, money in circulation remained at approximately the level of the corresponding months of 1926, and the effect of the gold inflow on the banks was neither counteracted nor accentuated by significant changes in the volume of currency outstanding. In April, however, the volume of money in circulation began to decline relative to the comparable figures of the previous year, and month by month it fell progressively further below the corresponding figures of 1926. By December it was 92 millions less than it had been a year earlier, and the losses in member-bank reserves occasioned by the 231 millions of gold exports had been offset by that amount.

The gold exports of 1927, together with the ear-markings, gave the United States a credit balance on international account of 154 millions, in addition to the credit balance of 588 millions arising from commodity trade and invisible items. Against this combined credit balance was a debit balance of 695 millions, occasioned by movements of long term capital and the large volume of foreign securities sold in the United States.[5]

However, it was the policy of the Federal Reserve System which was of primary significance for the credit situation, the condition of member banks, and the security markets in 1927. In January and February total Federal Reserve credit suffered its usual seasonal decline, and it remained at the level it then reached, about 1,050 millions, till August. From January to May there was no striking change in the composition of Federal Reserve assets, in the proportions of bills discounted, bills bought, and government securities held. But in June the Reserve Banks began to purchase government securities, and these purchases increased the System's holdings from 291 millions in May to 606 millions in December, a net rise of 315 millions.

---

[5] *The Balance of International Payments of the United States in 1928* (Trade Information Bulletin 625), pp. vi-vii. The discrepancy of 47 millions was described as "due to errors and omissions."

Until August these open-market operations brought no significant change in the total amount of Reserve credit outstanding,
since the usual seasonal decline in bills bought approximately
offset the purchases of securities. But in September the Reserve Banks began their customary autumn acquisition of acceptances, and thereafter Reserve credit increased very rapidly.
Between August and December it rose 475 millions, and since
rediscounts remained very stable all year,[6] almost all of this
advance was in the form of acceptances and government securities.[7]

These various developments had the net result of making the
position of member banks substantially and progressively easier
during the year. Although 231 millions of gold was lost between April and December, concurrently with the gold exports
money in circulation began to decline, as compared with the
previous year, so that by December the gold losses had been
offset by the fall in money in circulation to the extent of 92
millions, leaving a net loss of only 139 millions. The restrictive
influence which these developments might have had upon member banks was more than compensated for by the Federal Reserve purchases in the summer and fall of government securities
and acceptances. These purchases increased total Reserve
credit about 475 millions in the last half of the year, and placed
in the hands of member banks more than three times the amount
of funds they lost through gold exports.

The effect which these funds produced upon the total credit
of reporting member banks was very striking. After a seasonal
decline in the first two months of the year it grew very rapidly,
more rapidly than in any other year in the post-war decade
except 1924. From 19,690 millions in January 1927 it increased to 21,490 millions in January 1928, a net rise for the
year of 1,800 millions. Since business activity did not advance
during the year — it even declined somewhat — there was no

[6] In January 1927 rediscounts amounted to 481 millions, and by December
they had risen only to 529 millions.
[7] Between May and December the Reserve holdings of acceptances and governments increased 460 millions, an amount almost exactly equivalent to the
475 million increase in total Reserve credit that took place between August and
December.

increased demand for loans for industrial and commercial purposes, and 1,790 millions of the 1,800 million increase took the form of security loans and investments.

The motives that produced the Federal Reserve's policy of easy credit in 1927 have occasioned a great amount of discussion and altercation,[8] but they do not seem to have pertained directly to the internal financial situation in the United States. There had been no credit restrictions in 1925 and 1926 that needed alleviation in 1927, nor was the slight decline in business activity during the year sufficient to warrant so vigorous a policy of expansion as was undertaken. The explanation of the policy seems to be, at least in part, the desire of the Reserve authorities to check gold imports, particularly imports of such large proportions as prevailed in the early months of the year, and their desire to relieve the international credit situation and to take pressure off sterling.

But whatever the reasons that led to the relaxation of credit conditions in 1927, they were of the greatest importance for both the banks and the security markets, then and in the following years, and it does not seem too much to say that 1927 was, for the bond market, the critical year in the entire postwar decade. The funds which were placed at the disposal of the member banks through the Federal Reserve open-market operations were — as always in the period of this study — used very largely to increase security loans and investments, and the purchases of bonds by financial institutions amounted to almost one-third the "net" volume of new issues in 1927, a larger proportion than in any year considered except 1922.[9] And it would seem that the support thus given the market was, to a large extent, directly responsible for the high prices, the great activity, and the unprecedented quantity of flotations of that year.

[8] Almost every writer and commentator on Federal Reserve policy has something to say in regard to the policy pursued in 1927, and the attention given it is second only to that paid Federal Reserve policy in the period 1928–1930.

[9] Life insurance companies bought more bonds in 1927 than in any other year covered by this study, and the purchases of city banks were exceeded only in 1922 and in 1930.

However, in spite of the heavy purchases of bonds by banks in 1927, made possible by the funds placed in their hands by the Federal Reserve System, and notwithstanding the fact that 1927 was the peak year in the post-war bond market, not all of the funds in the money market were absorbed by the bond market, nor was speculative attention fixed on it exclusively. The stock market, following its decline in the first part of 1926, had begun to rise in June of that year, and the advance continued in 1927, the averages advancing from month to month with hardly a setback. The Standard Statistics average, at 106 in January 1927, had, by December, increased to 133. The volume of new stock issues previous to 1927 — aside from the boom in the latter part of 1919 — had reached its post-war peak in the first quarter of 1926. But in the first quarter of 1927 it went to a new high level, and, after a small decline in the second and third quarters, to a still higher peak in the last quarter of the year. The boom that achieved such tremendous proportions in 1928 and 1929 was well begun, and with this advance began that extraordinary growth of brokers' loans and of "outside" loans that was later of such sinister significance.

The security markets were further congested in 1927 by the retirement of the Second Liberty Loan and the large flotations of government securities which the operation entailed. These offerings, which were the largest since 1922, began in March, when the Treasury first announced its refunding plans, and continued through September. By the exchange of the Second Libertys for five-year 3½ per cent notes offered in March, and for 3⅜ per cent Treasury bonds of 1943–1947 offered in June, and through purchases of Libertys for the sinking fund, the 3,105 millions of Second Libertys outstanding on March 1 were reduced to about 758 millions by November 15, when this remainder was redeemed.[10] This last operation was facilitated by the use of the 637 million Treasury surplus, the largest since the war.[11]

[10] *Annual Report of the Secretary of the Treasury,* 1927, pp. 37–41.

[11] "The surplus of 1927 was an anomaly, resulting from a combination of unusual and nonrecurring items in both receipts and expenditures. Almost two-

Since 1927 was the peak year in the post-war bond market, the climax of the period, the course of the market in that year has a particular interest. The increase of bond trading of the second half of 1926 carried past the turn of the year, and the curve of actual trading touched its peak in January, although the twelve-month moving-average did not reach its maximum till May. During the remainder of the year bond trading declined, but bond prices continued their long five-year advance, interrupting it only to a very slight extent in the three months May, June, and July as short rates stiffened. The weakness of bond prices, however, was probably caused as much by the tremendous volume of issues that had been brought out in the first six months of the year as by the slight increase in short rates. However, in August the Reserve Bank of New York lowered its discount rate to 3.50 per cent, short rates fluctuated downward, and long rates resumed their fall. By December the yields of Aaa and Baa bonds had declined to 4.46 and 5.32 per cent, as compared with 4.66 and 5.61 in the preceding January. They remained at this level, almost without a change, till May 1928. This was the lowest point reached by the yield of the Baa bonds in the period of this study; the yield of the Aaa bonds dropped slightly below this level in September and October 1930.

The first two months of 1927 brought very large quantities of new issues into the market, as the seasonal decline in Federal Reserve and member-bank credit combined with the very large gold imports to ease money rates. The one billion volume of new issues in the first six weeks of the year was an unprecedented amount, but bond prices continued to rise.

In March governments soared as the Treasury announced its plans for refunding the Second Liberty Loan, and lifted the whole list with them. Atchison General 4's broke through a 4.20 yield basis for the first time in many years, and the Dow-Jones average made a new high record of 97.16. Gold imports continued large this month, money in circulation began to decline,

---

thirds of the surplus of $635,000,000 was due to receipts on account of capital assets, of back collections in excess of tax refunds, and other items of a fast-disappearing or nonrecurring character" (*ibid.*, p. 21).

and member-bank credit started the advance that was to continue throughout the year. The gold imports of April carried the stock of money gold to the highest point it had yet reached, and to a point not exceeded till 1931, and the Dow-Jones average again made a high record of 97.49.

May, June, and July saw bond prices weaken and long rates increase slightly as gold exports began. In April the yields of the Aaa and Baa bonds had been 4.58 and 5.48 per cent, but by July these had increased to 4.60 and 5.55. In June and July time money and commercial paper also tightened in an unseasonable firmness, though the customers' rate continued to decline. The softness of bond prices was currently attributed to the extraordinarily large volume of issues floated in the past six months and to "indigestion" in the market, rather than to the rise of short rates. This "indigestion" brought a certain amount of public criticism of the habit, then common in certain issuing houses, of classifying an issue as "all sold" when blocks of it still remained in the hands of subsidiary distributors in Wall Street.[12] In June the city of New York placed an issue of 60 millions on the very cheap basis of 3.50–3.90 per cent, new offerings continued large, and brokers' loans, which had been growing steadily since the first of the year, passed the previous high record made in 1926.[13] In July comment on the "marked oversupply of bonds" continued as the flotations of the first six months of 1927 were found to be approximately as large as the total offerings of 1926.

In August the situation changed. Both long and short rates receded as the Federal Reserve Bank of New York lowered its rate to 3.50 per cent and total Reserve credit began to increase. The talk in the market surveys of the "oversupply" of bonds and the market's "indigestion" was superseded by a discussion that lasted throughout the summer as to the advisability of

[12] *Chronicle*, CXXV, 3718 (June 25, 1927).

[13] The figures used for brokers' loans are taken from *Facts and Figures Relating to the American Money Market* (1931). The series used is "Brokers' Loans Reported by the N. Y. Stock Exchange" (p. 82); it is a more comprehensive series than that taken from reports of reporting member banks in New York City (given in *Facts and Figures*, p. 80), though it does not extend back so far as does the reporting member-bank series.

establishing a clearing house for bonds.[14] In September total
Federal Reserve credit began to grow rapidly as the system
bought acceptances, and the Dow-Jones average made a new
high of 98.30. In October Federal Land Bank bonds were
brought out with a 4 per cent coupon rate for the first time,
and the Dow-Jones average went up to 98.76. The market
moved smartly ahead again in November, as the retirement of
the Second Liberty Loan was completed. Although the Federal
Reserve stopped its policy of expansion in December, short
rates were little affected and long rates continued to decline.

The year 1927 was a crucial one, not only in the history of
the bond market, but also in the post-war financial history of
the United States. In the early months of the year gold imports carried the stock of money gold up to the highest point
it had yet reached; and although after April substantial quantities of gold were exported, funds placed in the hands of member banks through the very large purchases of government
securities by the Reserve Banks more than made up for such
strain as these exports might have occasioned. Consequently,
credit remained easy and short rates did not rise — they were,
in fact, distinctly lower at the end of the year than at the beginning. Low interest rates and the large supply of banking
funds seeking employment in the security markets permitted,
perhaps it can be said caused, the continued fall in long rates
and the flotation of an unprecedented volume of securities. In
the boom of 1927 bond prices and offerings reached the highest
level of the post-war period, but the influence of easy money
and cheap credit was not confined to the bond market. Stock
prices and offerings also increased to record levels, and though
the levels of that year subsequently were left far behind, the
boom that culminated in 1929 had its beginnings in 1927, if
not earlier. This rise of the stock market intimately affected
the bond market, and to it and the new financial situation it
created can be attributed in large measure the termination of
the bond-market boom in the early months of 1928.

[14] *Chronicle,* CXXV, 869 (Aug. 13, 1927).

CHAPTER IX

1928–1930

UNTIL its culmination, the stock-market boom in 1928 and 1929 was the great dominating influence in the business world and of controlling importance in every sphere of commercial and financial activity. The speculative fever that carried share values up and up, in spite of the high and rising interest rates, in spite of the low yield of stocks that high prices had already brought, in spite of the efforts of the Reserve System to control the movement, was the central factor in the financial world in this period. It overshadowed all other developments, and analysis of these years must be based upon the actions of the stock market. Nor were the consequences of the market's movement confined to the boom period. After the stock market broke in October 1929 the fall in security values severely augmented the business depression that developed, and in many ways was of almost equal significance.

The effect that the boom and its subsequent collapse had upon the bond market was such as to group these three years into a single phase of recession. Although bond prices remained steady and offerings large in the early months of 1928, the growing interest in the stock market and the rise of short rates that came with the turn of the year foreshadowed the rise of long rates, the higher cost of borrowing, and the consequent decline of new offerings that presently developed. This downward movement of bond prices and of new flotations continued till the stock market broke in the autumn of 1929. In the first part of 1930, as business indices ceased to fall and stock prices temporarily rallied, bond prices — and to some extent new issues — recovered, but the revival did not last. In the latter part of the year bond prices and new offerings renewed their decline at an accelerated pace, in spite of the low and falling interest rates. The fall was not primarily motivated by those factors which usually influence the bond market directly, such

as the relationship of short and long rates and Federal Reserve
policy, but by psychological and political influences, and all
those forces which come to the fore as the depression phase of

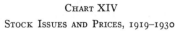

CHART XIV

STOCK ISSUES AND PRICES, 1919–1930

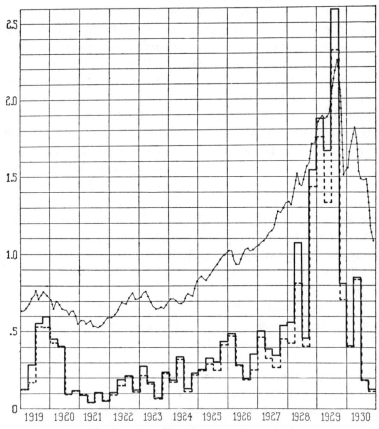

——— Total Issues, by Quarters, in Millions.
- - - - New Capital Issues, by Quarters, in Millions.
..... Stock Prices, Standard Statistics Company Average,
     by Months, in Relatives, 1926 = 100.

a business cycle develops. However, since the actions of the
stock market were of more importance during the greater part
of these three years than were those of either the bond market
or anything else, analysis of the years 1928, 1929, and 1930 is
most readily achieved in terms of the stock market's move-

ments, and the advances and recessions of stock prices divide this interval into a number of fairly distinct periods.

At the end of 1927 business was not inflated; during the year it had remained below the levels of 1925 and 1926, and a decline in the latter months had carried some of the indices below normal. Although commodity prices had recovered to some extent during the year, they also were below normal and well below the peak of 1925. In spite of the gold exports in the latter part of the year and the restrictive effect which they tended to exert, short term rates continued low in the final months of 1927, with a slight downward tendency; their low level was, of course, largely attributable to Federal Reserve policy. In short, these indices gave little evidence of the presence of a large speculative movement, or of an abnormal situation. However, their evidence was not complete.

The Federal Reserve had pursued a rigorous policy of expansion in 1927, and it was apparent by the end of the year that the policy of the past six months had induced a substantial degree of speculation. The strength and activity of the bond market during the year had been unparalleled; the stock market had made new post-war highs almost every month, and the year's advance — as measured by the Standard Statistics Company average — had been the greatest in any year since the war; the loans — particularly the security loans — and investments of member banks had increased persistently; and the volume of brokers' loans had reached almost unprecedented proportions. Believing that this situation required a change of policy, the Federal Reserve System shifted its position with the turn of the year and instituted restrictive measures; and the first phase of the 1928–1930 period seems to extend from December 1927, when the new policy was instituted, to the summer of 1928, when the rise of the stock market [1] was temporarily checked.

In January [2] the Reserve Banks began to sell governments on

[1] For a very careful and thorough discussion of Federal Reserve policy in these years, and the changes which developed in the banking situation, see Seymour Harris, *Twenty Years of Federal Reserve Policy* (1933), II.

[2] The Federal Reserve policy of expansion was reversed in December 1927, but the results of the change did not become apparent till January 1928. (See

a large scale, and on February 3 the discount rate at New York was raised from 3½ to 4 per cent. These developments were immediately reflected in the action of short rates, stock prices, brokers' loans, and reporting member-bank credit. In January time money and the customers' rates, and in February commercial paper rates, began advances that continued, subject to fluctuation, until October 1929. The stock market gained only one point in January and dropped back two in February, and brokers' loans receded slightly in these months from the peak they had reached in December. The increase of reporting member banks' security loans and investments to new high levels in January pushed total reporting member-bank credit to a new peak that month; but in February and March their security loans declined sharply, so that their total credit, in spite of the continued growth in investments, checked its advance. Concurrently with the change in Federal Reserve policy the Treasury took the first step toward the refunding and retirement of the Third Liberty Loan due September 15, 1928, of which 2,148 millions were outstanding at the end of 1927. On January 16, 1928, the Treasury offered 3½ per cent 3–5 year Treasury notes in exchange for the Liberty Bonds, and about 607 millions of such bonds were so refunded.[3]

The restrictive effects of the Federal Reserve policy, however, were partially vitiated by a number of factors. First, gold exports almost ceased in January and February, and, although they recommenced in March, the stock of money gold remained almost constant in these two months and member banks were temporarily relieved of the strain that the exports had imposed. Second, the seasonal drop of money in circulation in January, some 326 millions, was unusually large, and money in circulation in the early months of 1928 was some 150 millions less than in the corresponding period of the previous year.[4] Third,

---

Annual Report of the Federal Reserve Board, 1928, pp. 3–4; *Annual Report of the Secretary of the Treasury,* 1928, p. 5; *Sen. Res. 71,* p. 141, statement of Dr. A. C. Miller.)

　[3] *Annual Report of the Secretary of the Treasury,* 1928, pp. 25–28.

　[4] The volume of money in circulation in 1928 was considerably less than the amount in circulation in 1927 in all but the last two months of the year. The

and most important, the Federal Reserve System continued, from January through May, to buy sufficient acceptances to maintain their holdings close to the seasonal peak of December 1927. In December 1927 their acceptance holdings amounted to 378 millions, and in May were still 349 millions. Ordinarily Federal Reserve holdings of acceptances decline very rapidly from the seasonal peak reached at the year-end to a low point in August, and the continued purchases of acceptances in the spring of 1928 must, it would seem, have substantially lessened the tightening effect that the sales of government securities would otherwise have tended to have upon credit conditions. The restrictive influence of the Federal Reserve policy was further weakened by the fact that from May 18, 1928, when the New York discount rate was raised to 4½ per cent, till the spring of 1929 buying rates for acceptances at the New York Reserve Bank were always below the discount rates.[5]

Finally, it may be noted that during the spring of 1928 the member banks showed little of that dislike for remaining in debt to the Reserve Banks upon which the Reserve authorities had relied and upon which the success of their restrictive policy was predicated. Rediscounts grew from 465 millions in January, when they were at their low point for the year and amounted to about 34 per cent of total Reserve credit, to 1,090 millions in July, when they reached their high point for the year and accounted for about 71 per cent of total Reserve credit.

---

average amount in circulation in 1928 was 4,793 millions, and in 1927 4,897 millions. The *Annual Report of the Federal Reserve Board* for 1928 says that it is not clear why money in circulation declined in 1927 and the early part of 1928. It hazards the suggestion that the business recession of 1927 may have been the original cause and that the continued fall, after business improved in 1928, was brought by the continued low prices for some commodities and the tendency of banks to hold less vault cash in 1928 than in 1927 (p. 18). The business revival and speculative boom of 1928 would have tended, it would seem, to increase the volume in circulation that year.

[5] At the beginning of 1928 buying rates for acceptances at the New York Bank for maturities up to 90 days were 3–3⅜ per cent. The rates began to rise at the end of January; on May 18, when the discount rate was raised to 4½ per cent, buying rates were increased to 4 per cent; they were advanced again to 4¼ per cent on July 13, when the discount rate went to 5 per cent. Although buying rates for these maturities were raised again on July 26 to 4½–4⅝ per cent, the differential in favor of acceptances continued till the spring of 1929.

Instead of a liquidation of clients' accounts being forced by the pressure which Reserve operations put upon member banks, member banks' borrowings rapidly advanced — no doubt in part because of the profitable differential existing between the rediscount rate and open-market rates —, and the funds which they lost because of Federal Reserve sales of governments were replaced, in part, by the funds which they borrowed from the Reserve Banks.

The situation in the spring of 1928 was further complicated by a vigorous revival of business activity and wholesale prices. This advance, subject to some fluctuation, continued till the summer of 1929. The precise effect which it had upon the speculative movement and the financial situation is somewhat obscure, but no doubt the recovery increased the confidence of the business world and appeared to form a firm foundation for the speculative boom at the same time that it increased the demand for banking accommodation and, consequently, the dependence of the member banks upon the Reserve System.[6]

On May 18, however, the discount rate at New York was raised to 4½ per cent, and in the latter part of the month the System stopped its purchases of acceptances and let its holdings decline very rapidly. Concurrently, the rise of brokers' loans, stock prices, and the security loans and total credit of reporting member banks came to an end. The stock market broke sharply. The June average was 7 points below that of May, and in July it dropped another point, though stock offerings continued to increase, and in the second quarter, at 1,073 millions, were almost double the volume of the first quarter.

This check in the advance of stock prices ended the first phase of this three-year period. During this phase both the volume and number of bond offerings were very large, though not so large as in the previous year, and bond prices remained almost constant at the high level reached at the end of 1927. In December 1927 the yield of Moody's Aaa and Baa bonds were, respectively, 4.46 and 5.32 per cent; in April they were

---

[6] Commercial loans of reporting member banks increased persistently in 1928 and 1929.

still 4.46 and 5.33 per cent, and New York City was able to
float an issue of 23 millions at the lowest rate in seventeen
years.[7] The rise of short rates, however, carried time money
and the customers' rate above the yield of Moody's Aaa bonds
in March, and in June the commercial paper rate also went
above the yield of the Aaa bonds as time money, advancing to
5.70 per cent, moved above the yield of the Baa bonds. This
changed relationship, as well as the shift of financial attention
to the stock market, checked in April the long five-year decline
in bond yields; and in May, as credit tightened, they turned
up. So far as may be judged, bond trading, after the first two
or three months of the year, fluctuated downward through 1928.

In July 1928 it might have seemed reasonable to believe that
the restrictive measures of the Federal Reserve System had
proved effective and had checked the speculative boom.[8] Since
December 393 millions of governments had been sold by the Reserve Banks, and by July their holdings of acceptances had
declined to 185 millions, an amount in line with the quantity
held in July in previous years and almost 200 millions less
than the holdings of the first four months of the year. Credit
conditions had been further tightened by gold exports that had
lowered the stock of money gold 266 millions since December.
Rediscounts had more than doubled since the first of the year,
and in July amounted to 71 per cent of total Reserve credit
outstanding. Short term interest rates were rising; on July 13
the rediscount rate of the New York Reserve Bank was raised,
for the third time since January, to 5 per cent; and even the
advance of business activity seemed to hesitate.[9] Moreover,
stock prices were distinctly lower than they had been in May,
and bond yields were rising, ending their long five-year decline.
The best municipals, which earlier in the year had sold on a
3.85 basis had dropped to one of 4.10–4.25,[10] and even gov-

[7] *National City Bank Monthly Letter*, April 1928.
[8] Harris admits that "From June to August reserve policy seemed to be verg-
ing on success" (*Twenty Years*, II, 446).
[9] The Federal Reserve index receded in June and July, and the Harvard Economic Society index dropped sharply in the latter month; the Brookmire index
continued to advance, however.
[10] *National City Bank Monthly Letter*, August 1928.

ernments were weak, although the Treasury was retiring large amounts of the Third Liberty Loan.[11]

However, a new situation developed in the summer of 1928, and the forces affecting the financial world rearranged themselves. Gold exports came to an end in June, the stock of money gold remained almost constant in the last six months of the year, and the member banks were no longer under the strain the exports had imposed. In August the Federal Reserve sales of governments and acceptances ceased, and, although Federal Reserve holdings of governments changed little during the remainder of the year, such was not the case with acceptances.[12]

Since a differential in favor of acceptance rates as compared with the discount rate had existed since the spring, the seasonal increase in credit requirements in the fall brought a very rapid growth in this form of credit.[13] On August 13 authority was given the Reserve Banks by the Reserve Board to buy sufficient acceptances to accommodate the increased credit needs of

[11] On May 11 a public offer was made by the Treasury to purchase at the option of the holders up to 50 millions of Third Libertys at 100 $\frac{8}{32}$ plus accrued interest, and some 51 millions were so retired. On June 11 a similar offer was made to purchase up to 125 millions at 100 $\frac{2}{32}$ plus accrued interest, and 104 millions were sold to the Treasury under this offer. On July 5 the Treasury offered 3⅜ per cent 12–15 year bonds in exchange for Third Libertys, and 108 millions were refunded in this operation. The sinking fund retired some 60 millions of Third Libertys in July, and on August 1 the Treasury offered to purchase Third Libertys in indefinite quantities at 100 $\frac{1}{32}$ up to September 14, and 66 millions were repurchased under this offer. A further 103 millions were exchanged for the nine-months 4¼ per cent Treasury certificates offered September 7, and 35 millions were bought at par on September 15. Provision for the few bonds remaining outstanding was made from the cash receipts of the eleven-months 4¾ per cent certificates sold on October 15, 1928 (*Annual Report of the Secretary of the Treasury*, 1928, pp. 25–28).

[12] The change in Federal Reserve policy in the fall of 1928 Harris refers to as "a disastrous reversal of policy" (*Twenty Years*, I, 528). Certainly the cessation of the restrictive measures of the spring was followed by a new burst of violent speculation. What motives lay behind this change of policy is not clear. Harris suggests (pp. 437–438) that political pressure for easier credit, disappointment with the results of the policy of the previous six months — notably the fact that high call-money rates had brought quantities of "outside" money into the market —, and fear of the repercussions from high rates in Europe all played a part in the change. Perhaps the success that seemed to have attended the restrictive policy in the spring, and the consequent belief that speculation had been checked, is part of the explanation of the change.

[13] The total volume of acceptances outstanding increased from 952 millions in August to 1,284 millions in December (*Facts and Figures*, p. 61).

the autumn,[14] and since the low rates rendered acceptances unattractive to investors, the Reserve Banks, beginning in September, bought very large quantities. These purchases by December amounted to 305 millions, and had increased the bill portfolio of the Reserve Banks to 483 millions, a figure about 25 per cent higher than the year-end average of the previous four or five years.[15] These purchases appear to have exceeded the seasonal increase in credit requirements,[16] for in October and November — ordinarily months when credit is tight and interest rates firm — reporting member banks were able to reduce their rediscounts 167 millions, and short rates temporarily softened. It would thus appear that part of the increase in the Federal Reserve discount portfolio of the first half of the year, caused by sales of government securities, was in the second half of the year shifted to the acceptance portfolio because of the low acceptance rates; and, consequently, it would seem that the restrictions which had been imposed in the spring were, to that extent, relaxed in the fall. In December, however, rediscounts again increased and, together with the growth in acceptances bought, pushed total Reserve credit to the highest figure since 1921.

During the summer and fall of 1928 security loans and total credit of reporting member banks fluctuated in a narrow range, slightly below the peak of the previous May, though their investments steadily declined. But in December, as short rates resumed their advance, reporting member-bank security loans and total credit again increased and passed the levels of the early part of the year.[17] Although commercial banks bought

---

[14] *Sen. Res. 71*, pp. 166–167, statement of the Hon. C. S. Hamlin.

[15] Before 1928 changes in Federal Reserve holdings of acceptances were almost entirely seasonal; there was practically no year-to-year change (*Annual Report of the Federal Reserve Board*, 1928, pp. 13–14). In December 1928 the Reserve Banks held for their own account and for the account of foreign correspondents roughly three-fourths of all acceptances outstanding — a considerably larger proportion than they had ever held before.

[16] *Sen. Res. 71*, pp. 166–167, statement of the Hon. C. S. Hamlin. Also *Annual Report of the Federal Reserve Board*, 1928, pp. 6–7.

[17] Hardy states: "The result of the combination of gold inflow, increased rediscounts, increased acceptance buying, and stable holdings of government securities was to restore to member-bank reserves about two-thirds of the funds which had been squeezed out in the first half of the year" (*Credit Policies*, p. 131).

few bonds in 1928, the purchases of life insurance companies and savings banks were substantial; but approximately two-thirds of total "net" offerings were left for others than financial institutions to absorb.

In spite of the tight credit conditions, the high and rising interest rates, and the restrictive policy of the Reserve Banks, stock prices and brokers' loans had tentatively renewed their advance in August. This advance rapidly gathered momentum. The Standard Statistics Company stock average, at 144 in July, had risen to 171 by December. Brokers' loans increased in the same period from 4,837 millions to 6,440 millions. The larger part of this increase was furnished by "outside" funds flowing into the New York money market,[18] attracted by the high level of call money, which averaged 7.07 per cent between July and December and went to 12 per cent at the year-end. Although short rates, already higher than long rates, continued to rise — except for a temporary softening in October and November as Federal Reserve purchases of acceptances eased the credit situation —, bond prices, apparently sympathetically influenced by the soaring stock prices, advanced from August through November, although in the last month of the year they turned down in a decline that continued till October 1929.

The advance of stock prices and the concurrent ease of selling stock issues in the latter part of 1928 brought tremendous quantities of new offerings into the market. Although the volume of issues in the third quarter receded in the usual seasonal decline from the level of the previous quarter, the volume of flotations in the last three months of the year shot up to the unprecedented total of 1,541 millions. Both the number and volume of bond flotations, as stock prices and offerings began their rapid increase in the latter half of 1928, declined sharply to about half the volume of the first half of the year. "Net" issues fell precipitately, as more bonds were retired than issued, and their index dropped to the largest negative figure in the

---

[18] Of the 1,603 million increase in brokers' loans between July and December, 1,128 millions were "For the Account of Out of Town Banks," "For the Account of Others," and from private banks, corporations, etc. (*Facts and Figures*, pp. 81–82).

period of this study. In the last quarter of 1928 total issues were smaller than stock flotations for the first time in the period of this study,[19] although 71 new issues were listed on the Exchange during the year. The decline in corporate and foreign government issues in the third quarter of 1928 was particularly abrupt; although corporate offerings rallied somewhat in the last quarter of 1928 and the first two quarters of 1929, there were practically no foreign issues brought out in the last half of 1928 or in 1929.

The advance of stock prices, issues, and brokers' loans that had begun in August 1928 continued, with only a temporary check in the spring of 1929, till October of that year and constituted the culminating phase of speculation. There were, however, significant movements of other economic forces during this time that must be summarized before considering the termination of the boom.

The United States Department of Commerce estimated that in 1928 the United States had, in international transactions, credit balances of 650 millions on commodity trade and miscellaneous invisible items account, and 272 millions on gold export account; against this are to be set debit balances of 708 millions on long term capital account and 226 millions on short term capital account, leaving a net discrepancy of 12 millions caused by errors and omissions.[20] The export of long term capital in 1928, 708 millions, was greater than that of any other year considered in this study, although the total of foreign issues underwritten in the United States was not so great as in 1927. The discrepancy was caused, apparently, by the resale to Europe of European securities and by the very large increase in 1928 in the amount of United States securities bought back from foreigners. However, more than two-thirds of the foreign

---

[19] Bond flotations continued to be smaller than stock flotations in the first, second and third quarters of 1929. In Ellsworth's series of new bond issues, which included only long term, new capital, corporate financing, bond offerings were smaller than stock offerings in the second, third, and fourth quarters of 1919, the first and second quarters of 1920, the third and fourth quarters of 1928, and in all four quarters of 1929 (Ellsworth, "Investments," p. 103).

[20] *The Balance of International Payments of the United States in 1929* (Trade Information Bulletin 698), pp. vi–vii.

securities underwritten in the United States in 1928 were issued in the first half of the year,[21] and in the second half of the year, as interest rates rose, foreign long term borrowing was sharply curtailed, and the necessary financing of international trade was, apparently, done by short term borrowing.[22]

The developments of 1929 that formed the background for the culmination of the boom can be described briefly. Business indices continued to fluctuate upward, making their high points in midsummer; [23] although they receded in the late summer and early fall, the decline did not become precipitate till after October. Wholesale prices remained through the summer at approximately the level of 1928, but in the autumn began a decline that carried through 1930 and 1931. Money in circulation stayed at about the same level as in 1928, its movements chiefly influenced by seasonal factors. The rising interest rates and the stock-market boom reduced sharply the United States' export of long term capital to 319 millions, less than half the amount of 1928, and at the same time attracted considerable quantities of gold and of short term funds from abroad.[24] Gold began to flow into the United States in February, principally from Europe, and before the imports ceased in October the stock of money gold had been raised to 4,386 millions, an increase of 259 millions. This inflow, the Treasury pointed out, was "not reflected in a reduction of member-bank

[21] *The Balance of International Payments of the United States in 1928* (Trade Information Bulletin 625), p. 40.   [22] *Ibid.*, p. 49.

[23] The Brookmire index made its high of 115.0 in June; the Federal Reserve index its high of 110 in July; the Harvard Economic Society index its high of 2.04 in July.

[24] The United States Department of Commerce estimated that in 1929 the United States' net credit balance on merchandise trade and invisible miscellaneous items account was contracted to 377 millions, little more than half the figure for 1928, and that imports of short term capital gave the United States a credit balance on this account of 13 millions, compared with a debit balance of 226 millions in 1928. Against these credit balances are to be set debit balances of 319 millions on long term capital account and 120 millions on account of gold imports, leaving a net discrepancy of 49 millions (*The Balance of International Payments . . . in 1930*, Trade Information Bulletin 761, pp. viii–ix). These estimates are for the entire year, and, since gold was exported and foreign balances withdrawn in the last three months of 1929, short term lending and gold imports in the first nine months of the year were larger than these net figures.

discounts at the reserve banks, but was taken up largely in the liquidation of acceptance holdings, which carried a higher rate of interest than discounts, and in part by further sales of United States securities by the reserve banks." [25] Rediscounts, in fact, remained at the level of the latter part of 1928, fluctuating between 850 and 1,100 millions. The Federal Reserve Banks' holdings of governments dropped from 263 millions in December to 147 millions in July, a net decline of 116 millions, while in the same period their holdings of acceptances fell from 483 millions to 75 millions, a net decline of 408 millions. This fall in acceptance holdings was considerably greater than the usual seasonal decline, and the low point of 75 millions reached in July was about 125 millions below the seasonal low point of previous years. The large decline in acceptance holdings reduced total reserve credit from 1,824 millions in December 1928 to 1,380 millions in July and, since rediscounts stayed at about the same level, increased their proportion of total Federal Reserve credit to about 80 per cent.

The open-market operations of the Federal Reserve System in the spring of 1929, however, were not of great moment, and were not the principal means by which the System endeavored to control the situation. The policy of the spring of the previous year had failed, in the sense that stock prices and brokers' loans had renewed their advance in the fall of 1928, and hence it was, perhaps, logical to abandon it. Moreover, the security portfolio of the Reserve System was, by 1929, so reduced that the sale of the small remaining quantity of government bonds would hardly have affected the situation. Also, further increases in the discount rate were looked upon with disfavor by many of the Reserve authorities, partly because of the effect that such increases would have presumably produced upon business,[26] partly because of certain differences of opinion as to how and when such rates, if imposed, should be introduced, and partly because of certain doubts as to the efficacy of such

---

[25] *Annual Report of the Secretary of the Treasury,* 1930, pp. 19–20.

[26] It appeared self-evident to certain Reserve authorities that increases in rediscount rates in the spring of 1929 sufficient to check speculation in the

rates, unless very large, since much of the money supporting speculation was "outside" money and was thought to be less sensitive to Reserve policy than New York bank credit. In these circumstances the System turned to the policy of "direct pressure" and "moral suasion."

This policy, about which so much has been said and written, marked a considerable change in Federal Reserve doctrine and procedure. It represented a shift from the "quantitative" control of credit, upon which Reserve authorities had previously relied, to a "qualitative" control, that is, to a regulation of the uses to which member banks put Federal Reserve funds.[27] Although the policy was, in a general way, an effort to control speculation, it had, as a more immediate goal, the object of making money "high" when used for "speculative" purposes and (relatively) "low" when used for the purposes of "legitimate business."

The policy had been foreshadowed in the *Annual Report of the Federal Reserve Board* of 1928 in the distinction made there between "credit" and "banking" policy,[28] and on November 22, 1928, the Federal Reserve Council at its meeting in Washington advised that the Reserve authorities ask the member banks for "coöperation" in the attempt to control speculation — that is, that the Federal Reserve System embark on a policy

---

stock market would necessarily be so great as to prostrate business. Also, it was felt that such increases would be very hard to justify in view of the provisions of the Federal Reserve Act and in view of the fact that the reserve ratio was above 65 per cent in January 1929 and grew steadily during the spring. There was not, however, unanimity among Reserve authorities as to the desirability of abandoning the policy of rate increases, and, as is well known, the New York Bank differed sharply with the Reserve Board on this point.

[27] See, for instance, Hardy, *Credit Policies*, pp. 124–137, on this point.

[28] "Influence exerted by a reserve bank on the loan and investment policy of an individual member bank is ordinarily exercised only over banks that are borrowers from the reserve banks. It is in the nature of banking supervision, and is akin in many respects to the bank examination function of the reserve system. This phase of reserve bank policy may be called banking policy. . . . The importance of banking policy lies in promoting the soundness of member banks, and coöperation of these banks with the Federal reserve system in carrying out banking policy is essential to the maintenance of sound banking conditions. For influencing general credit conditions, however, the Federal reserve system relies on credit policy rather than on banking policy" (*Annual Report of the Federal Reserve Board*, 1928, pp. 9-10).

of direct pressure.[29] On February 2, 1929, the Reserve Board
addressed a letter to all the Reserve Banks in which its views
as to the proper conduct for Reserve Banks in the existing circumstances were expressed. This letter was supplemented on
February 7 by a statement to the public, which briefly discussed
the current situation and the relation of the Reserve Banks to
the member banks and incorporated part of the letter of February 2. In this statement the policy of direct pressure was
outlined very forcibly. Although the letter stated that the
Federal Reserve Board "neither assumes the right nor has it
any disposition to set itself up as an arbiter of security speculation or values," yet it nevertheless went on to say that when
the Board finds conditions arising which obstruct the functioning of the Reserve Banks, "it is its duty to inquire into them
and to take such measures as may be deemed suitable and
effective in the circumstances to correct them; which, in the
immediate situation, means to restrain the use, either directly
or indirectly, of Federal reserve credit facilities in aid of growth
of speculative credit. . . . A member bank is not within its
reasonable claims for rediscount facilities at its Federal reserve
bank when it borrows either for the purpose of making speculative loans or for the purpose of maintaining speculative
loans."[30] On February 15 the Federal Advisory Council approved the Board's letter of February 2 and even suggested
that stronger methods of pressure be taken.[31]

This policy of direct pressure was continued till the end of
May.[32] It would appear that for a time it met with a certain

---

[29] *Sen. Res. 71*, p. 168, statement of the Hon. C. S. Hamlin.

[30] *Annual Report of the Federal Reserve Board*, 1929, pp. 2–4. To this statement may be added another made in the *Federal Reserve Bulletin* of March
1929: "It is a generally recognized principle that reserve bank credit should
not be used for profit, and that continued indebtedness at the reserve banks,
except under unusual circumstances, is an abuse of reserve bank facilities. In
cases where individual banks have been guilty of such abuse Federal reserve
authorities have taken the matter up with the officers of offending banks and
made it clear to them that their reserve position should be adjusted by liquidat-
ing part of their loan or investment account, rather than through borrowing"
(p. 177).

[31] *Federal Reserve Bulletin*, XV, 176 (March 1929).

[32] Although the discount rate at the New York Reserve Bank was not put

measure of success.[33] In April [34] reporting member-bank security loans checked the advance that had begun the previous October; their investments had already begun in February a decline that continued for a year; and in April and May their security loans and total credit receded sharply. In these two months, also, brokers' loans contracted about 150 millions,[35] and call rates, advancing rapidly as speculative loans ceased to grow, touched 20 per cent the last week of April. Under these influences, and with congestion currently developing in the bond market,[36] the stock market slipped back two points in April and failed to advance in May, and stock flotations in the second quarter of the year dropped 210 millions below the level of the first quarter.

But on May 21 the Federal Advisory Council recommended that such Reserve Banks as wished to raise their rates be permitted to do so,[37] and on May 31 Mr. McGarrah wrote the Federal Reserve Board from the New York Bank, stating "that under the so-called direct pressure the banks were really afraid

---

up, buying rates for acceptances were raised, removing the differential that had existed in favor of acceptances since the previous spring. By March 21, rates for 60–90 day paper had reached 5⅜ per cent, and on March 25 the rates for paper of shorter maturities were raised to that point. From this level the rates were steadily brought down. On August 9, the day the discount rate of New York was finally raised to 6 per cent, rates for all maturities up to 90 days were reduced from 5¼ to 5⅛ per cent, and a new differential in favor of acceptances was created.

[33] Mr. Hamlin expressed the opinion that the policy was a success, though this opinion was not shared by all the Reserve authorities. He used as evidence the fact that between February 8 and June 8, 1929, the security loans of all reporting member banks decreased 361 millions and their investments 262 millions, while in the same period total Federal Reserve credit declined only 193 millions (*Sen. Res.* 71, pp. 168–169, statement of the Hon. C. S. Hamlin).

[34] It was during March, on Monday the twenty-fifth, that call money shot up to 20 per cent, and the National City Bank, under the leadership of Mr. Mitchell, dramatically rushed 25 millions into the call market to stave off the break that seemed so imminent.

[35] Reporting member banks in New York City appear to have coöperated substantially with the Federal Reserve Banks. Their loans "For Own Account" dropped from 1,082 millions in February to 861 millions in May; loans "For Account of Others," however, grew steadily (*Facts and Figures*, p. 81).

[36] On March 16, 1929, the *Journal of Commerce* reported that bonds on dealers' shelves were currently estimated at 500–600 millions compared with 250–300 millions considered normal.

[37] *Federal Reserve Bulletin*, XV, 362 (June 1929).

to borrow at all, and that there was coming a time very soon when there would be an absolute necessity for more Federal Reserve credit." As a result of this letter, "the board practically agreed then that it would suspend the direct pressure for the purpose of enabling banks to get the credit they needed. . . ." [38] In other words, by June it had become apparent that the objective of "high" money for "speculative purposes" and "low" money for "legitimate business" had not been achieved, that it was not likely to be achieved, and that for other, additional reasons the policy had become unsatisfactory. Consequently, at the end of May the policy of direct pressure came to an end, though the change was not officially announced.

With the termination of this policy the speculative advance was resumed. The Standard Statistics Company stock average advanced three points in June to 191, sixteen points in July, and by September had reached 225, in spite of the increase of the discount rate at New York to 6 per cent on August 9. Security loans and total credit of reporting member banks resumed their growth, together with their rediscounts at the Federal Reserve, and although the advance was not rapid, the extraordinary increase in the turnover of bank deposits, especially in New York City evidenced the renewed speculation.[39] Outside money continued to flow into the New York market, and increased brokers' loans to the phenomenal total of 8,549 mil-

---

[38] *Sen. Res. 71*, p. 164, statement of the Hon. C. S. Hamlin.

[39] Reed takes the position that the culminating phase of the stock-market boom in the latter part of 1928 and 1929 was largely financed by the increased velocity of credit, rather than by the absorption in the stock market of credit taken from commerce and industry (Reed, *Federal Reserve Policy*, Chaps. V, VI). W. R. Burgess gives the following figures illustrating the increased velocity of bank credit ("The Money Market in 1929," *Review of Economic Statistics*, XII, 15–20, February 1930):

VELOCITY OF BANK DEPOSITS

ANNUAL RATE OF TURNOVER WITH SEASONAL ADJUSTMENT

	New York City	140 Cities outside of New York City
1927 average	75	35
January 1929	111	40
September 1929	133	44
Increase (Jan.–Sept. 1929)	20%	10%

lions.[40] Interest rates continued to mount,[41] and call rates in the first nine months of 1929 averaged 8.29 per cent, although the differential established in favor of acceptance rates on August 9 eased credit conditions somewhat and, apparently, as in the previous year, allowed member banks to shift some of their borrowings from the Federal Reserve discount portfolio to the acceptance portfolio.[42]

Stock flotations, after their slight recession in the second quarter of the year, shot up in the third quarter, directly contrary to the usual seasonal movement, to the tremendous figure of 2,587 millions. Bond offerings remained small in 1929, of less volume than stock offerings in the first three-quarters of the year, and their numbers declined sharply. As stock flotations reached their peak in the third quarter bond offerings

---

[40] Of this total only 1,048 millions were made by reporting member banks in New York City "For Own Account" (*Facts and Figures*, p. 81). In regard to the increase of brokers' loans in 1929 the *Federal Reserve Bulletin* noted: "The increase in the demand for credit to finance security operations, therefore, during the past year has not been met to any considerable extent by domestic banks, but by others, including foreign banks, individuals, and corporations" (XV, 360, June 1929). For a thorough and illuminating discussion of the composition of brokers' loans see Harris, *Twenty Years*, vol. II, Chap. XXXV.

[41] The table given in the *Annual Report of the Secretary of the Treasury*, 1929 (p. 5), showing the rise of rates for certificates of indebtedness from June 1928 to June 1929, illustrates the situation.

COUPON RATES FOR CERTIFICATES OF INDEBTEDNESS

June 1928	September 1928	Oct. 1928 and Mar. 1929	June 1929
3⅞–4	4½	4¾	5⅛

It was probably the rise in short rates and the increased price of government borrowing that it necessitated that brought at this time the amendment to the Second Liberty Bond Act which permitted the Treasury to sell bills at a discount, and relieved the Treasury of the necessity of doing its short term financing by certificates with a fixed coupon rate. On June 17, 1929, the President approved H. R. 1648, which allowed the Treasury to sell for cash, under competitive conditions, Treasury bills not exceeding twelve months maturity on a discount basis (*Annual Report of the Secretary of the Treasury*, 1929, p. 38). On June 17, 1929, this amendment was again amended, exempting this type of security from the capital gains and losses provisions of the income tax laws (*Annual Report of the Secretary of the Treasury*, 1930, p. 23). On December 10, 1929, the first tender of such bills was made. The offering was for 100 millions, dated December 17, 1929, with a 90-day maturity. Bids for 224 millions were received, and the average price accepted was 99.181, equivalent to a bank discount rate of 3.376 per cent (*ibid.*, p. 14).

[42] Federal Reserve acceptance holdings mounted very rapidly, and rediscounts decreased slightly in August, September, and October.

dropped abruptly to 862 millions, the smallest quarterly total since 1923; "net" offerings became a minus quantity as more bonds were retired than offered; and only forty-four new issues were listed on the Exchange during the year. All types of banks sold securities in 1929, and these sales augmented the total "net" offerings coming into the market by more than 750 millions.

Stock prices reached their highest point in the early part of September; the industrial average touched 381.17 on September 3,[43] and the railroad average reached its maximum the next week. During the remainder of the month stock prices slipped back from these levels, and at the same time brokers' loans increased rapidly, evidencing, as the Secretary of the Treasury pointed out, "the movement of securities from holders with large equities to holders with smaller equities, or from stronger to weaker hands." [44] On September 26 the Bank of England raised its rate for the second time since January, from 5½ to 6½ per cent, and in the same week the news of the Hatry failure in London further shook confidence in the international money markets. The withdrawal of foreign balances from New York began, the "creeping bear market" developed, and on October 3 the stock market declined abruptly. Although prices recovered the next week, the market declined very sharply on the sixteenth, many issues made new lows for the year, and 12,894,650 shares changed hands, an amount 50 per cent higher than the previous record made in March 1929, and double the record of earlier years. On October 29 the market suffered the most severe break of its history; 16,410,000 shares were sold, and individual stock prices dropped 10, 15, and 20 points between sales.[45]

The stock market break of October was followed by two months of almost chaotic conditions in the financial world. Business indices, which had been declining, began to fall precipitately. The Brookmire index dropped below normal in No-

[43] *Barron's,* X, 20 (Jan. 6, 1930).
[44] *Annual Report of the Secretary of the Treasury,* 1930, p. 20.
[45] Most of the figures in this paragraph are taken from *Bradstreet's,* Sept. 7–Nov. 2, 1929.

vember, as did the Federal Reserve index in December, though the Harvard Economic Society index remained above normal till June 1930. Short rates went into an almost vertical decline;[46] the rediscount rate at the New York Bank was reduced twice in November, from 6 to 4.50 per cent; and long rates, reversing their trend in October, began to fall as bond prices rose. The inflow of gold was also suddenly reversed, and in November and December 102 millions were exported as foreign balances were hurriedly withdrawn. These exports, however, were more than offset by the action of the Reserve Banks, which rushed into the market and bought 292 millions of government securities in the last two months of the year. Security loans of reporting member banks advanced sharply in October and November, raising total reporting member-bank credit to a new peak in November, as the banks, in an endeavor to allay the panic, took over a considerable portion of the brokers' loans that had been carried by outside money.[47] It has been estimated that New York banks took over 1,500–2,000 millions of call loans in the week ended October 30.[48] But in December security loans and total credit of reporting member banks began to fall rapidly. Total brokers' loans dropped from 8,549 millions in September to 6,109 millions in October, and to 4,017 millions in November. The Standard Statistics Company stock average fell 71 points in these months in the most rapid decline ever known, and new stock offerings amounted to only

---

[46] Short term interest rates:

	October 1929 per cent	December 1929 per cent
Commercial paper rates	6.01	5.00
Time-money rates	8.64	4.72
The customers' rate	6.08	5.74

Reed suggests that call money, which averaged 8.50 per cent in September, 6.43 in October, 5.44 in November, and 4.83 in December, would have dropped much more rapidly if it had not been pegged on the Exchange, since outside money was often obtainable in these months at 3 per cent or less (*Federal Reserve Policy*, p. 187).

[47] Brokers' loans of reporting member banks in New York City "For Account of Out of Town Banks" and "For Account of Others" dropped about 2,600 millions in October and November, while loans "For Own Acount," after increasing 200 millions in October, receded about the same amount in November (*Facts and Figures*, p. 81).

[48] *Federal Reserve Bulletin*, XV, 755–757 (December 1929). Also, *Sen. Res.* 71, p. 95, statement of Governor Harrison.

811 millions in the last quarter of the year, compared with 2,587 millions in the third quarter.

In December and January, however, the remedial measures of the Federal Reserve System and of the New York banks began to take effect, and the acute phase of the crisis passed. The first four or five months of 1930, in fact, witnessed a substantial degree of recovery. In December the stock market stopped its headlong fall and began an advance that continued till May and which was supported, after January, by a large increase of brokers' loans. Business indices also ceased their almost perpendicular decline and remained relatively steady through April, though commodity prices continued to fall uninterruptedly. Although new stock flotations receded to 406 millions in the first quarter of 1930 — in spite of the recovery of stock prices — in the second quarter they increased to 850 millions. The volume of bond offerings increased substantially, to the highest level since the early months of 1928, though the rise was not so pronounced in their number. Presumably this recovery was stimulated by the substantial rise in bond prices and the cheaper borrowing the advance permitted, by the current considerable repatriation of foreign bonds, and by the fact that in January time-money and in February commercial paper rates dropped below the yield of first grade bonds.[49]

Moreover, the situation was further strengthened by the cessation of gold exports in December and by the resumption of imports from the Orient and South America on a substantial scale in February. These imports were induced by the drop in the price of raw materials exported by these areas, rather than by a difference between short rates in New York and in other centers, such as had caused gold imports in 1929.[50] The Reserve System, as the situation improved, reduced its purchases of governments in January, bought none in February, and on February 7 reduced the rediscount rate in New York to 4 per cent.[51]

[49] The customers' rate did not fall below the yield of first grade bonds till July 1930.
[50] *Annual Report of the Federal Reserve Board*, 1930, p. 6.
[51] On March 25, 1930, the Federal Reserve Open Market Investment Committee was replaced by the Open Market Policy Conference (*Sen. Res. 71*, p. 158, statement of Dr. A. C. Miller).

The purchases of government securities by the Reserve Banks in the past two months had greatly eased the position of the reporting member banks, and rediscounts had declined from 953 millions in November, when they were about 58 per cent of total Reserve credit, to 231 millions in April, when they constituted only about 22 per cent of Federal Reserve credit. In February the improved position of the reporting member banks brought to an end the rapid decline in their security loans and total credit that had begun in December, as well as the fall in their investments that had begun a year earlier, and in the next month all three of these asset items began to increase.

By April the Standard Statistics Company stock price average had climbed back to 181, 30 points above its November level; and in the same period brokers' loans had increased 1,046 millions. April, however, marked the limit of the recovery, although new offerings of stocks and bonds remained large and the security loans of reporting member banks continued to expand through June.

In March and April "indigestion" was noted in the bond market,[52] and in May stock prices, brokers' loans, and business indices turned down in a decline that continued almost without interruption throughout the year. This decline took place in spite of the steady fall in short rates and the continued reduction of rediscount rates at the Reserve Banks,[53] in spite of the very large acquisitions of securities by member banks,[54] and in spite of the ease of credit conditions that these developments evidenced. This ease resulted from the decreased pressure for commercial loans — occasioned by the rapid decline of business activity —, from the renewed gold imports, from the very considerable drop in money in circulation,[55] and after May, from the resumption by the Reserve System of very large pur-

---

[52] *National City Bank Monthly Letter,* April and May, 1930.

[53] By the end of the year successive reductions had brought the discount rate at New York down to 2 per cent, the lowest rate in the period of this study.

[54] Reporting member banks bought more securities in 1930 than in any year considered, and city banks more than in any year except 1922. Total purchases by financial institutions were one-half the total "net" offerings for the year.

[55] The average volume of money in circulation was 211 millions less in 1930 than in 1929, apparently because of lower prices and smaller pay rolls.

chases of securities. By December Federal Reserve holdings of government securities had increased to 644 millions, as compared with 446 millions twelve months earlier and 154 millions in October 1929.

In the second half of the year, as security loans of reporting member banks turned down and stock prices and brokers' loans fell, flotations of both stock and bond issues dropped abruptly, though seventy-three new bond issues were listed on the Stock Exchange. Stock offerings fell to 190 millions in the third quarter of the year, and to 122 millions in the final quarter, the lowest quarterly total since 1922. Bond offerings receded to 1,188 millions in the third quarter and to 991 millions in the final quarter, the total for the two quarters being only about one-half the volume of the first six months of the year. Municipal offerings were the only type that did not decline — they remained at substantially the level of 1927 till the end of 1931 —, and corporate issues began to recede from the high ratio to total issues that they had maintained since 1927.

Foreign issues particularly were curtailed in the latter part of 1930; and the United States Department of Commerce estimated that the net debit balance of the United States on long term capital account was only 290 millions in 1930, compared with 319 millions in 1929 and 708 millions in 1928. The reduction of long term capital exports, however, was accompanied by a tremendous increase in exports of short term capital. The Department of Commerce estimated that in 1930, because of the withdrawal of foreign balances, the United States had a debit balance of 443 millions, compared with a credit balance of 13 millions in the previous year.[56]

[56] The Department of Commerce estimated for 1930 a credit balance of 617 millions on commodity trade and miscellaneous invisible items account; debit balances of 290 millions on long term capital account, 443 millions on short term capital account, and 258 millions on account of gold movements. These estimates left the extraordinarily large balancing item of 374 millions as a credit item, an amount a great deal larger than that of previous years (*The Balance of International Payments of the United States in 1930,* Trade Information Bulletin 761, pp. viii–ix). Mr. R. O. Hall, who prepared most of the report, and who prepared the reports of previous years, resigned upon its publication, claiming that the figures of the report had been falsified. He alleged, among other things, that the merchandise imports of the United States had been

The sharp decline in bond offerings in the last quarter of 1930 reflected the sudden fall of bond prices that began in October. From October 1929 through September 1930 bond prices had risen, the market had been strong, and long rates had steadily declined. But in September, in spite of the ease of credit conditions and the declining short rates, bond prices weakened and long rates began a rise that continued beyond the limits of this study, and which, in the case of second grades, was most precipitate. This fall was occasioned by factors that overcame the influence of the cheap credit policy of the Federal Reserve System, the gold imports, and the low and falling short rates. It was caused by fear, engendered by the decline in business indices and stock prices; by the threat that the steep recession of business activity brought to the security of second grade bonds; by political developments abroad, especially in South America, that unsettled the market for foreign bonds; by the "distress selling" of financial institutions that needed to liquidate and found it impossible to realize upon assets other than securities. Such factors, of course, played a progressively greater part in the action of the market in 1931 and 1932.

By the end of 1930 business indices had broken through the low points of 1921 and were still going down. Wholesale prices had dropped far below any level touched since the war and were still decreasing. Stock prices, on the average, had fallen almost 50 per cent since April and well over 50 per cent since September 1929; in the case of certain issues the drop had been much greater, and prices were still declining. The bond market had recently gone into a very sharp decline that was, for second grades, of unprecedented rapidity.

On the other hand, the general financial situation was not such as to give great immediate concern. The gold imports of the latter part of the year had raised the stock of money gold almost to the peak of 1924, and the continued imports of 1931 were to carry it far above that level. These imports, the con-

much overvalued and that the capital exports had been greatly exaggerated (*New York Times*, July 13, 1931). If the valuation of the merchandise imports and the capital exports were reduced, the unusually large balancing figure of 374 millions would, obviously, be reduced.

tinued purchases of government securities by the Reserve System, and the decline of business activity had brought money rates down to the lowest level reached in the period of this study and had permitted member banks to liquidate a large part of their borrowings. The Treasury had ended its fiscal year on June 30 with receipts of 4,177 millions, a figure 145 millions greater than that for 1929; but since expenditures had also gone up by about the same amount, the surplus of 185 millions was approximately the same as for the preceding year.[57] The banking system as a whole did not appear to be under a dangerous amount of strain, though in certain districts banks were in difficulties. The hoarding of money, which became so ominous in the following years, had hardly begun,[58] and although bank failures had been numerous during the year, their number was not yet alarming, and the failures for the most part, were currently considered as "readjustments" made necessary by unsound banking in the past.[59] It was not until 1931, when continued bank failures and receding confidence brought hoarding of money on a large scale, when the international credit structure appeared to be falling apart, and when banks, in a desperate effort to remain liquid, quadrupled their rediscounts and dumped their investments on a sinking bond market, that the financial situation became acute.

[57] *Annual Report of the Secretary of the Treasury,* 1930, pp. 2, 8, 11.

[58] The seasonal peak of money in circulation in December 1930 was below that of 1929, but the increase of money in circulation in the last two months of the year was almost 500 millions, a much greater increase than was customary.

[59] Bank suspensions. Figures compiled from the Annual Reports of the Federal Reserve Board for the years 1928, 1929, 1930.

	1927	*1928*	*1929*	*1930*
Number of suspensions	662	491	642	1,345
Deposits of suspended banks (*in millions of dollars*)	194	139	235	865

CHAPTER X

CONCLUSION

IN THE financial as in the political world the World War brought many and profound changes, and the post-war situation has differed in many respects from that which existed prior to 1914. It is perhaps not yet possible to analyze and evaluate in their entirety all of the new conditions and relationships inherited from the conflict, in spite of the considerable investigations of this period which have been made. Yet it is apparent that in the United States, at least, the twenties were a time of very great capital accumulation. A tremendous volume of investment took place, capital goods were created on a grand scale, the productive capacity of the country was rapidly expanded, and the standard of living of a large part of the population was raised in something less than ten years to a level never hitherto reached. To many contemporary eyes it appeared that the Millennium had dawned, and the current developments were hailed as "the New Era." This period of prosperity, of great material success, was followed by a depression whose severity is probably unparalleled in the experience of the modern world and whose ultimate effects can not yet be estimated.

The economic mechanism, in short, passed through a cyclical movement of great length and amplitude in the post-war period, in spite of intermediate fluctuations and notwithstanding the optimistic forecasts made in the middle of the decade. No part of the economic structure was unaffected. Business activity, employment, the security markets, commodity prices — though here the movement was perhaps not so apparent — all participated.

As in any cycle, the fluctuations, the transactions, and the behavior of the bond market were integral parts of the movement. Much of the investment during the upswing was in the form of bonds, and much of the increase of capital goods and productive capacity was financed by bond issues. In the crash both bonds and the bond market were intimately affected, and as the depression deepened, its effects upon them became increasingly serious. Ultimately both bonds and the bond market ceased, in large measure, to perform their proper economic functions. As earnings shrank it became, in many instances, impossible for industry to pay the fixed charges it had assumed in issuing obligations, and, consequently, the conditions upon which they had been sold were violated, and the security they should have afforded their owners disappeared. Bond prices declined, not only for defaulted issues but for those on which interest payments were maintained, to such a point that their market values bore little relation to their values as determined by other tests,[1] and the pricing function of the market in this sense ceased to work properly. At times the continuity of bids, offers, and sales — upon which the existence of the market depends — was broken, so that the essential market process, the continuous evaluation of capital investments and the maintenance of their liquidity, was interrupted. New increments of savings failed to appear in the market, new issues of securities were almost entirely halted, and the market no longer served as a mechanism for providing industry with fresh funds.

When the post-war decade is viewed in its entirety, it seems apparent that the long upward sweep in the annual volumes of new bond issues that began in 1920 and continued, in spite of interruptions, till 1927 was instigated in its beginning by the needs for capital equipment, particularly in the construction field, which had accumulated during the war. It also seems apparent that, in a general way, the movement was supported and carried on by the ease of credit conditions, by the abundance and cheapness of funds available to the bond market which prevailed after 1922.

The principal basis for the abundance of cheap funds was

---

[1] It is always a question what test, other than market value, can legitimately be applied to a capital instrument. At many times, and for many purposes, no other test can properly be used. What is meant here is that large numbers of bonds at various times during the depression sold at prices very far below their values as determined by such measures as their price range over a long period of time, the generally accepted valuations of the assets supporting them, or the capitalization of their interest payments at the current short term rates.

the great increase in the gold holdings of the United States which the war brought, and the large gold imports during the twenties. Other factors, of course, contributed to the ease of credit conditions. The continued use, after the war, of government securities as collateral for member-bank borrowing, together with the great increase in the volume of these securities outstanding, provided an additional basis for member-bank loans. The rapid growth of time deposits in these years relieved the position of the banks, since a lower reserve was required for them than for demand deposits. The tremendous fall in the volume of money in circulation in 1920 and 1921 strengthened the banks, as did its slow decline from 1925 through 1930. The steady reduction in the government debt supplied a continuous flow of funds that were, presumably, for the most part largely reinvested directly in the securities markets rather than spent for consumption goods. But the underlying cause of the abundance of loanable funds seems to have been the great and growing gold reserves of the United States.

These various forces which tended to make loanable funds cheap and plentiful are, it would seem, to be considered as analogous to certain of those "monetary factors" which Keynes describes as capable of inducing a boom and creating a state of disequilibrium.[2] In this case the change was, of course, an increase in the credit base. It does not appear, however, that either the ways in which the boom developed or the characteristics of the position of disequilibrium were in exact conformance with Keynes's expectations.

Although the effect of the increased gold holdings resulting from the war was delayed, or obscured, for a time after the Armistice by the boom of 1919 and the depression of 1920 and 1921, as business returned to a more stable basis in 1922 the large and increasing holdings were reflected, in spite of the efforts of the Federal Reserve System to control any inflationary tendencies, by low interest rates, by the high reserve ratio of the System,[3] and by the excess reserves of member banks. The

[2] J. M. Keynes, *A Treatise on Money* (1930), I, 259.
[3] After October 1921 till the end of 1930 the reserve ratio was above 70 per

easiness of credit conditions, of course, directly influenced the level of short and long term rates, and tended to lower both. This tendency on the part of both short and long rates to decline was, of course, in accordance with the teachings of experience and the expectations of theory.

It may be noted parenthetically that the disposition of short and long term rates to move together is so well known as to be taken for granted in many theories of banking and investment — in Keynes's, for instance. And it must be admitted that the forces which operate to keep movements of short and long rates harmonious are so strong, persistent, and comprehensive as to give this relationship a "normal" character, in the sense that when this relationship weakens or disappears the financial mechanism is not acting in its usual manner. When a diversity of movement does appear it can be taken as evidence that the financial mechanism is subject to unusual influences. Moreover, this customary harmony of movement between short and long rates is of the greatest importance for the economic structure. Since movements of short rates are largely controlled, on the one hand, by factors significant in the banking structure — such as gold movements, changes in reserve ratios, and Federal Reserve policy — and on the other hand by the demand for short term loans used in industry and in the commodity and security markets, the connection which exists between short and long term rates relates these banking and industrial forces to those others which are significant in the bond market, particularly the volume of saving and the demand for long term capital. Hence this relationship is of considerable consequence for the economic system; and the maintenance of the usual links between the various parts of the economic fabric is contingent upon the maintenance of harmony between movements of short and long term rates. The history of this relationship in the years since the war consequently has a good deal of bearing upon the interpretation of the financial history of the period, and appears to be an

---

cent almost all the time, going above 80 per cent for considerable periods in 1924 and 1928, and falling as low as 63 per cent only once (*Annual Report of the Federal Reserve Board*, 1928, p. 40).

aspect of it which has been largely neglected in most analyses of the decade.

From the beginning of 1919 until, roughly, the middle of 1921, during the post-Armistice inflation and deflation, movements of short and long rates, although similar, did not exactly synchronize.[4] But there were so many unusual elements present at this time, during the return of the country to a peace basis and in the boom and collapse that followed the end of the war, that it is not surprising that customary financial relationships were not strictly adhered to.

From the middle of 1921 till the latter part of 1924 there was very close conformity between the movements of long and short rates. The periods of advance and recession corresponded, and the turning points of the two series fell in practically the same months. The greatest similarity of movement was shown at this time, as indeed at almost all times, by the customers' rate and the yield of the Baa bonds.[5]

In 1923, however, the situation changed. In that year short term interest rates dropped to very low levels, into that very low range which they held until 1928. Long term rates began that long, five-year decline that was so striking a feature of the post-war period. And in the next year, in 1924, there began that diversity in the movements of short and long rates that is so noticeable in the years 1924–1928.

---

[4] Charts I and X, pp. 28 and 59. Although long rates advanced almost steadily after June 1919, till they reached temporary high points in June and July 1920, short rates, if money is disregarded, did not show a definite upward tendency till November 1919. Time money was 6 per cent or above from June 1919 till September 1921, and consequently was not an adequate index in this period. After reaching their high points in the middle of 1920, long rates fell abruptly till November, but in that month they rose sharply to their earlier levels, and remained there, with some fluctuations, till June 1921, when they definitely began to decline. Commercial paper and the customers' rate, on the other hand, continued through 1920, almost without interruption, the advance that had begun in 1919. Commercial paper reached its high of 8 per cent in August and held that level till November, when it began to fall; the customers' rate did not begin to decline till March 1921. This decline of short rates continued throughout 1921 and the greater part of 1922, and, as noted, was accompanied after June 1921 by a fall in long rates.

[5] The customers' rate apparently conforms more closely to long rates than do the other short rates because it is less sensitive than other short rates.

The yield of the Aaa bonds began to decline in April 1923, although short term rates and the yields of the Baa bonds advanced till the last quarter of the year, when they too started down. The fall in long rates carried through 1924, although short rates advanced in the latter part of that year; and it continued till the first quarter of 1928. At that time long rates finally reversed their movement, as short rates increased their rate of advance, and short and long rates again moved together till the final months of 1930, although the similarity of their movements was not so great as in the period 1921 to 1924. In October 1930 bond prices broke and long rates rose rapidly, although the fall in short rates that had begun in November 1929 continued.

This five-year decline in long rates, from 1923 to the middle of 1928, appears to have been of considerable moment, both for the bond market and for the whole financial structure. The fall was almost continuous — only twice was it interrupted for more than one month [6] — and it was almost unaffected by fluctuations of short rates. Short rates, of course, from 1924 through 1927 were at a very low level and fluctuated in a very narrow range — the level was lower and the range narrower than in either the preceding or succeeding period. But neither their distinct upward trend from the middle of 1925 till the last quarter of 1926, nor their intermediate movements, were reflected in the action of long rates. Such behavior on the part of interest rates appears to indicate that certain "normal" or customary relationships were relaxed at this time, and the consequent "abnormal" situation is, perhaps, to be taken as evidence of a situation of "disequilibrium," in the ordinary economic meaning of the term.

Other evidence of the presence of an unusual situation in the capital markets in these years can be found. From 1920 through 1923 movements in the yields of short and long term government obligations outstanding, as computed by the Fed-

---

[6] In the middle of 1925 and in the middle of 1927 the fall was interrupted, but the interruption lasted only for two months in each case.

eral Reserve Board, were harmonious and sympathetic.[7] As has been noted, other short and long rates moved together during this time. But as a diversity of movement between short and long rates developed in 1924, the actions of the prices and yields of short and long term governments became dissimilar. The yield of short term governments tended to follow the movements of other short term rates, the yield of long term governments moved in close conformity with that of other long term investments, and practically no similarity in the action of these two types of securities is discernible. In 1928, as other short and long rates came into conformity, a degree of harmony in the movements of the yields of long and short term governments was reëstablished.

Moreover, the five-year decline in long rates was accompanied by a very striking decrease in the spread between the yields of first and second grade bonds.[8] This decrease continued as long as did the fall in long rates. The spread shrank from 2.30 per cent in August 1923, the month of approximately the widest spread, to .86 per cent in March 1928, the month of approximately the narrowest spread.

The low level at which short rates remained in these years, the steady fall in long rates, the continued narrowing of the spread betwen yields of first and second grade bonds all indicate that funds, particularly those available to the securities markets, were unusually abundant and cheap during this time. The rapid growth of reporting member-bank security loans in this same period, particularly in 1924, 1925, and 1927, and of member-bank security investments, particularly in 1924 and 1927, also indicates that such a situation prevailed, since such growth evidences the presence of funds at the disposal of the banks which commerce and industry do not wish to or can not profitably absorb. In 1929 the Federal Reserve Board, survey-

---

[7] For a discussion of this point see C. C. Abbott, "A Note on the Government Bond Market, 1919–1930," *Review of Economic Statistics*, XVII, 7–12 (January 1935).

[8] Chart I, p. 28. The greatest part of this shrinkage took place in the years 1924–1926; in December 1923 the spread was 2.28 per cent; in December 1926 it amounted to only .99 per cent.

ing the developments of the preceding decade, declared in its Annual Report: "The entire period from 1922 to 1927 was . . . characterized by a relatively low level of money rates and an abundance of credit." [9]

If the developments just discussed are considered in the light of Keynes's analysis certain points seem evident. Various "monetary factors," notably an increase in gold holdings, tended to make credit conditions extremely easy in the United States in the years following the war. The abundance and cheapness of funds initiated a boom, a position of disequilibrium, as would be expected in Keynes's theory. Much the greater part of the boom was felt in the rise of prices of securities (and of real estate) and in the increase in their issue, rather than in a rise in commodity prices, which remained relatively stable. Such a situation is not contemplated in the three types of cycles which Keynes discusses,[10] but it can, perhaps, be reconciled with other parts of his analysis. Nor is such a diversity in the movements of short and long term interest rates, as developed in 1923 and 1924, dealt with adequately in his work, though certain of his statements can, perhaps, be interpreted as recognizing such a possibility.[11]

This situation of disequilibrium appears, in Keynes's terminology, to have been primarily a "capital" and a "profit" inflation, since security prices rose and the volume of new issues

[9] *Annual Report of the Federal Reserve Board*, 1929, p. 5.

[10] Keynes discusses his three types of cycles in volume I, chapter XVIII, of his *Treatise*. He does not contemplate, in this discussion, that the commodity price level will remain constant during the upswing of the cycle, as it appears to have done in the United States during the twenties, and this is the aspect of the period most difficult to reconcile with Keynes's analysis. His own attempt does not seem to the author particularly happy. His statement (II, 259) that the gold imports of 1921–1923 did not produce inflationary results subsequent to 1923 because of the "remarkable growth during the same period in the volume of bank-money required by the American public" does not seem to the author an adequate explanation. Nor does his argument (I, 190) that the period from 1925 to the spring of 1928 was "an example rare in monetary history, namely, one in which high rates of productive activity and of investment were developed without the rate of savings falling behind" appear to the author to be one that can be supported. This proposition is, of course, the one that can most readily be reconciled with his analysis.

[11] For further elaboration of this point, see pp. 151–152.

increased, rather than a "commodity inflation," since commodity prices did not rise. This situation of disequilibrium, this boom, was accompanied by a rapid increase in "investment." In Keynes's analysis a "boom" is, perhaps, to be defined as a situation in which "investment" increases faster than "savings." It seems altogether probable that the volume of new issues did increase more rapidly than the savings available to take them off the market during the post-war period, although this proposition is not susceptible of absolute proof, since an adequate index of savings does not exist.[12] There is, however, a certain amount of indirect evidence which indicates that the supply of new investments was outrunning the demand for them as expressed in the form of savings.

In the first place, the rapid increase in the volume of security loans of member banks in 1924, 1925, and 1927, and the rapid rise of call loans in 1928 and 1929 show that a progressively larger volume of securities was being carried by bank loans, and was not being absorbed by new increments of savings. Although such loans are used for the purchase of stocks as well as bonds, their increase, together with the fact that annual volumes of new bond issues increased rapidly till 1928, suggests that they served to take off of the market a growing volume of bonds. Further, although no good index of savings available for the purchase of securities exists, it is generally believed that savings increase at a pretty steady rate, and, if this is the case, the increasing volume of new investments was probably steadily outdistancing the new increments of savings.[13] Until 1928 most of this increase was in the form of bonds; in 1928 and 1929 the

[12] To determine definitely the relationship of savings to investment it would be necessary to have an index of savings to compare with our indices of new security issues. Such an index, to be accurate, would need to be based upon the resources of all types of savings banks and upon the savings and time deposits of state and member banks (although insofar as time deposits are merely slow demand accounts classified as time deposits they should not be included), upon the resources of life insurance and building and loan associations, upon that part of corporate savings which are used for the permanent or semi-permanent purchase of bonds, and upon the savings of private individuals, including the savings of trusts, foundations, and estates. Such an index does not exist.

[13] In this connection many of the findings of F. C. Mills in his *Economic Tendencies in the United States* (1932) are most suggestive.

volume of new stock issues became larger than the volume of new bond issues as such issues, after 1927, declined in the face of rising interest rates. It thus seems evident that the low level of interest rates that prevailed after 1923, particularly the steady decline in long term rates, furnished the basis for the rapid increase in bond issues. As has been noted, long term rates declined from 1923 till 1928 and were practically unaffected by the fluctuations of short rates.

But it also seems evident that the flow of new issues was even more directly stimulated by the abundance of credit, particularly by the open-market purchases of the Federal Reserve System, than it was by the low level of long term interest rates. The years in which the Federal Reserve Banks bought government bonds in large quantities — 1922, 1924, 1927, and 1930 — were also the years in which commercial banks increased substantially their security portfolios. Likewise it was in these years that the indices of total, new capital, and "net" bond issues rapidly advanced — even though such advances were not always accompanied by unusually rapid declines in long term rates and rises in bond prices[14]—, and it was in these years that the index of bond trading reached the four peaks it attained in the 1920–1930 period. The funds which the Federal Reserve placed at the disposal of the banks through its purchases of open-market obligations thus seem to have had an immediate effect on the bond market and to have directly stimulated the flow of new issues.

Such a relationship is not specifically contemplated in Keynes's theory of investment, although certain passages in his work indicate that he is not oblivious to such a possibility. When he states that "changes in Bank-rate primarily affect the short rate of interest, whereas open market operations — so far as they relate to the Central Bank's holdings of long dated securities —

[14] In 1922 long term rates, continuing the decline that had started in the middle of 1921, fell until the last quarter of the year; in 1924 and 1927 long term rates declined, though at no more rapid a pace than that which prevailed in the latter part of 1923, in 1925, and in 1926; in 1930 long term rates continued, during the first three quarters of the year, the fall that had begun subsequent to the stock-market crash of 1929.

influence the long-rate of interest," [15] he recognizes that open-market operations have a particular significance for long term rates, and hence — it follows in his analysis — upon the rate of investment. Nevertheless he does not seem to envisage the possibility of such operations so strengthening the market as to stimulate directly the flow of new issues, without producing any very discernible effect upon long rates, as seems to have happened in 1924 and 1927. Still more suggestive is his discussion of the "fringe of unsatisfied borrowers"— those persons who are quite ready to borrow at the going rate of interest, but who are not accommodated, since they "are not considered to have the first claims on a bank's favors," although the "bank would be quite ready to lend [to them] if it were to find itself in a position to lend more." [16] At the beginning of this passage he states: "The relaxation or contraction of credit by the Banking System does not operate, however, merely through a change in the rate charged to borrowers; it also functions through a change in the abundance of credit." [17] This idea is not elaborated to any great extent, and it is unfortunate that the theory is not carried further, since the relative abundance or scarcity of credit supplied by the Federal Reserve System seems to have had a more direct bearing in this period on the flow of new issues than did the movements of short term interest rates.

When the bond market in the 1920–1930 period is surveyed from the point of view of industry, the salient fact is that a very large, even a major, part of the financing in the post-war decade was done by business corporations. Such flotations increased, both absolutely and relative to total issues, from a low point in 1920 to a maximum in 1927; they accounted for slightly more than half the total volume of issues in these years; [18] and the

[15] Keynes, *A Treatise*, II, 252.
[16] *Ibid.*, II, 365.
[17] *Ibid.*, II, 364.
[18] Charts XII and XIII, pp. 67 and 69. The absolute growth of corporate securities began in 1920 and continued till 1927, when it reached its maximum; in the following years it decreased sharply. The growth of corporate financing relative to total issues began in 1923 and reached its high point in the years 1926–1928; it continued at a high proportionate level till 1931, in spite of the large absolute decline in corporate issues in 1929 and 1930.

annual rate of increase of such issues appears to have been distinctly more rapid than it was before the war.[19] Much of this financing, it seems probable, was made possible, if not caused, by the new situation which existed in the security markets after the war, notably the increased number of security purchasers which the Liberty Loans produced and the unusual ease in selling securities which prevailed from 1922 to 1929.

Not all of this large increase in the bond issues of business corporations, of course, was a net increase in debt. Very large quantities of bonds were refunded, and the growth of long term financing was accompanied by a decrease in bank loans and short term accommodation. Business, influenced among other factors by the cheapness and abundance of long term funds, turned more and more in this period to the security markets for its capital requirements, and relied less and less upon the banking structure, so that commercial loans declined as bond — and stock — issues increased. The member banks, as the volume of their commercial loans decreased, were forced to invest a larger and larger proportion of their assets in security loans and investments.

This change in the financial policy of business corporations and in the investment policy of banks tended to become a cumulative process. Many business enterprises, induced by the ease of selling securities to increase their capitalization, came into control of funds which they either did not need in their immediate operations or which they could not profitably employ in seasons when activity was low. Such funds they either temporarily invested in securities or placed in the call market — with the result that the security markets were given further support — or left on deposit in the banks. Even in the latter case — and especially if such funds were left as time deposits, as they often were — the bond market was strengthened. For the banks found it necessary to employ such funds, and security loans and in-

---

[19] It is estimated by Ellsworth that the annual rate of increase for all corporate securities, both stocks and bonds, was 3.48 per cent for the years 1906–1917 and 11.40 per cent for the years 1919–1930. With investment-trust financing excluded, the rate of growth in the post-war years was only 10.49 per cent a year (Ellsworth, "Investments," pp. 24–27).

vestments became of more importance as an outlet for their resources as commercial loans declined. The bond and stock
markets were thus given further support, so that the inducement
to further issues became steadily greater. Such funds as were
raised by investment trusts and holding companies were, of
course, also put back into the security markets, either directly
or indirectly through the call-money market, and still further
enhanced security prices and the ease of selling securities. Although in most of the years covered in this study the larger
part of the new funds necessary to absorb the "net" volume of
bond issues was furnished by the classification described as "the
general public," [20] there seems little doubt, when the growth of
brokers' loans and security loans of member banks is considered,
that a substantial portion of these funds was lent to the public
by the banks.

This growth of indebtedness was significant in a variety of
ways, social and economic. It marked a change in the methods
of business financing, with more reliance placed upon the public
security markets and less upon the closed market of the commercial banker's loan. It altered the character of the assets
of commercial banks, as a larger proportion was invested in
securities and security loans and a smaller proportion lent to
private clients. It involved the public at large more immediately
in the fortunes of "big business" than had ever been the case
before, and it placed the industrial structure under heavy obligations to this myriad of bond holders. It put a great strain
upon the mechanism which absorbs new securities, directly upon
the banking and brokerage system, and more remotely upon
the savers of the country. It made the cost structure of
industry more rigid and more resistant to adjustment than it
had hitherto been. It placed great quantities of funds in the
hands of a relatively small number of business men, and enabled
them to extend their operations greatly, both in the acquisition
of existing plant and equipment and in the creation of new productive capacity.

Many of these changes are by their nature intangible and in-

[20] Chart VIII, p. 38.

commensurable, and their content and importance can only be estimated. Others are more susceptible to statistical measurement. In Chart XV [21] an attempt is made to trace certain of

CHART XV

GROWTH OF ALL CORPORATE BOND ISSUES AND OF "NET" CORPORATE BOND ISSUES, COMPARED WITH GROWTH OF INTEREST PAYMENTS AND NET INCOMES OF ALL CORPORATIONS PAYING INCOME TAXES, AND WITH MILLS' INDEX OF PRODUCTION OF CAPITAL ELEMENTS, 1920–1930, IN RELATIVES 1926 = 100

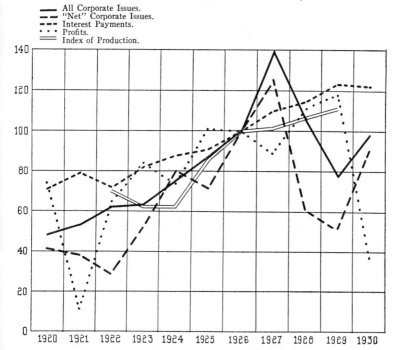

these changes in economic relationships which appear to be of particular moment. Like the problem with which it deals, the chart is complex and appears confused; and the statistics upon which it is based are not so authoritative as would be desirable. But it permits the extraction of a certain amount of information, and a number of tentative conclusions can be drawn from it.

The chart is plotted in relatives, 1926 always being used as the base year, in order to compare the rates of growth of various

[21] The figures from which this chart is drawn are given in Appendix O.

economic magnitudes. Represented are the rates of growth of all corporate bond issues, of "net" corporate bond issues, of net incomes of all corporations paying income taxes and the interest payments of such corporations, together with Mills's index of the Production of Capital Elements.[22] The curve of all corporate bond issues is taken from the classification of the *Commercial and Financial Chronicle,* used throughout this study. The curve of "net" corporate issues is drawn from statistics obtained by subtracting the total of corporate issues called and matured each year from the volume of new corporate issues, and represents in a rough way the rate at which the amount of new funds necessary to absorb new corporate issues increased, on the hypothesis — by no means exact — that funds released by corporate issues called and matured were reinvested in new corporate issues. The curve for all corporate issues is significant in that it indicates the increasing rate at which corporate bonds were issued from 1922 through 1927, and the effect produced upon corporate bond issues by the post-war cycle. The curve of "net" issues reflects the cyclical nature of the demand for new funds for corporate purposes. It is more irregular than the curve of total issues, since the volume of called bonds varies widely [23] from year to year, depending upon money market conditions. The statistics from which the curve of interest payments is drawn were compiled from the Statistics of Income published by the United States government. These statistics unfortunately include both bond interest and interest on short term obligations, since it was not possible to segregate the bond interest in the statistics as compiled nor to estimate what proportion it was of the total. Consequently the slope of this curve is not directly comparable to the rate of increase of corporate indebtedness. However, the steady rise of this curve, and its smoothness — which is more pronounced than that in any of the other curves drawn — appears to be distinctly significant. The figures from which the curve of net incomes is drawn are

[22] Mills, *Economic Tendencies,* p. 278, Table 117. This index has been shifted, in order to use 1926 as the base year.

[23] The volume of called bonds varies much more from year to year than does the volume of matured bonds, which remains relatively constant.

taken from S. H. Nerlove's *A Decade of Corporate Incomes* (1932).[24] This curve is the most irregular of those represented in the chart; the cyclical element in it is strongly marked; and the indication which it gives of the rise and fall of profits during the cycle is, when considered in conjunction with the other curves, of very considerable importance. Mills's index of the Production of Capital Elements, shifted to a 1926 base, is included in the chart — although it unfortunately extends only from 1922 through 1929 — in order to furnish some evidence of how the rate of production of capital goods increased, compared with the rates at which bonds were issued, profits made, and interest paid.

This chart illustrates, in certain respects, the relation of the corporate bond market to other economic factors during the twenties. Advancing from a very low level in 1920, the rate at which corporate bonds were issued increased rapidly and steadily till 1927. As the volume of corporate issues increased during the upswing of the cycle the volume of funds necessary to absorb new corporate issues increased, and the curve of "net" corporate issues rose at approximately as rapid a rate as did that of total issues, though not as consistently. Both of these curves reached their high points in 1927 — some two years before the boom was at its peak and the other curves of the chart touched their maxima. After 1927, as the bull market in stocks developed, the rate at which corporate bonds were issued fell off, and the curves of total and of "net" issues declined rapidly. Although this decline was checked in 1930 it of course continued later.

The rate at which the curves of bond issues advanced seems to have been somewhat — though not a great deal — more rapid than the rate at which profits, interest payments, and the production of capital goods increased. After the rapid rise of

[24] Page 13. The figures are defined as "the difference between 'gross' incomes as defined by the Revenue Act and deductions allowed from these incomes by the Act. . . . Corporate net incomes, then, are profits, as usually defined by the economist, plus interest and rent charge on owned capital and land" (p. 12). They have been adjusted to include net incomes of personal service corporations in 1920 and 1921 and the special deductions allowed life insurance companies.

profits in 1922, profits, interest payments, and the production of capital goods all seem, significantly enough, to have risen at about the same rate. Although the fluctuations in the rates at which these magnitudes rose differ among themselves, the general slope of the three curves seems to be about the same, and they all reached their high points in 1929, at the culmination of the boom.[25] It is, perhaps, worth noting that the rate at which profits increased (or decreased) seems to have had no effect whatever upon the rate at which bonds were issued.

When this chart is looked at from another point of view it seems evident that the cycle, on its upward swing from 1921 through 1927, was accompanied by a rapid increase in the rate at which corporate bonds were issued. Corporate bonds, for the most part, are used to finance the construction of capital goods, and, as would be expected, the increase in corporate indebtedness was attended by an advance in the index of the Production of Capital Elemente, though this index does not seem to have risen so rapidly as did the rate at which corporate bonds were issued.[26] With the rise in corporate indebtedness corporate interest payments also increased, although the presence of short term interest payments in the statistics from which this curve is drawn precludes a direct comparison of the rate of increase of debt with the rate of increase of interest payments. This increased volume of interest payments, however, does not seem to have weighed heavily on business during the upswing of the cycle, since profits rose, even though erratically, at about the same rate.

Nor does it appear that the increase in capital goods during the decade brought any great amount of overexpansion or overcapacity to American industry. According to the most careful investigation made of this subject [27] there was, with the exception of a few particular instances, notably the transportation in-

[25] Although the index of the Production of Capital Elements extends only through 1929, it seems altogether probable that this index declined in the following years.
[26] A number of explanations can be found for this discrepancy of movement. One of the most pertinent is that the statistics from which the curve for corporate issues is drawn include refunding issues, the sale of which does not usually result in new capital equipment.
[27] E. G. Nourse and others, *America's Capacity to Produce* (1934), pp. 421–422.

dustry, little or no tendency for excess industrial capacity to grow during the decade. Thus, in these respects, the boom of the twenties does not seem to have brought serious maladjustments to the economic mechanism.

However, if the rates at which capital goods, profits, and interest payments were increasing in 1929 seem to have been in about the same general relationship as they were six or seven years earlier, it nevertheless is apparent that the industrial mechanism was, in 1929, in a much more vulnerable position than it was in 1922 and 1923. The increased volume of capital goods did not bring a serious amount of overcapacity, nor did the larger volume of interest payments place a severe burden upon business, so long as the quantity of goods which industry was adjusted to produce could be sold at suitable prices, so long as profits were maintained, and so long as the economic process functioned smoothly. But in the event that markets shrank, that profit margins declined, that the even operation of the economic process was broken — and all of these developments occurred in the years following 1929 —, the increased capacity of industry and its enlarged fixed charges inevitably placed it in a very serious situation. The increases of plant and of interest payments that had been accepted readily enough during the upswing of the cycle achieved a new and disquieting aspect with the coming of the depression.

Although the cycle appears to have had a very considerable effect upon the rate at which corporate bonds, both total and "net," were issued, it seems to have had much less influence upon the rate at which bonds of all types were brought out. In Chart XVI [28] is plotted the rate at which all kinds of bonds — including governments, municipals, corporates, and foreigns — were brought out, and the rate at which the "net" volume of bonds of all types — that is, total bonds offered less those called and matured — were issued. The chart is drawn in relatives, 1926 = 100, upon the same basis as that of Chart XV, and the two sets of curves may be directly compared.

[28] The figures from which this chart is drawn are given in Appendix P.

In the curves of Chart XVI the cyclical element is much less evident than in those of Chart XV. After the curves of Chart XVI recover from the low levels of 1920 the upward trend, so apparent in the curves of corporate issues, is not very clear, although these curves of Chart XVI do reach their high points

CHART XVI

GROWTH OF ALL BOND ISSUES AND OF "NET" BOND ISSUES, 1920–1930, IN RELATIVES, 1926 = 100

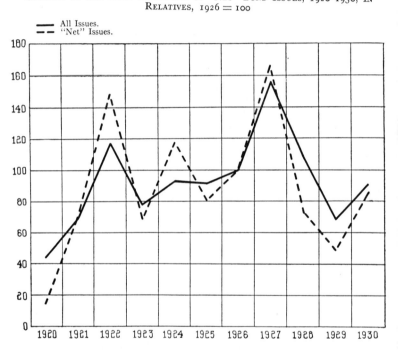

in 1927, and then recede, as in the case of corporate issues. The intermediate fluctuations, however, are much more marked in the case of total than in the case of corporate issues. In 1922, 1924, 1927, and 1930 the curves for total issues rise to very considerable peaks. These were the years in which the Federal Reserve System bought bonds in the open market, and the effect which such operations produced upon the issue of all types of bonds appears to have been much greater than the effect produced upon the flow of new corporate bonds.

In this last chapter some slight attempt has been made to summarize the principal developments — described at length in the preceding chapters — which took place in the post-war bond market, and to indicate some of the changes which these developments occasioned in various financial and economic relationships. Primarily the object has been to trace connections which existed during the twenties between the happenings in the bond market and the chief occurrences in the credit system, the structure of interest rates, and the methods of corporate financing. Some small consideration has been given to the relation of these events to current theories of investment, and the bearing which they had upon a number of magnitudes of importance in the industrial fabric has been touched upon. Such an undertaking, inevitably complex, has been made the more embarrassing by the deficiencies of many statistics which, in the absence of better, have had to be relied upon. The real difficulty in such an undertaking as is comprised in this work, however, lies in the fact that in the present stage of economic knowledge many of the points that must be dealt with are largely matters of opinion and judgment, rather than of fact, and the author is quick to acknowledge his shortcomings in these respects. But it is hoped that this study will further to some extent our comprehension of the post-war years, which constitute so fascinating a subject for investigation and which are of such importance in the understanding, and solution, of the problems that confront society at the present time.

APPENDICES

APPENDIX A

BOND YIELDS, 1919–1930, BY MONTHS *

Date		Average Yield of Moody's Aaa Bonds	Average Yield of Moody's Baa Bonds
1919	Jan.	5.35	7.12
	Feb.	5.35	7.20
	Mar.	5.39	7.15
	Apr.	5.44	7.23
	May	5.39	7.09
	June	5.40	7.04
	July	5.44	7.06
	Aug.	5.56	7.13
	Sept.	5.60	7.27
	Oct.	5.54	7.34
	Nov.	5.66	7.54
	Dec.	5.73	7.77
1920	Jan.	5.75	7.78
	Feb.	5.86	7.94
	Mar.	5.92	7.97
	Apr.	6.04	8.17
	May	6.25	8.39
	June	6.38	8.39
	July	6.34	8.52
	Aug.	6.30	8.39
	Sept.	6.22	8.14
	Oct.	6.05	7.99
	Nov.	6.08	8.21
	Dec.	6.26	8.56
1921	Jan.	6.14	8.50
	Feb.	6.08	8.42
	Mar.	6.08	8.55
	Apr.	6.06	8.53
	May	6.11	8.52
	June	6.18	8.56
	July	6.12	8.48
	Aug.	5.99	8.51
	Sept.	5.93	8.34
	Oct.	5.84	8.34
	Nov.	5.60	7.88
	Dec.	5.50	7.61
1922	Jan.	5.34	7.70
	Feb.	5.29	7.55
	Mar.	5.23	7.45
	Apr.	5.15	7.14

* Source of figures: Moody's Investors Service.

Appendix A (*Continued*)

Date		Average Yield of Moody's Aaa Bonds	Average Yield of Moody's Baa Bonds
	May	5.13	6.89
	June	5.08	6.97
	July	5.00	6.89
	Aug.	4.96	6.85
	Sept.	4.93	6.75
	Oct.	4.97	6.78
	Nov.	5.09	6.98
	Dec.	5.08	7.02
1923	Jan.	5.04	6.98
	Feb.	5.07	6.97
	Mar.	5.18	7.09
	Apr.	5.22	7.17
	May	5.16	7.17
	June	5.15	7.21
	July	5.14	7.34
	Aug.	5.08	7.38
	Sept.	5.12	7.38
	Oct.	5.11	7.46
	Nov.	5.09	7.40
	Dec.	5.09	7.38
1924	Jan.	5.09	7.24
	Feb.	5.09	7.14
	Mar.	5.10	7.08
	Apr.	5.08	7.03
	May	5.04	6.97
	June	4.99	6.82
	July	4.95	6.67
	Aug.	4.95	6.69
	Sept.	4.95	6.73
	Oct.	4.92	6.62
	Nov.	4.94	6.54
	Dec.	4.95	6.46
1925	Jan.	4.95	6.44
	Feb.	4.95	6.36
	Mar.	4.91	6.36
	Apr.	4.87	6.41
	May	4.83	6.30
	June	4.83	6.18
	July	4.87	6.20
	Aug.	4.90	6.24
	Sept.	4.87	6.20
	Oct.	4.85	6.17
	Nov.	4.84	6.17
	Dec.	4.85	6.15

Appendix A (*Continued*)

Date		Average Yield of Moody's Aaa Bonds	Average Yield of Moody's Baa Bonds
1926	Jan.	4.82	6.09
	Feb.	4.77	6.02
	Mar.	4.79	6.05
	Apr.	4.74	5.98
	May	4.71	5.86
	June	4.72	5.80
	July	4.71	5.79
	Aug.	4.72	5.81
	Sept.	4.72	5.79
	Oct.	4.71	5.81
	Nov.	4.68	5.77
	Dec.	4.68	5.68
1927	Jan.	4.66	5.61
	Feb.	4.67	5.59
	Mar.	4.62	5.54
	Apr.	4.58	5.48
	May	4.57	5.50
	June	4.58	5.55
	July	4.60	5.55
	Aug.	4.56	5.48
	Sept.	4.54	5.42
	Oct.	4.51	5.38
	Nov.	4.49	5.35
	Dec.	4.46	5.32
1928	Jan.	4.46	5.35
	Feb.	4.46	5.33
	Mar.	4.46	5.32
	Apr.	4.46	5.33
	May	4.49	5.42
	June	4.57	5.55
	July	4.61	5.58
	Aug.	4.64	5.61
	Sept.	4.61	5.59
	Oct.	4.61	5.58
	Nov.	4.58	5.55
	Dec.	4.61	5.60
1929	Jan.	4.62	5.63
	Feb.	4.66	5.66
	Mar.	4.70	5.79
	Apr.	4.69	5.80
	May	4.70	5.80
	June	4.77	5.94
	July	4.77	5.95
	Aug.	4.79	6.04

Appendix A (*Continued*)

Date		Average Yield of Moody's Aaa Bonds	Average Yield of Moody's Baa Bonds
	Sept.	4.80	6.12
	Oct.	4.77	6.11
	Nov.	4.76	6.03
	Dec.	4.67	5.95
1930	Jan.	4.66	5.92
	Feb.	4.69	5.89
	Mar.	4.62	5.73
	Apr.	4.60	5.70
	May	4.60	5.72
	June	4.57	5.78
	July	4.52	5.77
	Aug.	4.47	5.73
	Sept.	4.42	5.65
	Oct.	4.42	5.94
	Nov.	4.47	6.25
	Dec.	4.52	6.71

APPENDIX B

Bonds Traded on the New York Stock Exchange, 1920–1930, by Months *

Date		Bonds Traded on the New York Stock Exchange	Twelve-Month Moving-Average of Bonds Traded †
		(in millions)	
1920	Jan.	362	346
	Feb.	300	344
	Mar.	310	341
	Apr.	342	341
	May	367	342
	June	320	340
	July	238	329
	Aug.	215	324
	Sept.	286	318
	Oct.	332	309
	Nov.	320	302
	Dec.	562	291
1921	Jan.	296	291
	Feb.	225	291
	Mar.	227	292
	Apr.	231	296
	May	243	298
	June	311	306
	July	243	294
	Aug.	228	304
	Sept.	338	311
	Oct.	347	328
	Nov.	412	347
	Dec.	418	358
1922	Jan.	417	360
	Feb.	315	365
	Mar.	420	372
	Apr.	461	368
	May	382	369
	June	333	358
	July	307	342
	Aug.	310	331
	Sept.	296	328
	Oct.	365	314
	Nov.	272	296
	Dec.	222	286

* Source of figures: *Annalist*, seriatim.
† Average centered on the first of the month.

Appendix B (*Continued*)

Date		Bonds Traded on the New York Stock Exchange	Twelve-Month Moving-Average of Bonds Traded †
		(in millions)	
1923	Jan.	288	279
	Feb.	261	268
	Mar.	268	256
	Apr.	242	244
	May	268	232
	June	244	228
	July	178	229
	Aug.	158	235
	Sept.	157	232
	Oct.	225	236
	Nov.	227	238
	Dec.	237	238
1924	Jan.	354	250
	Feb.	235	265
	Mar.	282	278
	Apr.	282	287
	May	279	292
	June	395	306
	July	349	319
	Aug.	314	320
	Sept.	263	327
	Oct.	291	329
	Nov.	395	329
	Dec.	388	335
1925	Jan.	364	326
	Feb.	319	318
	Mar.	313	310
	Apr.	276	308
	May	346	306
	June	284	293
	July	265	284
	Aug.	218	279
	Sept.	240	272
	Oct.	262	268
	Nov.	243	271
	Dec.	270	262
1926	Jan.	304	261
	Feb.	242	256
	Mar.	269	264
	Apr.	306	249
	May	239	246
	June	267	258

† Average centered on the first of the month.

Appendix B (*Continued*)

Date		Bonds Traded on the New York Stock Exchange	Twelve-Month Moving-Average of Bonds Traded †
		(*in millions*)	
	July	214	261
	Aug.	182	268
	Sept.	192	271
	Oct.	227	275
	Nov.	276	275
	Dec.	311	279
1927	Jan.	382	282
	Feb.	278	283
	Mar.	317	284
	Apr.	303	288
	May	284	290
	June	261	289
	July	215	286
	Aug.	245	278
	Sept.	242	276
	Oct.	255	276
	Nov.	263	276
	Dec.	277	275
1928	Jan.	290	275
	Feb.	242	274
	Mar.	320	270
	Apr.	307	266
	May	272	264
	June	260	260
	July	206	254
	Aug.	181	251
	Sept.	199	246
	Oct.	235	236
	Nov.	220	229
	Dec.	207	226
1929	Jan.	248	220
	Feb.	181	232
	Mar.	213	238
	Apr.	216	239
	May	229	249
	June	236	255
	July	304	261
	Aug.	258	258
	Sept.	215	259
	Oct.	352	271
	Nov.	291	274
	Dec.	277	274

† Average centered on the first of the month.

Appendix B (*Continued*)

Date	Bonds Traded on the New York Stock Exchange	Twelve-Month Moving-Average of Bonds Traded †
	(*in millions*)	
1930 Jan.	208	274
Feb.	201	264
Mar.	348	256
Apr.	268	258
May	221	250
June	226	241
July	191	240
Aug.	170	244
Sept.	226	244
Oct.	268	234
Nov.	187	222
Dec.	266	224

† Average centered on the first of the month.

AVERAGE VOLUME OF BONDS TRADED PER YEAR IN TEN–YEAR PERIODS, 1911–1929 *

1911–20	1,552,369,260
1912–21	1,813,894,534
1913–22	2,156,342,637
1914–23	2,381,577,708
1915–24	2,717,489,882
1916–25	2,961,716,717
1917–26	3,148,522,662
1918–27	3,375,442,527
1919–28	3,460,079,552
1920–29	3,384,959,504

* Source of figures: *New York Stock Exchange Year Book*, 1929–30.

APPENDIX C

Number of Bond Issues, 1923–1932, by Months and by Quarters *

Date		By Months		By Quarters	
		Actual Totals	Corrected for Seasonal Fluctuation	Actual Totals	Corrected for Seasonal Fluctuation
1923	Jan.	94	91		
	Feb.	76	92	275	267
	Mar.	105	101		
	Apr.	61	57		
	May	106	99	288	269
	June	121	122		
	July	103	103		
	Aug.	59	75	238	253
	Sept.	76	78		
	Oct.	87	78		
	Nov.	127	113	314	328
	Dec.	100	99		
1924	Jan.	96	93		
	Feb.	95	114	316	307
	Mar.	125	120		
	Apr.	120	111		
	May	129	121	388	362
	June	139	140		
	July	160	160		
	Aug.	85	108	369	393
	Sept.	124	128		
	Oct.	151	136		
	Nov.	126	112	437	455
	Dec.	160	158		
1925	Jan.	167	162		
	Feb.	149	180	463	450
	Mar.	147	141		
	Apr.	155	144		
	May	152	142	479	447
	June	172	174		
	July	177	177		
	Aug.	112	142	428	455
	Sept.	139	143		
	Oct.	163	147		
	Nov.	169	151	481	500
	Dec.	149	148		
1926	Jan.	138	134		
	Feb.	107	129	421	409

* Source of figures: A special compilation by the Standard Statistics Company.

Appendix C (*Continued*)

Date			By Months		By Quarters	
			Actual Totals	Corrected for Seasonal Fluctuation	Actual Totals	Corrected for Seasonal Fluctuation
	Mar.	....	176	169		
	Apr.	....	162	150		
	May	....	147	137	481	450
	June	....	172	174		
	July	....	166	166		
	Aug.	....	109	138	415	442
	Sept.	....	140	144		
	Oct.	....	156	141		
	Nov.	....	146	130	440	459
	Dec.	....	138	137		
1927	Jan.	....	197	191		
	Feb.	....	156	188	544	528
	Mar.	....	191	184		
	Apr.	....	165	153		
	May	....	199	186	527	491
	June	....	163	165		
	July	....	207	207		
	Aug.	....	139	176	478	509
	Sept.	....	132	136		
	Oct.	....	160	144		
	Nov.	....	184	164	476	496
	Dec.	....	132	131		
1928	Jan.	....	82	80		
	Feb.	....	189	239	419	406
	Mar.	....	148	142		
	Apr.	....	142	131		
	May	....	249	231	541	505
	June	....	150	152		
	July	....	162	162		
	Aug.	....	96	121	348	370
	Sept.	....	90	93		
	Oct.	....	135	122		
	Nov.	....	122	109	341	356
	Dec.	....	84	83		
1929	Jan.	....	156	151		
	Feb.	....	97	117	340	330
	Mar.	....	87	84		
	Apr.	....	90	83		
	May	....	79	74	253	236
	June	....	84	85		
	July	....	85	85		
	Aug.	....	59	75	190	210
	Sept.	....	46	47		

Appendix C (*Continued*)

Date		By Months		By Quarters	
		Actual Totals	Corrected for Seasonal Fluctuation	Actual Totals	Corrected for Seasonal Fluctuation
	Oct.	51	46		
	Nov.	29	26	151	157
	Dec.	71	70		
1930	Jan.	72	70		
	Feb.	51	61	210	202
	Mar.	87	84		
	Apr.	88	82		
	May	63	59	211	197
	June	60	61		
	July	81	81		
	Aug.	28	35	166	177
	Sept.	57	59		
	Oct.	47	42		
	Nov.	38	34	113	118
	Dec.	28	28		
1931	Jan.	50	49		
	Feb.	32	39	137	133
	Mar.	55	53		
	Apr.	49	45		
	May	39	37	128	120
	June	40	40		
	July	27	27		
	Aug.	27	34	74	79
	Sept.	20	21		
	Oct.	7	6		
	Nov.	15	13	35	37
	Dec.	13	13		
1932	Jan.	13	12		
	Feb.	9	11	38	37
	Mar.	16	15		
	Apr.	14	13		
	May	9	8	28	26
	June	5	5		
	July	11	11		
	Aug.	15	19	38	40
	Sept.	12	12		
	Oct.	18	16		
	Nov.	9	8	38	40
	Dec.	11	11		

APPENDIX D

VOLUME OF BOND ISSUES, 1919–1931, BY QUARTERS
(*in Millions*)

Year	C. & F. Chronicle New Capital Figures	C. & F. Chronicle Refunding Figures	Government Issues of Maturity of Longer than One Year *	Total Issues
1919				
	514	189		703
	910	79	4,498	5,487
	1,031	241	657	1,929
	1,107	299		1,406
1920				
	578	109		687
	735	39		774
	533	128		661
	754	63		817
1921				
	720	134		854
	758	319	311	1,388
	766	59	391	1,216
	1,063	105		1,168
1922				
	1,067	184	1,220	2,471
	1,334	316	335	1,985
	690	241	487	1,418
	640	140	1,233	2,013
1923				
	1,167	210	367	1,744
	934	211	668	1,813
	547	161		708
	997	26		1,023
1924				
	1,049	208		1,257
	1,311	134		1,445
	1,076	224		1,300
	1,328	157	757	2,242
1925				
	1,356	259	340	1,955
	1,348	164		1,512
	1,039	254		1,293
	1,263	133		1,396
1926				
	1,329	184	619	2,132
	1,467	307		1,774

* Figures from the Annual Reports of the Secretary of the Treasury.

Appendix D (*Continued*)

Year	C. & F. Chronicle New Capital Figures	C. & F. Chronicle Refunding Figures	Government Issues of Maturity of Longer than One Year *	Total Issues
	1,111	128		1,239
	1,256	330		1,586
1927				
	1,583	468	1,360	3,411
	1,790	614	467	2,871
	1,178	207	647	2,032
	1,730	589		2,319
1928				
	1,404	681		2,085
	1,551	521	607	2,679
	758	48	359	1,156
	1,331	71		1,402
1929				
	1,106	204		1,310
	1,250	221		1,471
	737	125		862
	1,004	27		1,031
1930				
	1,739	128		1,867
	1,881	182		2,063
	959	229		1,188
	915	76		991
1931				
	1,158	328	594	2,080
	845	414	871	2,130
	583	96	800	1,479
	210	39		249

* Figures from the Annual Reports of the Secretary of the Treasury.

APPENDIX E

"Net" Volume of Bonds Issued, 1920–1930, by Quarters *
(in Millions)

Year	Total Issues	Total Issues Called and Matured	"Net" Issues
1920			
	687	578	109
	774	718	56
	661	915	*254* †
	817	254	563
1921			
	854	516	338
	1,388	319	1,069
	1,216	669	547
	1,168	719	449
1922			
	2,471	489	1,982
	1,985	799	1,186
	1,418	762	656
	2,013	780	1,233
1923			
	1,744	597	1,147
	1,813	744	1,069
	708	771	*63*
	1,023	835	188
1924			
	1,257	379	878
	1,445	665	780
	1,300	672	628
	2,242	542	1,700
1925			
	1,955	698	1,257
	1,512	1,002	510
	1,293	779	514
	1,396	914	482
1926			
	2,132	690	1,442
	1,774	736	1,038
	1,239	1,261	*22*
	1,586	627	959
1927			
	3,411	1,410	2,001

* Source of figures: See footnote 7, p. 34.
† Italic figures are minus quantities.

Appendix E (*Continued*)

Year	Total Issues	Total Issues Called and Matured	"Net" Issues
	2,871	803	2,068
	2,032	838	1,194
	2,319	1,963	356
1928			
	2,085	1,099	986
	2,679	1,310	1,369
	1,156	1,742	*586* †
	1,402	697	705
1929			
	1,310	579	731
	1,471	722	749
	862	945	*83*
	1,030	743	287
1930			
	1,867	644	823
	2,063	853	1,210
	1,188	600	588
	991	664	327

† Italic figures are minus quantities.

APPENDIX F

TOTAL ISSUES, NEW CAPITAL ISSUES, AND "NET" ISSUES CORRECTED. FOR SEASONAL FLUCTUATION, 1920–1930, BY QUARTERS

(in Millions)

Year	Total Issues	New Capital Issues	"Net" Issues
1920			
	636	555	79
	666	655	46
	818	684	*255* *
	861	718	1,061
1921			
	791	692	242
	1,195	675	882
	1,501	983	636
	1,230	1,012	847
1922			
	2,292	1,025	1,425
	1,710	1,190	970
	1,750	885	764
	2,140	610	2,314
1923			
	1,616	1,120	825
	1,566	833	882
	875	701	*63*
	1,080	948	355
1924			
	1,165	1,009	631
	1,245	1,170	640
	1,605	1,380	731
	2,360	1,263	3,210
1925			
	1,810	1,303	905
	1,305	1,201	418
	1,599	1,332	597
	1,470	1,202	910
1926			
	1,972	1,278	1,038
	1,530	1,309	851
	1,530	1,423	*22*
	1,670	1,197	1,809
1927			
	3,160	1,522	1,440

* Italic figures are minus quantities.

Appendix F (*Continued*)

Year	Total Issues	New Capital Issues	"Net" Issues
	2,438	1,598	1,697
	2,502	1,510	1,389
	2,480	1,648	672
1928			
	1,930	1,351	710
	2,301	1,383	1,121
	1,440	973	*586* *
	1,478	1,268	1,330
1929			
	1,211	1,062	526
	1,290	1,113	614
	1,064	945	*83*
	1,085	956	541
1930			
	1,729	1,670	592
	1,775	1,679	992
	1,468	1,228	684
	1,042	872	617

* Italic figures are minus quantities.

APPENDIX G

Annual Totals of "Net" Bond Issues, 1920–1930, Compared with Year-to-Year Changes in Bond Holdings of Life Insurance Companies, Savings Banks, City Banks, Country Banks *

(*in Millions*)

Year	Increases (or Decreases) during Year in Bond Holdings		Total "Net" Issues	Funds Necessary to Absorb "Net" Issues Furnished by Others
1920	Life Insurance Companies	95		
	Savings Banks	253		
	City Banks	641 †		
	Country Banks	69		
	Total	362	474	836
1921	Life Insurance Companies	21		
	Savings Banks	84		
	City Banks	134		
	Country Banks	7		
	Total	78	2,403	2,325
1922	Life Insurance Companies	246		
	Savings Banks	377		
	City Banks	1,141		
	Country Banks	386		
	Total	2,150	5,057	2,907
1923	Life Insurance Companies	99		
	Savings Banks	224		
	City Banks	248		
	Country Banks	246		
	Total	321	2,341	2,020
1924	Life Insurance Companies	231		
	Savings Banks	28		
	City Banks	902		
	County Banks	257		
	Total	1,418	3,986	2,568
1925	Life Insurance Companies	278		
	Savings Banks	196		
	City Banks	131		
	Country Banks	210		
	Total	553	2,763	2,210

* Source of figures: See pp. 37–39.
† Italic figures are decreases in bond holdings.

Appendix G (*Continued*)

Year	Increases (or Decreases) during Year in Bond Holdings		Total "Net" Issues	Funds Necessary to Absorb "Net" Issues Furnished by Others
1926	Life Insurance Companies	270		
	Savings Banks	129		
	City Banks	25 †		
	Country Banks	92		
	Total	466	3,417	2,951
1927	Life Insurance Companies	464		
	Savings Banks	33		
	City Banks	923		
	Country Banks	447		
	Total	1,867	5,619	3,752
1928	Life Insurance Companies	438		
	Savings Banks	236		
	City Banks	79		
	Country Banks	89		
	Total	842	2,474	1,632
1929	Life Insurance Companies	273		
	Savings Banks	21		
	City Banks	*433*		
	Country Banks	*313*		
	Total	*494*	1,684	2,178
1930	Life Insurance Companies	356		
	Savings Banks	93		
	City Banks	1,126		
	Country Banks	79		
	Total	1,654	2,948	1,294

† Italic figures are decreases in bond holdings.

APPENDIX H

INDICES OF BUSINESS ACTIVITY AND WHOLESALE COMMODITY PRICES, 1919–1930, BY MONTHS

Date		Harvard Economic Society — Index of Business Curve B *	Federal Reserve Bank of New York Volume of Trade Index, I †	Brookmire Economic Service — Business Index ‡	U. S. Bureau of Labor Revised Wholesale Commodity Price Index, in Relatives, 1926=100
1919	Jan.	− .88		98.0	134.4
	Feb.	−1.14		97.3	129.8
	Mar.	−1.46		94.0	131.3
	Apr.	−1.23		94.1	133.0
	May	− .40		93.3	135.3
	June	− .16		96.0	135.6
	July	.35		103.3	141.1
	Aug.	.54		105.8	144.3
	Sept.	.18		105.9	141.1
	Oct.	.26		103.8	141.6
	Nov.	.34		105.1	144.5
	Dec.	.76		107.3	150.5
1920	Jan.	1.07	109	111.0	157.7
	Feb.	.95	106	112.6	157.1
	Mar.	1.20	107	113.0	158.6
	Apr.	1.44	104	105.1	165.5
	May	1.76	105	104.7	167.2
	June	1.94	104	107.5	166.5
	July	2.02	104	106.0	165.8
	Aug.	1.68	103	105.8	161.4
	Sept.	1.50	99	100.1	155.2
	Oct.	.84	97	94.3	144.2
	Nov.	.35	97	90.6	133.4
	Dec.	− .01	95	86.1	120.7
1921	Jan.	− .58	92	78.9	114.0
	Feb.	− .88	90	80.3	104.9
	Mar.	−1.27	89	78.2	102.4
	Apr.	−1.25	90	78.7	98.9
	May	−1.09	90	78.8	96.2
	June	−1.14	91	79.3	93.4
	July	−1.42	91	77.9	93.4
	Aug.	−1.16	91	80.8	93.5
	Sept.	−1.08	91	79.4	93.4

* As changed by the revisions of May 1923, April 1926, and November 1928.
† Third revision, dated September 28, 1931.
‡ Revised as of November 1930.

Appendix H (*Continued*)

Date		Harvard Economic Society — Index of Business Curve B *	Federal Reserve Bank of New York Volume of Trade Index, I †	Brookmire Economic Service — Business Index ‡	U. S. Bureau of Labor Revised Wholesale Commodity Price Index, in Relatives, 1926=100
	Oct.	−1.09	92	81.8	94.1
	Nov.	−1.35	90	81.6	94.2
	Dec.	−1.44	91	80.5	92.9
1922	Jan.	−1.66	92	80.8	91.4
	Feb.	−1.34	93	82.9	92.9
	Mar.	−1.25	94	86.1	92.8
	Apr.	−1.20	95	86.4	93.2
	May	− .64	97	90.5	96.1
	June	− .38	100	97.4	96.3
	July	− .38	99	94.9	99.4
	Aug.	− .08	97	94.8	98.6
	Sept.	− .14	99	93.2	99.3
	Oct.	− .10	101	97.9	99.6
	Nov.	− .34	102	103.4	100.5
	Dec.	.10	104	105.8	100.7
1923	Jan.	.52	104	105.6	102.0
	Feb.	.71	104	103.3	103.3
	Mar.	.69	105	106.2	104.5
	Apr.	.72	106	109.5	103.9
	May	.98	106	109.4	101.9
	June	.62	104	111.7	100.3
	July	.20	102	108.3	98.4
	Aug.	.38	101	105.7	97.8
	Sept.	− .13	101	103.2	99.7
	Oct.	− .06	100	106.0	99.4
	Nov.	− .30	102	106.5	98.4
	Dec.	− .16	103	103.1	98.1
1924	Jan.	− .10	102	106.8	99.6
	Feb.	.22	103	107.0	99.7
	Mar.	.12	100	103.6	98.5
	Apr.	− .07	100	99.1	97.3
	May	− .29	98	93.0	95.9
	June	− .42	97	92.2	94.9
	July	− .36	97	90.1	95.6
	Aug.	.10	98	92.3	97.0
	Sept.	− .14	100	95.3	97.1
	Oct.	.20	100	97.8	98.2
	Nov.	.56	103	99.6	99.1
	Dec.	.79	103	100.9	101.5

* As changed by the revisions of May 1923, April 1926, and November 1928.
† Third revision, dated September 28, 1931.
‡ Revised as of November 1930.

Appendix H (*Continued*)

Date		Harvard Economic Society — Index of Business Curve B *	Federal Reserve Bank of New York Volume of Trade Index, I †	Brookmire Economic Service — Business Index ‡	U. S. Bureau of Labor Revised Wholesale Commodity Price Index, in Relatives, 1926=100
1925	Jan.	1.36	104	103.0	102.9
	Feb.	1.32	105	103.9	104.0
	Mar.	1.51	104	104.9	104.2
	Apr.	.96	103	105.7	101.9
	May	1.04	103	102.8	101.6
	June	1.24	102	104.1	103.0
	July	1.40	103	103.8	104.3
	Aug.	1.47	103	100.9	103.9
	Sept.	1.40	104	102.5	103.4
	Oct.	1.48	106	111.7	103.6
	Nov.	1.43	108	113.2	104.5
	Dec.	1.31	108	113.5	103.4
1926	Jan.	1.65	107	110.4	103.6
	Feb.	1.28	105	109.1	102.1
	Mar.	1.12	104	108.5	100.4
	Apr.	1.07	104	108.7	100.1
	May	1.02	104	107.8	100.5
	June	1.00	104	109.2	100.5
	July	1.16	106	108.7	99.5
	Aug.	.84	106	110.1	99.0
	Sept.	.76	105	110.7	99.7
	Oct.	1.00	105	109.3	99.4
	Nov.	.55	104	109.2	98.4
	Dec.	.66	104	106.0	97.9
1927	Jan.	.82	104	107.6	96.6
	Feb.	.76	104	106.6	95.9
	Mar.	.72	105	107.7	94.5
	Apr.	.76	105	106.5	93.7
	May	.80	105	106.6	93.7
	June	.66	104	105.8	93.8
	July	.77	104	103.8	94.1
	Aug.	.64	105	104.2	95.2
	Sept.	.99	104	101.2	96.5
	Oct.	.90	102	98.8	97.0
	Nov.	.80	101	98.6	96.7
	Dec.	.84	101	97.9	96.8
1928	Jan.	.76	102	102.5	96.3
	Feb.	.66	102	104.0	96.4
	Mar.	.98	104	103.0	96.0

* As changed by the revisions of May 1923, April 1926, and November 1928.
† Third revision, dated September 28, 1931.
‡ Revised as of November 1930.

Appendix H (*Continued*)

Date		Harvard Economic Society — Index of Business Curve B *	Federal Reserve Bank of New York Volume of Trade Index, I †	Brookmire Economic Service — Business Index ‡	U. S. Bureau of Labor Revised Wholesale Commodity Price Index, in Relatives, 1926 = 100
	Apr.	1.23	105	104.2	97.4
	May	1.50	106	105.8	98.6
	June	1.52	105	106.3	97.6
	July	1.14	104	107.7	98.3
	Aug.	1.16	104	108.6	98.9
	Sept.	1.46	107	111.2	100.1
	Oct.	1.33	106	111.6	97.8
	Nov.	1.20	107	109.3	96.7
	Dec.	1.55	108	108.9	96.7
1929	Jan.	1.40	109	113.2	97.2
	Feb.	1.31	109	112.8	96.7
	Mar.	1.64	109	112.0	97.5
	Apr.	1.54	108	114.2	96.8
	May	1.26	108	114.3	95.8
	June	1.39	109	115.0	96.4
	July	2.04	110	114.2	98.0
	Aug.	1.96	110	112.0	97.7
	Sept.	1.74	109	110.8	97.5
	Oct.	1.81	108	106.3	96.3
	Nov.	1.28	102	98.4	94.4
	Dec.	.56	98	93.9	94.2
1930	Jan.	.31	97	96.5	93.4
	Feb.	.16	98	96.6	92.1
	Mar.	.14	97	93.7	90.8
	Apr.	.10	98	95.9	90.7
	May	.02	96	92.9	89.1
	June	− .33	95	90.4	86.8
	July	−1.04	91	85.7	84.0
	Aug.	−1.23	89	83.3	84.0
	Sept.	−1.34	87	81.8	84.2
	Oct.	−1.74	85	79.5	82.6
	Nov.	−2.24	83	76.4	80.4
	Dec.	−2.50	82	75.4	78.4

* As changed by the revisions of May 1923, April 1926, and November 1928.
† Third revision, dated September 28, 1931.
‡ Revised as of November 1930.

APPENDIX I

SHORT TERM INTEREST RATES, 1919–1930, BY MONTHS

Date		Average Daily Rates for Prime 90–Day Commercial Paper *	Average Daily Time-Money Rates 90–Day Mixed Collateral *	Weighted Average of Rates Charged Customers by Banks in New York City †	Discount Rate of the Federal Reserve Bank of New York ‡	
1919	Jan.	5.50	5.25	5.54	4.75	
	Feb.	5.31	5.25	5.36	4.75	
	Mar.	5.31	5.50	5.46	4.75	
	Apr.	5.25	5.50	5.56	4.75	
	May	5.25	5.50	5.43	4.75	
	June	5.50	6.00	5.45	4.75	
	July	5.30	6.00	5.49	4.75	
	Aug.	5.50	6.00	5.49	4.75	
	Sept.	5.33	5.87	5.49	4.75	
	Oct.	5.25	6.00	5.63	4.75	
	Nov.	5.40	7.00	5.56	4.75	
	Dec.	5.75	7.00	5.61	4.75	
1920	Jan.	5.95	7.90	5.93	6.00	Jan. 23
	Feb.	6.62	9.25	6.00	6.00	
	Mar.	6.87	8.87	6.00	6.00	
	Apr.	6.65	8.50	6.09	6.00	
	May	7.18	8.50	6.00	6.00	
	June	7.75	8.50	6.00	6.00	
	July	7.75	8.50	6.43	6.00	
	Aug.	8.00	8.50	6.36	6.00	
	Sept.	8.00	8.00	6.57	6.00	
	Oct.	8.00	7.50	6.57	6.00	
	Nov.	7.93	7.87	6.71	6.00	
	Dec.	7.75	7.30	6.36	6.00	
1921	Jan.	7.62	6.87	6.71	6.00	
	Feb.	7.62	7.00	6.78	6.00	
	Mar.	7.50	7.00	6.70	6.00	
	Apr.	7.40	6.85	6.64	6.00	
	May	6.87	6.75	6.68	6.00	
	June	6.50	6.81	6.43	6.00	
	July	6.25	6.00	6.21	5.50	July 21
	Aug.	6.37	6.00	6.25	5.50	
	Sept.	6.25	5.80	6.11	5.00	Sept. 22
	Oct.	5.93	5.50	5.93	5.00	

* Figures from *Facts and Figures.*
† Figures from *Annual Report of the Federal Reserve Board,* 1930, p. 83.
‡ Figures from *Standard Statistics Company Base Book; Facts and Figures.*
To July 21, 1921, the rate on 60/90 day commercial, agricultural, and livestock paper was used; thereafter the rate on all classes of paper.

Appendix I (*Continued*)

Date		Average Daily Rates for Prime 90–Day Commercial Paper *	Average Daily Time-Money Rates 90–Day Mixed Collateral *	Weighted Average of Rates Charged Customers by Banks in New York City †	Discount Rate of the Federal Reserve Bank of New York ‡	
	Nov.	5.50	5.25	5.96	4.50	Nov. 3
	Dec.	5.50	5.00	5.68	4.50	
1922	Jan.	5.00	4.75	5.50	4.50	
	Feb.	4.82	5.00	5.48	4.50	
	Mar.	4.50	4.80	5.43	4.50	
	Apr.	4.31	4.50	5.46	4.50	
	May	4.31	4.25	5.06	4.50	
	June	4.10	4.25	4.93	4.00	June 22
	July	4.00	4.15	5.16	4.00	
	Aug.	4.00	4.15	4.66	4.00	
	Sept.	4.18	4.50	4.70	4.00	
	Oct.	4.50	4.94	4.74	4.00	
	Nov.	4.62	5.00	4.82	4.00	
	Dec.	4.68	5.00	4.86	4.00	
1923	Jan.	4.43	4.75	4.82	4.00	
	Feb.	4.58	4.84	4.91	4.50	Feb. 23
	Mar.	5.00	5.50	4.98	4.50	
	Apr.	5.00	5.50	5.32	4.50	
	May	5.00	5.25	5.27	4.50	
	June	5.00	5.00	5.21	4.50	
	July	4.86	5.25	5.29	4.50	
	Aug.	5.20	5.25	5.18	4.50	
	Sept.	5.30	5.50	5.33	4.50	
	Oct.	5.36	5.34	5.37	4.50	
	Nov.	5.00	5.25	5.39	4.50	
	Dec.	4.91	5.00	5.21	4.50	
1924	Jan.	4.75	4.79	5.21	4.50	
	Feb.	4.75	4.70	5.07	4.50	
	Mar.	4.75	4.67	5.06	4.50	
	Apr.	4.55	4.62	4.98	4.50	
	May	4.32	4.12	4.89	4.00	May 1
	June	3.94	3.31	4.64	3.50	June 12
	July	3.38	2.90	4.21	3.50	
	Aug.	3.19	2.92	4.09	3.00	Aug. 8
	Sept.	3.16	3.12	4.20	3.00	
	Oct.	3.04	3.12	4.41	3.00	
	Nov.	3.28	3.33	4.13	3.00	

* Figures from *Facts and Figures*.
† Figures from *Annual Report of the Federal Reserve Board*, 1930, p. 83.
‡ Figures from *Standard Statistics Company Base Book; Facts and Figures*.
To July 21, 1921, the rate on 60/90 day commercial, agricultural, and livestock paper was used; thereafter the rate on all classes of paper.

Appendix I (*Continued*)

Date		Average Daily Rates for Prime 90–Day Commercial Paper *	Average Daily Time-Money Rates 90–Day Mixed Collateral *	Weighted Average of Rates Charged Customers by Banks in New York City †	Discount Rate of the Federal Reserve Bank of New York ‡	
	Dec.	3.74	3.72	4.29	3.00	
1925	Jan.	3.12	3.52	4.16	3.00	
	Feb.	3.12	3.50	4.43	3.50	Feb. 27
	Mar.	4.00	4.00	4.53	3.50	
	Apr.	4.00	3.87	4.48	3.50	
	May	4.00	3.75	4.38	3.50	
	June	4.00	3.75	4.36	3.50	
	July	4.00	3.85	4.46	3.50	
	Aug.	4.00	4.18	4.36	3.50	
	Sept.	4.15	4.40	4.57	3.50	
	Oct.	4.25	4.50	4.62	3.50	
	Nov.	4.25	4.87	4.61	3.50	
	Dec.	4.25	4.87	4.70	3.50	
1926	Jan.	4.25	4.74	4.64	4.00	Jan. 8
	Feb.	4.25	4.52	4.68	4.00	
	Mar.	4.25	4.75	4.62	4.00	
	Apr.	4.21	4.39	4.62	3.50	Apr. 23
	May	4.00	4.00	4.66	3.50	
	June	4.00	4.13	4.58	3.50	
	July	4.00	4.39	4.38	3.50	
	Aug.	4.31	4.66	4.62	4.00	Aug. 13
	Sept.	4.46	4.90	4.81	4.00	
	Oct.	4.55	5.02	4.85	4.00	
	Nov.	4.53	4.74	4.79	4.00	
	Dec.	4.50	4.62	4.79	4.00	
1927	Jan.	4.36	4.55	4.66	4.00	
	Feb.	4.02	4.50	4.56	4.00	
	Mar.	4.19	4.50	4.56	4.00	
	Apr.	4.06	4.50	4.63	4.00	
	May	4.02	4.42	4.63	4.00	
	June	4.05	4.46	4.60	4.00	
	July	4.18	4.47	4.56	4.00	
	Aug.	4.00	4.20	4.41	3.50	Aug. 5
	Sept.	4.00	4.10	4.44	3.50	
	Oct.	4.00	4.23	4.49	3.50	
	Nov.	4.00	4.18	4.35	3.50	
	Dec.	4.00	4.11	4.50	3.50	

* Figures from *Facts and Figures*.
† Figures from *Annual Report of the Federal Reserve Board*, 1930, p. 83.
‡ Figures from *Standard Statistics Company Base Book; Facts and Figures*.
To July 21, 1921, the rate on 60/90 day commercial, agricultural, and livestock paper was used; thereafter the rate on all classes of paper.

Appendix I (*Continued*)

Date		Average Daily Rates for Prime 90–Day Commercial Paper *	Average Daily Time-Money Rates 90–Day Mixed Collateral *	Weighted Average of Rates Charged Customers by Banks in New York City †	Discount Rate of the Federal Reserve Bank of New York ‡	
1928	Jan.	3.94	4.30	4.56	3.50	
	Feb.	4.02	4.45	4.44	4.00	Feb. 3
	Mar.	4.21	4.51	4.59	4.00	
	Apr.	4.15	4.85	4.72	4.00	
	May	4.46	5.22	4.97	4.50	May 18
	June	4.70	5.70	5.09	4.50	
	July	5.71	5.94	5.38	5.00	July 13
	Aug.	5.37	6.35	5.56	5.00	
	Sept.	5.50	7.03	5.63	5.00	
	Oct.	5.50	7.11	5.63	5.00	
	Nov.	5.25	7.00	5.56	5.00	
	Dec.	5.49	7.48	5.63	5.00	
1929	Jan.	5.00	7.50	5.74	5.00	
	Feb.	5.00	7.64	5.73	5.00	
	Mar.	5.72	7.87	5.81	5.00	
	Apr.	5.88	8.63	5.85	5.00	
	May	5.80	8.53	5.88	5.00	
	June	6.00	7.95	5.93	5.00	
	July	6.00	7.66	5.88	5.00	
	Aug.	6.09	8.79	6.05	6.00	Aug. 9
	Sept.	6.00	8.85	6.06	6.00	
	Oct.	6.01	8.64	6.08	6.00	
	Nov.	5.42	5.51	5.86	5.00	Nov. 1
					4.50	Nov. 15
	Dec.	5.00	4.72	5.74	4.50	
1930	Jan.	4.81	4.57	5.64	4.50	
	Feb.	4.52	4.50	5.35	4.00	Feb. 7
	Mar.	4.12	3.82	5.22	3.50	Mar. 14
	Apr.	3.75	3.78	4.91	3.50	
	May	3.52	3.25	4.74	3.00	May 2
	June	3.43	2.74	4.59	2.50	June 20
	July	3.05	2.59	4.48	2.50	
	Aug.	3.00	2.25	4.41	2.50	
	Sept.	3.00	2.33	4.29	2.50	
	Oct.	2.73	1.93	4.26	2.50	
	Nov.	2.75	2.00	4.17	2.50	
	Dec.	2.77	2.24	4.16	2.00	Dec. 24

* Figures from *Facts and Figures.*
† Figures from *Annual Report of the Federal Reserve Board,* 1930, p. 83.
‡ Figures from *Standard Statistics Company Base Book; Facts and Figures.*
To July 21, 1921, the rate on 60/90 day commercial, agricultural, and livestock paper was used; thereafter the rate on all classes of paper.

APPENDIX J

FEDERAL RESERVE BANK CREDIT, CREDIT OF REPORTING MEMBER BANKS IN
LEADING CITIES, STOCK OF MONEY GOLD, AND MONEY IN CIRCULATION,
1919–1931, BY MONTHS

Date	Reporting Member Banks in Leading Cities — Monthly Averages of Weekly Figures (in billions)*			Federal Reserve Banks — Monthly Averages of Daily Figures (in millions)†				Stock of Money Gold — End of Month Figures (in millions) ‡	Money in Circulation (in millions) ‡
	Total Loans and Investments	Total Investments	Security Loans	Total Federal Reserve Credit	Bills Bought in the Open Market	U. S. Gov't. Securities	Bills Discounted		
1919									
Jan.	14.23	4.30		2,359	278	200	1,731	3,162	4,919
Feb.	14.31	4.54		2,341	274	186	1,765	3,165	4,922
Mar.	14.63	4.80		2,480	261	195	1,863	3,165	4,948
Apr.	14.61	4.76		2,451	207	213	1,920	3,177	4,943
May	14.94	4.91		2,498	187	228	1,976	3,177	4,918
June	15.02	4.36		2,467	247	236	1,840	3,113	4,877
July	14.86	4.06		2,599	358	249	1,864	3,064	4,870
Aug.	15.26	4.29		2,559	372	270	1,798	3,125	4,948
Sept.	15.63	4.29		2,636	351	341	1,776	3,147	5,037
Oct.	16.01	4.11		2,847	343	296	2,068	3,103	5,127
Nov.	16.19	4.00		3,038	455	307	2,140	3,044	5,269
Dec.	16.39	3.98	4.70	3,203	549	327	2,115	2,994	5,378
1920									
Jan.	16.68	3.94	4.74	3,205	570	326	2,136	2,930	5,177
Feb.	16.65	3.76	4.50	3,314	541	309	2,297	2,887	5,360
Mar.	16.85	3.61	4.45	3,413	480	344	2,377	2,850	5,391
Apr.	16.98	3.64	4.39	3,364	413	332	2,431	2,841	5,409
May	16.99	3.64	4.30	3,385	411	302	2,536	2,856	5,452
June	16.97	3.55	4.25	3,382	400	347	2,456	2,865	5,468
July	16.92	3.41	4.18	3,344	362	319	2,513	2,862	5,454
Aug.	16.91	3.39	4.08	3,353	324	304	2,596	2,851	5,548
Sept.	17.06	3.37	4.11	3,495	310	339	2,667	2,873	5,616
Oct.	17.19	3.30	4.16	3,522	303	305	2,780	2,868	5,698
Nov.	16.87	3.29	4.07	3,467	276	320	2,762	2,897	5,643
Dec.	16.74	3.31	4.11	3,442	242	339	2,718	2,926	5,612
1921									
Jan.	16.45	3.28	4.04	3,110	200	298	2,523	2,966	5,303
Feb.	16.18	3.25	3.96	2,918	169	287	2,400	3,000	5,273
Mar.	16.07	3.28	3.92	2,798	137	296	2,297	3,086	5,124
Apr.	15.78	3.27	3.85	2,564	110	277	2,129	3,164	5,080
May	15.51	3.24	3.84	2,386	84	303	1,959	3,231	5,015
June	15.36	3.33	3.81	2,211	54	302	1,811	3,275	4,911
July	15.07	3.21	3.74	2,049	26	261	1,719	3,347	4,797
Aug.	14.92	3.23	3.67	1,863	38	249	1,548	3,439	4,740
Sept.	14.90	3.23	3.67	1,767	40	254	1,442	3,519	4,744
Oct.	14.94	3.28	3.72	1,669	56	207	1,371	3,572	4,695
Nov.	14.84	3.43	3.72	1,544	79	208	1,228	3,627	4,651
Dec.	14.84	3.42	3.77	1,548	105	226	1,180	3,660	4,690
1922									
Jan.	14.69	3.49	3.71	1,326	98	238	962	3,685	4,441
Feb.	14.69	3.66	3.67	1,233	88	357	769	3,723	4,491
Mar.	14.62	3.58	3.64	1,207	92	459	638	3,750	4,497
Apr.	14.69	3.69	3.66	1,210	93	520	572	3,764	4,468
May	14.97	3.92	3.83	1,208	103	603	479	3,771	4,455
June	15.24	4.22	3.91	1,192	136	591	437	3,785	4,463
July	15.25	4.30	3.90	1,170	153	547	425	3,829	4,424
Aug.	15.37	4.43	3.86	1,102	159	497	396	3,855	4,480
Sept.	15.45	4.38	3.91	1,180	212	486	417	3,873	4,608
Oct.	15.73	4.39	4.06	1,246	252	448	486	3,888	4,646

* Source of figures: *Annual Report of the Federal Reserve Board,* 1931, Table 2, 1928 Revision.

† Source of figures: *ibid.,* Table 57, 1929 Revision.

‡ Source of figures: *Standard Statistics Company Base Book.*

Appendix J (*Continued*)

Date	Reporting Member Banks in Leading Cities — Monthly Averages of Weekly Figures (*in billions*)*			Federal Reserve Banks — Monthly Averages of Daily Figures (*in millions*)†				Stock of Money Gold — End of Month Figures (*in millions*)‡	Money in Circulation (*in millions*)‡
	Total Loans and Investments	Total Investments	Security Loans	Total Federal Reserve Credit	Bills Bought in the Open Market	U. S. Gov't. Securities	Bills Discounted		
Nov.	15.82	4.42	4.10	1,265	260	325	623	3,906	4,704
Dec.	16.01	4.56	4.12	1,377	259	380	660	3,929	4,817
1923									
Jan.	16.23	4.67	4.19	1,249	218	421	547	3,953	4,614
Feb.	16.23	4.63	4.12	1,205	190	356	608	3,963	4,703
Mar.	16.37	4.57	4.12	1,228	234	316	628	3,970	4,747
Apr.	16.44	4.52	4.17	1,214	272	229	658	3,982	4,759
May	16.49	4.49	4.22	1,222	271	193	705	4,028	4,797
June	16.43	4.52	4.16	1,178	224	153	741	4,050	4,823
July	16.40	4.49	4.15	1,179	186	97	834	4,079	4,787
Aug.	16.20	4.41	3.99	1,127	175	90	809	4,111	4,876
Sept.	16.31	4.38	4.03	1,184	174	102	845	4,136	4,945
Oct.	16.38	4.35	4.05	1,204	185	91	873	4,167	4,929
Nov.	16.29	4.31	4.06	1,204	265	83	799	4,207	5,018
Dec.	16.32	4.33	4.14	1,260	324	106	771	4,244	5,044
1924									
Jan.	16.32	4.33	4.25	1,041	300	118	574	4,289	4,777
Feb.	16.32	4.32	4.17	955	273	135	514	4,323	4,887
Mar.	16.44	4.31	4.18	990	228	244	476	4,364	4,899
Apr.	16.57	4.35	4.22	981	170	274	489	4,411	4,853
May	16.62	4.46	4.22	879	80	324	433	4,455	4,905
June	16.82	4.57	4.31	886	50	416	370	4,488	4,849
July	17.13	4.73	4.48	879	44	467	315	4,511	4,756
Aug.	17.45	4.85	4.58	881	30	539	268	4,521	4,859
Sept.	17.76	5.03	4.68	983	92	575	262	4,511	4,863
Oct.	18.22	5.26	4.73	1,057	180	585	240	4,509	4,942
Nov.	18.36	5.39	4.74	1,135	268	588	228	4,527	5,052
Dec.	18.47	5.38	4.92	1,288	358	554	301	4,499	5,047
1925									
Jan.	18.50	5.32	5.00	1,125	329	464	267	4,423	4,802
Feb.	18.44	5.21	5.06	1,094	314	384	340	4,369	4,853
Mar.	18.52	5.20	5.12	1,122	298	376	390	4,346	4,818
Apr.	18.55	5.26	5.10	1,110	287	355	403	4,350	4,789
May	18.53	5.23	5.17	1,100	279	361	397	4,361	4,841
June	18.64	5.27	5.29	1,118	263	345	437	4,365	4,815
July	18.72	5.25	5.37	1,118	231	338	480	4,370	4,795
Aug.	18.78	5.22	5.38	1,143	205	329	545	4,383	4,867
Sept.	18.98	5.18	5.45	1,227	226	335	594	4,382	4,916
Oct.	19.24	5.18	5.56	1,321	298	328	619	4,407	4,969
Nov.	19.33	5.15	5.70	1,352	352	332	597	4,397	5,044
Dec.	19.41	5.17	5.84	1,507	369	359	688	4,399	5,104
1926									
Jan.	19.36	5.16	5.87	1,279	324	368	520	4,412	4,841
Feb.	19.32	5.18	5.77	1,218	305	335	526	4,423	4,904
Mar.	19.42	5.25	5.65	1,216	268	336	557	4,442	4,860
Apr.	19.39	5.25	5.58	1,204	234	371	537	4,438	4,907
May	19.50	5.34	5.59	1,200	232	398	511	4,433	4,923
June	19.60	5.36	5.69	1,185	243	408	473	4,447	4,885
July	19.56	5.32	5.74	1,221	230	380	549	4,471	4,909
Aug.	19.59	5.28	5.77	1,203	245	353	555	4,473	4,930
Sept.	19.78	5.28	5.85	1,278	265	316	640	4,466	4,978
Oct.	19.78	5.23	5.74	1,322	295	306	663	4,473	5,021
Nov.	19.67	5.19	5.63	1,318	348	302	615	4,477	5,037
Dec.	19.74	5.17	5.77	1,445	385	322	688	4,492	5,095
1927									
Jan.	19.69	5.15	5.92	1,186	343	310	481	4,564	4,846
Feb.	19.56	5.21	5.78	1,043	304	307	393	4,586	4,885
Mar.	19.99	5.45	5.87	1,055	253	345	425	4,597	4,862
Apr.	20.07	5.50	5.93	1,087	248	341	447	4,610	4,891
May	20.27	5.61	6.02	1,041	233	291	473	4,608	4,893

* Source of figures: *Annual Report of the Federal Reserve Board*, 1931, Table 2, 1928 Revision.

† Source of figures: *ibid.*, Table 57, 1929 Revision.

‡ Source of figures: *Standard Statistics Company Base Book.*

Appendix J (*Continued*)

Date	Reporting Member Banks in Leading Cities — Monthly Averages of Weekly Figures (*in billions*)*			Federal Reserve Banks — Monthly Averages of Daily Figures (*in millions*)†				Stock of Money Gold — End of Month Figures (*in millions*)‡	Money in Circulation (*in millions*)‡
	Total Loans and Investments	Total Investments	Security Loans	Total Federal Reserve Credit	Bills Bought in the Open Market	U.S. Gov't. Securities	Bills Discounted		
June	20.51	5.66	6.22	1,081	205	398	429	4,587	4,851
July	20.40	5.62	6.19	1,115	190	381	454	4,580	4,846
Aug.	20.36	5.53	6.20	1,093	173	439	409	4,588	4,854
Sept.	20.65	5.59	6.30	1,187	216	501	422	4,571	4,948
Oct.	20.92	5.66	6.40	1,254	282	506	424	4,541	4,946
Nov.	21.11	5.80	6.49	1,377	336	579	415	4,451	4,952
Dec.	21.33	5.93	6.68	1,568	378	606	529	4,379	5,003
1928									
Jan.	21.49	6.05	6.81	1,388	373	512	465	4,373	4,677
Feb.	21.32	6.09	6.61	1,264	360	406	471	4,362	4,690
Mar.	21.50	6.13	6.59	1,295	343	415	513	4,305	4,749
Apr.	21.94	6.14	6.92	1,405	358	351	661	4,226	4,748
May	22.15	6.19	7.08	1,472	349	257	836	4,160	4,744
June	22.06	6.19	6.96	1,531	244	232	1,019	4,109	4,797
July	22.01	6.11	6.96	1,531	185	213	1,090	4,113	4,701
Aug.	21.81	5.98	6.82	1,485	178	210	1,061	4,123	4,803
Sept.	21.87	5.97	6.84	1,581	226	240	1,064	4,125	4,846
Oct.	21.94	5.93	6.87	1,621	368	237	975	4,143	4,807
Nov.	21.98	5.89	7.08	1,653	471	238	897	4,128	4,990
Dec.	22.19	5.94	7.20	1,824	483	263	1,013	4,141	4,973
1929									
Jan.	22.32	6.02	7.51	1,613	473	229	859	4,127	4,657
Feb.	22.26	6.00	7.52	1,502	385	184	889	4,153	4,698
Mar.	22.47	5.98	7.58	1,481	265	197	969	4,188	4,748
Apr.	22.39	5.92	7.39	1,377	156	165	1,004	4,259	4,676
May	22.11	5.84	7.22	1,303	145	153	956	4,301	4,738
June	22.23	5.75	7.33	1,317	99	179	978	4,324	4,746
July	22.48	5.53	7.72	1,380	75	147	1,096	4,341	4,717
Aug.	22.47	5.50	7.58	1,376	124	155	1,043	4,360	4,840
Sept.	22.65	5.45	7.65	1,427	229	165	969	4,372	4,819
Oct.	23.12	5.42	8.10	1,450	337	154	885	4,386	4,838
Nov.	23.66	5.62	8.25	1,631	296	315	953	4,367	4,929
Dec.	23.01	5.57	7.97	1,643	320	446	803	4,284	4,865
1930									
Jan.	22.37	5.55	7.79	1,357	314	485	501	4,293	4,562
Feb.	22.08	5.54	7.67	1,181	285	480	378	4,355	4,579
Mar.	22.35	5.61	7.96	1,095	246	540	274	4,423	4,549
Apr.	22.66	5.76	8.27	1,072	226	530	231	4,491	4,476
May	22.66	5.84	8.31	996	182	529	247	4,517	4,551
June	23.02	5.98	8.56	1,000	141	571	251	4,534	4,522
July	23.10	6.19	8.39	1,003	154	583	226	4,517	4,426
Aug.	23.13	6.29	8.35	998	153	599	214	4,501	4,533
Sept.	23.22	6.36	8.38	1,016	197	597	189	4,511	4,501
Oct.	23.41	6.58	8.24	1,020	185	602	196	4,535	4,493
Nov.	23.46	6.78	7.90	1,033	184	599	221	4,571	4,660
Dec.	23.12	6.78	7.78	1,273	257	644	338	4,593	4,890
1931									
Jan.	22.66	6.77	7.50	1,129	206	647	253	4,643	4,610
Feb.	22.66	7.10	7.32	936	102	603	216	4,665	4,620
Mar.	22.84	7.39	7.30	921	123	604	176	4,697	4,608
Apr.	22.94	7.75	7.16	952	173	600	155	4,726	4,652
May	22.71	7.82	7.00	926	144	599	163	4,798	4,702
June	22.44	7.82	6.77	945	121	610	188	4,956	4,822
July	22.39	7.80	6.63	954	79	674	169	4,949	4,837
Aug.	22.09	7.71	6.48	1,107	135	712	222	4,995	5,052
Sept.	22.08	7.80	6.41	1,313	259	736	280	4,741	5,246
Oct.	21.43	7.78	5.97	2,088	692	733	613	4,292	5,540
Nov.	21.02	7.58	5.86	2,035	560	727	695	4,414	5,536
Dec.	20.75	7.55	5.76	1,950	340	777	774	4,460	5,647

* Source of figures: *Annual Report of the Federal Reserve Board*, 1931, Table 2, 1928 Revision.

† Source of figures: *ibid.*, Table 57, 1929 Revision.

‡ Source of figures: *Standard Statistics Company Base Book*.

APPENDIX K

Net Gold Movements, 1919–1931, by Months *

	1919	1920	1921	1922	1923	1924	1925
			(in millions)				
Jan.	− 1 †	−36	31	25	24	45	−76
Feb.	1	−38	42	38	10	34	−59
Mar.	7	−30	87	27	7	41	−25
Apr.	5	4	80	14	12	47	3
May	− 1	8	57	7	46	44	15
June	−57	21	43	14	22	33	3
July	−53	− 2	61	44	29	23	7
Aug.	−43	−10	84	26	32	10	15
Sept.	−28	22	64	18	25	−10	0
Oct.	−39	91	40	15	31	− 2	25
Nov.	−49	37	61	18	40	18	−10
Dec.	−33	28	30	23	37	−28	2

	1926	1927	1928	1929	1930	1931
Jan.	13	72	− 6	−14	7	50
Feb.	11	22	−11	26	62	22
Mar.	19	11	−57	35	70	32
Apr.	− 4	13	−39	72	68	29
May	− 5	− 2	−106	41	26	72
June	14	−21	−51	23	18	158
July	24	− 7	4	17	−18	− 7
Aug.	2	8	10	19	−16	46
Sept.	− 7	−17	2	12	10	−254
Oct.	7	−30	17	14	24	−449
Nov.	4	−90	−14	−19	36	122
Dec.	15	−72	13	−83	22	46

* Source of figures: United States Department of Commerce and Harvard Economic Society. Earmarkings included after 1922.

† Minus signs indicate exports.

APPENDIX L

Type	Totals (*in millions*)	As Percentages of the Whole
1919		
First Quarter		
Corporate	569	81
Municipal	106	15
Foreign Government	28	4
United States Government		
Farm Loan		
Second Quarter		
Corporate	545	10
Municipal	209	4
Foreign Government	35	
War Finance Corporation	200	4
United States Government	4,498	82
Farm Loan		
Third Quarter		
Corporate	844	44
Municipal	301	16
Foreign Government	120	6
United States Government	657	34
Farm Loan	7	
Fourth Quarter		
Corporate	781	56
Municipal	180	13
Foreign Government	332	24
United States Government		
Farm Loan	103	7
1920		
First Quarter		
Corporate	452	66
Municipal	184	27
Foreign Government	50	7
United States Government		
Farm Loan		
Second Quarter		
Corporate	558	73
Municipal	166	21
Foreign Government	50	6
United States Government		
Farm Loan		

Appendix L (*Continued*)

Type	Totals (*in millions*)	As Percentages of the Whole
Third Quarter		
Corporate	330	50
Municipal	186	28
Foreign Government	145	22
United States Government		
Farm Loan		
Fourth Quarter		
Corporate	555	68
Municipal	216	28
Foreign Government	46	6
United States Government		
Farm Loan		
1921		
First Quarter		
Corporate	559	66
Municipal	216	25
Foreign Government	79	9
United States Government		
Farm Loan		
Second Quarter		
Corporate	635	46
Municipal	274	20
Foreign Government	128	9
United States Government	311	22
Farm Loan	40	3
Third Quarter		
Corporate	386	32
Municipal	348	28
Foreign Government	83	7
United States Government	391	32
Farm Loan	8	1
Fourth Quarter		
Corporate	531	45
Municipal	473	40
Foreign Government	90	8
United States Government		
Farm Loan	74	7
1922		
First Quarter		
Corporate	629	26
Municipal	329	13
Foreign Government	189	8
United States Government	1,220	49
Farm Loan	104	4

Appendix L (*Continued*)

Type	Totals (*in millions*)	As Percentages of the Whole
	Second Quarter	
Corporate	842	43
Municipal	502	25
Foreign Government	159	8
United States Government	335	17
Farm Loan	147	7
	Third Quarter	
Corporate	513	36
Municipal	293	21
Foreign Government	22	2
United States Government	487	34
Farm Loan	103	7
	Fourth Quarter	
Corporate	465	23
Municipal	221	11
Foreign Government	62	3
United States Government	1,233	61
Farm Loan	32	2
	1923	
	First Quarter	
Corporate	894	51
Municipal	277	16
Foreign Government	75	4
United States Government	367	21
Farm Loan	132	8
	Second Quarter	
Corporate	603	33
Municipal	349	19
Foreign Government	31	2
United States Government	668	37
Farm Loan	162	9
	Third Quarter	
Corporate	340	48
Municipal	266	38
Foreign Government	95	13
United States Government		
Farm Loan	7	1
	Fourth Quarter	
Corporate	660	65
Municipal	230	22
Foreign Government	41	4
United States Government		
Farm Loan	92	9

Appendix L (*Continued*)

Type	Totals (*in millions*)	As Percentages of the Whole
1924		
	First Quarter	
Corporate	654	52
Municipal	309	25
Foreign Government	218	17
United States Government		
Farm Loan	76	6
	Second Quarter	
Corporate	755	52
Municipal	532	37
Foreign Government	103	7
United States Government		
Farm Loan	54	4
	Third Quarter	
Corporate	751	58
Municipal	424	33
Foreign Government	100	7
United States Government		
Farm Loan	25	2
	Fourth Quarter	
Corporate	811	36
Municipal	292	13
Foreign Government	357	16
United States Government	757	34
Farm Loan	25	1
1925		
	First Quarter	
Corporate	1,111	57
Municipal	345	18
Foreign Government	99	5
United States Government	340	17
Farm Loan	60	3
	Second Quarter	
Corporate	832	55
Municipal	474	32
Foreign Government	154	10
United States Government		
Farm Loan	50	3
	Third Quarter	
Corporate	650	52
Municipal	414	31
Foreign Government	215	16
United States Government		
Farm Loan	14	1

Appendix L (*Continued*)

Type	Totals (*in millions*)	As Percentages of the Whole
	Fourth Quarter	
Corporate	833	60
Municipal	322	23
Foreign Government	178	13
United States Government		
Farm Loan	63	4
1926		
	First Quarter	
Corporate	1,030	49
Municipal	394	19
Foreign Government	50	2
United States Government	619	29
Farm Loan	39	1
	Second Quarter	
Corporate	1,083	61
Municipal	463	26
Foreign Government	153	9
United States Government		
Farm Loan	76	4
	Third Quarter	
Corporate	851	69
Municipal	254	20
Foreign Government	122	10
United States Government		
Farm Loan	12	1
	Fourth Quarter	
Corporate	1,017	64
Municipal	374	24
Foreign Government	190	12
United States Government		
Farm Loan	5	
1927		
	First Quarter	
Corporate	1,390	41
Municipal	417	12
Foreign Government	211	6
United States Government	1,360	40
Farm Loan	32	1
	Second Quarter	
Corporate	1,558	54
Municipal	538	19
Foreign Government	199	7
United States Government	467	16
Farm Loan	110	4

Appendix L (*Continued*)

Type	Totals (*in millions*)	As Percentages of the Whole
	Third Quarter	
Corporate	922	45
Municipal	320	16
Foreign Government	138	7
United States Government	647	32
Farm Loan	5	
	Fourth Quarter	
Corporate	1,676	72
Municipal	382	16
Foreign Government	229	10
United States Government		
Farm Loan	32	2
	1928	
	First Quarter	
Corporate	1,423	68
Municipal	374	18
Foreign Government	283	14
United States Government		
Farm Loan	5	
	Second Quarter	
Corporate	1,382	52
Municipal	439	16
Foreign Government	219	8
United States Government	607	23
Farm Loan	32	1
	Third Quarter	
Corporate	498	43
Municipal	220	19
Foreign Government	85	8
United States Government	350	30
Farm Loan	3	
	Fourth Quarter	
Corporate	878	63
Municipal	426	30
Foreign Government	65	5
United States Government		
Farm Loan	24	2
	1929	
	First Quarter	
Corporate	1,016	77
Municipal	258	20
Foreign Government	36	3
United States Government		
Farm Loan		

Appendix L (*Continued*)

Type	Totals (*in millions*)	As Percentages of the Whole
	Second Quarter	
Corporate	1,014	69
Municipal	451	31
Foreign Government	6	
United States Government		
Farm Loan		
	Third Quarter	
Corporate	572	66
Municipal	267	31
Foreign Government	23	3
United States Government		
Farm Loan		
	Fourth Quarter	
Corporate	503	49
Municipal	523	51
Foreign Government	4	
United States Government		
Farm Loan		

1930

Type	Totals (*in millions*)	As Percentages of the Whole
	First Quarter	
Corporate	1,438	77
Municipal	337	18
Foreign Government	70	4
United States Government		
Farm Loan	22	1
	Second Quarter	
Corporate	1,270	61
Municipal	479	24
Foreign Government	305	15
United States Government		
Farm Loan	9	
	Third Quarter	
Corporate	775	65
Municipal	300	25
Foreign Government	98	8
United States Government		
Farm Loan	15	2
	Fourth Quarter	
Corporate	421	43
Municipal	519	52
Foreign Government	10	1
United States Government		
Farm Loan	41	4

Appendix L (*Continued*)

Type	Totals (*in millions*)	As Percentages of the Whole
1931		
	First Quarter	
Corporate	856	41
Municipal	448	22
Foreign Government	152	7
United States Government	594	29
Farm Loan	30	1
	Second Quarter	
Corporate	757	36
Municipal	404	19
Foreign Government	67	3
United States Government	871	41
Farm Loan	31	1
	Third Quarter	
Corporate	307	21
Municipal	287	19
Foreign Government	50	4
United States Government	800	54
Farm Loan	35	2
	Fourth Quarter	
Corporate	108	43
Municipal	111	44
Foreign Government		
United States Government		
Farm Loan	30	12

APPENDIX M

NUMBER OF INDIVIDUAL BOND ISSUES LISTED ON THE NEW YORK STOCK EXCHANGE, 1919–1930 *

1919	1,131
1920	1,114
1921	1,115
1922	1,156
1923	1,234
1924	1,262
1925	1,332
1926	1,367
1927	1,420
1928	1,491
1929	1,534
1930	1,607 †

* Source of figures: *New York Stock Exchange Year Book*, 1929–30.
† As of October 1.

APPENDIX N

STOCK PRICES, BY MONTHS, AND STOCK ISSUES, BY QUARTERS, 1919–1930

Date		Stock Prices by Months in Relatives, 1926=100 *	Stock Issues — by Quarters (in Millions) †	
			New Capital Issues	Total Issues
1919	Jan.	63		
	Feb.	63	122	122
	Mar.	65		
	Apr.	68		
	May	72	172	288
	June	74		
	July	77		
	Aug.	71	531	558
	Sept.	73		
	Oct.	76		
	Nov.	74	530	598
	Dec.	72		
1920	Jan.	71		
	Feb.	65	422	451
	Mar.	70		
	Apr.	69		
	May	65	401	407
	June	64		
	July	64		
	Aug.	61	96	97
	Sept.	63		
	Oct.	63		
	Nov.	60	116	116
	Dec.	55		
1921	Jan.	57		
	Feb.	57	88	89
	Mar.	55		
	Apr.	56		
	May	57	37	37
	June	53		
	July	53		
	Aug.	52	101	103
	Sept.	53		
	Oct.	54		
	Nov.	57	43	49
	Dec.	59		

* Standard Statistics Company average.
† Figures from *Commercial and Financial Chronicle.*

Appendix N (*Continued*)

Date		Stock Prices by Months in Relatives, 1926=100 *	Stock Issues — by Quarters (*in Millions*) †	
			New Capital Issues	Total Issues
1922	Jan.	59		
	Feb.	60	92	101
	Mar.	62		
	Apr.	66		
	May	69	159	189
	June	68		
	July	68		
	Aug.	71	212	214
	Sept.	73		
	Oct.	75		
	Nov.	71	110	120
	Dec.	71		
1923	Jan.	72		
	Feb.	75	212	278
	Mar.	76		
	Apr.	73		
	May	70	164	170
	June	67		
	July	65		
	Aug.	65	65	66
	Sept.	66		
	Oct.	65		
	Nov.	67	234	239
	Dec.	69		
1924	Jan.	71		
	Feb.	71	177	182
	Mar.	70		
	Apr.	68		
	May	68	322	332
	June	69		
	July	73		
	Aug.	75	111	128
	Sept.	74		
	Oct.	73		
	Nov.	78	220	224
	Dec.	82		
1925	Jan.	85		
	Feb.	86	245	253
	Mar.	84		
	Apr.	83		
	May	85	296	325

* Standard Statistics Company average.
† Figures from *Commercial and Financial Chronicle.*

Appendix N (*Continued*)

Date	Stock Prices by Months in Relatives, 1926=100 *	Stock Issues — by Quarters (*in Millions*) †	
		New Capital Issues	Total Issues
June	87		
July	89		
Aug.	91	253	300
Sept.	93		
Oct.	96		
Nov.	99	418	432
Dec.	100		
1926 Jan.	102		
Feb.	102	468	479
Mar.	96		
Apr.	93		
May	93	281	285
June	97		
July	100		
Aug.	103	184	196
Sept.	104		
Oct.	102		
Nov.	103	248	357
Dec.	105		
1927 Jan.	106		
Feb.	108	463	504
Mar.	109		
Apr.	111		
May	114	327	390
June	115		
July	117		
Aug.	122	263	347
Sept.	128		
Oct.	127		
Nov.	130	457	532
Dec.	133		
1928 Jan.	134		
Feb.	132	422	558
Mar.	138		
Apr.	146		
May	152	814	1,073
June	145		
July	144		
Aug.	148	401	455
Sept.	157		
Oct.	159		

* Standard Statistics Company average.
† Figures from *Commercial and Financial Chronicle*.

Appendix N (*Continued*)

Date		Stock Prices by Months in Relatives, 1926=100 *	Stock Issues — by Quarters (*in Millions*) †	
			New Capital Issues	Total Issues
	Nov.	171	1,434	1,541
	Dec.	171		
1929	Jan.	185		
	Feb.	187	1,743	1,872
	Mar.	189		
	Apr.	187		
	May	188	1,334	1,662
	June	191		
	July	207		
	Aug.	218	2,318	2,587
	Sept.	225		
	Oct.	202		
	Nov.	151	703	811
	Dec.	154		
1930	Jan.	156		
	Feb.	166	405	406
	Mar.	172		
	Apr.	181		
	May	171	838	850
	June	153		
	July	149		
	Aug.	148	189	190
	Sept.	149		
	Oct.	128		
	Nov.	117	114	122
	Dec.	109		

* Standard Statistics Company average.
† Figures from *Commercial and Financial Chronicle*.

APPENDIX O

VOLUME OF ALL CORPORATE BOND ISSUES, VOLUME OF "NET" CORPORATE BOND ISSUES, MILLS'S INDEX OF PRODUCTION OF CAPITAL ELEMENTS, INTEREST PAYMENTS AND NET INCOMES OF ALL CORPORATIONS PAYING INCOME TAXES, 1919–1930, BY YEARS

Date	Annual Totals of All Corporate Issues (in Millions)	Annual Totals of All Corporate Issues (in Relatives, 1926=100)	Annual Totals of "Net" Corporate Issues (in Millions)	Annual Totals of "Net" Corporate Issues (in Relatives, 1926=100)	Mills's Index of Production of Capital Elements, (Shifted 1926=100) *	Interest Payments of All Corporations Paying Income Taxes (in Millions) †	Interest Payments of All Corporations Paying Income Taxes (in Relatives, 1926=100)	Net Incomes of All Corporations Paying Income Taxes (in Millions) ‡	Net Incomes of All Corporations Paying Income Taxes (in Relatives, 1926=100)
1919	2,739	60				2,207	55	6,190	74
1920	1,895	48	1,091	41		2,835	71	970	11
1921	2,111	53	998	38		3,141	79	5,420	65
1922	2,449	62	775	29	70	3,069	72	7,060	84
1923	2,497	63	1,354	52	62	3,278	82	6,200	74
1924	2,971	75	2,102	80	62	3,445	86	8,490	101
1925	3,426	87	1,894	72	85	3,617	91	8,400	100
1926	3,981	100	2,647	100	100	3,989	100	8,400	100
1927	5,546	139	3,229	125	101	4,375	110	7,470	89
1928	4,181	105	1,604	61	106	4,581	115	9,340	111
1929	3,105	78	1,357	51	111	4,925	123	9,860	118
1930	3,904	98	2,380	90		4,861	122	3,100	37

* Figures from F. C. Mills, *Economic Tendencies in the United States.*

† Figures from *Statistics of Income.*

‡ Figures from S. H. Nerlove, *A Decade of Corporate Income.* These figures are defined by Nerlove as "The difference between 'gross' incomes as defined by the Revenue Act and all deductions allowed from these incomes by the Act. . . . Corporate net incomes, then, are profits, as usually defined by the economist, plus interest and rent charge on owned capital and land" (p. 12). These figures have been adjusted to include the net incomes of personal service corporations in 1920 and 1921, and the special deductions allowed life insurance companies since 1921.

APPENDIX P

VOLUME OF ALL BOND ISSUES AND OF "NET" BOND ISSUES, IN MILLIONS, AND IN RELATIVES, *1926 = 100*, 1919–1930, BY YEARS

Date	Annual Totals of All Bond Issues Including Refunding Issues (*in Millions*)	Annual Totals of All Bond Issues Including Refunding Issues (*in Relatives, 1926 = 100*)	Annual Totals of "Net" Bond Issues (*in Millions*)	Annual Totals of "Net" Bond Issues (*in Relatives, 1926 = 100*)
1919	9,525	141		
1920	2,939	44	474	14
1921	4,626	69	2,403	71
1922	7,887	117	5,057	148
1923	5,288	78	2,341	69
1924	6,244	93	3,986	117
1925	6,156	92	2,763	81
1926	6,731	100	3,417	100
1927	10,633	158	5,619	165
1928	7,322	109	2,474	73
1929	4,673	69	1,684	49
1930	6,109	91	2,948	86

APPENDIX Q

SEASONAL FLUCTUATION IN THE NUMBER AND VOLUME OF BOND ISSUES AND IN THE VOLUME OF BONDS CALLED AND MATURED, 1920–1930

THE statistical series of the number of new bond issues and of the volume of total, new capital, and "net" bond issues used in this study contain pronounced seasonal elements. Through the use of seasonal indices constructed by the link relative method an attempt was made to eliminate this type of fluctuation, in order that the cyclical movements of these series might be more clearly discerned, and the adjusted series are plotted in Charts III and VII. The character of the seasonal fluctuation in the number and volume of issues, however, possesses a certain interest of its own.

Both monthly and quarterly indices for the number of new issues were constructed.[1] The configuration of these is shown in Chart XVII, D. The monthly index has two low points, in the middle of the first and third quarters, and two high points, at the beginning of the second quarter and in the fourth quarter. The quarterly index is slightly above 100 in the first quarter, rises in the second quarter, falls below 100 in the third quarter, and recovers in the fourth quarter, though it does not return to the levels of the first two quarters.

Quarterly indices were also constructed for the total volume of offerings and for new capital offerings.[2] They are plotted in Chart XVII, A. Their configuration is very like that of the quarterly index of the number of bond issues. No difficulty was experienced in effecting these indices, and there is no reason to suspect that they are not approximately accurate.

A satisfactory index for "net" offerings was more difficult to obtain.

[1] Seasonal indices for the number of bond issues:

	By Months	By Quarters
Jan.	103	
Feb.	83	103
Mar.	104	
Apr.	108	
May	107	107
June	99	
July	100	
Aug.	79	94
Sept.	97	
Oct.	111	
Nov.	112	96
Dec.	101	

[2] Seasonal indices:

	First Quarter	Second Quarter	Third Quarter	Fourth Quarter
Total Issues	108	116	81	95
New Capital Issues	105	112	77	105
"Net" Issues	133	117	84	51

This series was subject to wider fluctuations than were the other two. It contained five negative amounts, which occasioned wide gaps in the chain relatives, and the distribution of the relatives was not always such as to

CHART XVII

SEASONAL INDICES FOR THE VOLUME OF TOTAL, NEW CAPITAL, AND "NET" BOND ISSUES, BY QUARTERS; THE VOLUME OF BONDS CALLED AND MATURED, BY QUARTERS; THE NUMBER OF BOND ISSUES

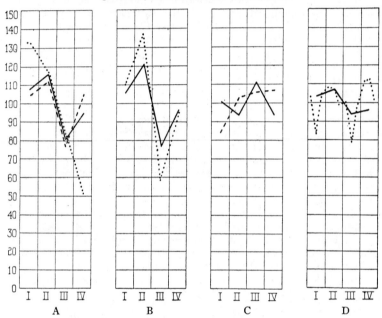

A   B   C   D

A: The Volume of Total, New Capital, and "Net" Bond Issues, Including Increases and Decreases in the Government Debt.
   —— Total Issues.
   - - - - New Capital Issues.
   . . . . . "Net" Issues.
B: The Volume of Total, and of "Net" Bond Issues, Excluding Increases and Decreases in the Government Debt.
   —— Total Issues.
   . . . . . "Net" Issues.
C: The Volume of Bonds Called and Matured.
   —— Excluding Decreases in the Government Debt.
   - - - - Including Decreases in the Government Debt.
D: The Number of Bond Issues.
   . . . . . By months.
   —— By quarters.

indicate the precise seasonal relationship. Various experiments were made in order to find as satisfactory an index as possible. The index finally chosen was one in which the relatives for three quarters only were used, the index **for** the other quarter (the third quarter which contained all the negative amounts) being estimated. The configuration of this index, plotted in Chart XVII, A, is quite different from that of total and new capital issues. It declines steadily from quarter to quarter, and appears to indicate that in the ordinary year in this period progressively greater amounts of bonds were called or matured from quarter to quarter, with the result that progressively smaller amounts of new funds were required by the market in each quarter. In adjusting the original series of "net" offerings with this index the negative amounts were not changed. Although this adjusted series appears fairly satisfactory in most years, the index has obviously produced exaggerated results in certain quarters, and great reliance can not be placed on it. It is by no means as satisfactory as are the other indices.

The wide divergence of the configuration of the seasonal index of "net" offerings from the configuration of the indices for total offerings and for new capital offerings involves consideration of the whole question of seasonal influence in this eleven-year period. The principal foreign factor in the bond market during this time, one not subject to influences which normally affect bond financing, was the debt operations of the Treasury. Neither flotations nor redemptions of government securities are primarily motivated by the same forces which affect similar operations for other types of bonds. The financial activity of the Treasury is in a category different from that in which the operations of private industry, or even those of municipalities and foreign governments, are to be placed. An attempt to estimate the influence of the Treasury's operations on the seasonal fluctuation, and to eliminate it, was made by constructing indices for the total volume of issues and for the "net" volume of issues exclusive of increases or decreases in the government debt.[3] The configuration of these indices, plotted in Chart XVII, B, is similar, though of a wider spread, to that of the index for total offerings that includes government financing and to the index for new capital. It seems, therefore, roughly accurate to say that what may be termed the normal seasonal influences affecting the bond market in these years tended to bring forth a large quantity of issues in the first quarter of the year, a somewhat larger quantity in the second quarter, a much reduced volume in the third quarter, which is followed in the fourth by an amount that is approximately equal to that of the first quarter; that this seasonal tendency was not seriously affected in the case of total issues by government financing, but that in the case of "net" offerings the activities of the Treasury completely changed the seasonal index.

This last conclusion is supported by the configuration of two seasonal indices which were constructed for called and matured bonds, one includ-

[3] Seasonal indices, exclusive of increases or decreases in the government debt:

	First Quarter	Second Quarter	Third Quarter	Fourth Quarter
Total Issues	106	121	77	96
"Net" Issues	110	137	59	94

Since the new capital series did not contain any government issues an additional seasonal index was not made for it.

ing, one excluding, decreases in the government debt.[4] These indices are also plotted in Chart XVII, C. The index that includes Treasury redemptions advances steadily throughout the year. The index that excludes them has a configuration approximately the reverse of that of the indices for total issues and for new capital issues.[5]

Elimination of the Treasury's operations in these years, and omission of government flotations and redemptions from these series of bond issues, would not give a result that could be called normal, nor one as significant as that obtained when such activities are included. The Treasury's operations were too important and formed too integral a part of the post-war bond market. Although there were no government issues in certain quarters, in other quarters the government issues amounted to over fifty per cent of the total offerings. However, as may be seen in Chart XII, where total issues are subdivided into types, the outline of these eleven years given by the series of total issues would be changed through the omission of government offerings mainly by a leveling of certain peaks.

[4] Seasonal indices for bonds called and matured:

	First Quarter	Second Quarter	Third Quarter	Fourth Quarter
Including decreases in the government debt	84	103	106	107
Excluding decreases in the government debt	101	94	111	94

[5] Ellsworth computed seasonal indices of bond offerings for the years 1907 through 1930. For the period 1907–1918 he used the *Journal of Commerce* figures; for the period 1919–1930 he used the figures of the *Commercial and Financial Chronicle* for long term, new capital, corporate financing. Issues other than corporate, and short term bonds and notes which are included in my new capital series, he did not use; nor did he use the figures for total financing, which include refunding issues. He notes: "The indices computed for the quarterly figures for 1907–16, by the median-link-relative method, are, in order: 151, 130, 46, 72. The same method applied to the post-war figures revealed a much smaller seasonal movement, the quarterly figures being: 117, 109, 79, 96. In both cases, though the distribution of the original link relatives was widely scattered, the deviation from 100 per cent was sufficiently great to warrant taking the median as fairly representative of the movement. It is worth remarking that for the later period, which exhibits a much less violent seasonal fluctuation, the scatter was notably less" (Ellsworth, "Investments," p. 113). His post-war index is to be contrasted with my index of new capital issues for 1920–1930; 105, 112, 77, 105. The greatest difference is that in my index the figure for the second quarter is slightly larger than the figure for the first quarter; in Ellsworth's index the figure for the second quarter is slightly smaller than the figure for the first quarter. This and other discrepancies are presumably to be attributed to the fact, noted above, that my index included other than corporate issues and also short term financing, and to the fact that his index is based on a period longer by one year than mine.

BIBLIOGRAPHY

BIBLIOGRAPHICAL NOTE

THIS bibliography makes no pretense of being complete or exhaustive. The literature concerned with the financial history of the United States in the post-war decade has so developed, even in the short space of seventeen years, and the number of sources of pertinent statistics has become so great, that it has not seemed feasible to include every title or statistical source connected with the bond market in the 1920–1930 period. Listed here are only those publications and statistical data which have been referred to in the text, and those others which seem to be of particular moment. For the sake of convenience the items have been divided into two parts. The first includes original material and statistical sources, notably those referred to in the appendices; the second includes secondary material, such as books and specific magazine articles.

BIBLIOGRAPHY
ORIGINAL SOURCES AND SOURCES OF STATISTICS

Abstract of Condition Reports of State Bank and Trust Company Members and of All Member Banks, 1919–1925.

American Underwriting of Foreign Securities in 1929 (Trade Information Bulletin, no. 688, United States Department of Commerce. Washington, D. C.).

Annalist, 1919–1931.

Annual Reports of the Comptroller of the Currency, 1919–1930 (Washington, D. C.).

Annual Reports of the Federal Reserve Board, 1919–1930 (Washington, D. C.).

Annual Reports of the Secretary of the Treasury, 1919–1931 (Washington, D. C.).

Annual Reports of the Superintendent of Insurance, State of New York, 1919–1930 (Albany).

The Balance of International Payments of the United States in 1922, 1924, 1926, 1928, 1929, 1930 (Trade Information Bulletins, nos. 144, 340, 503, 625, 698, 761; United States Department of Commerce. Washington, D. C.).

Barron's, 1919–1930.

Bond Buyer, 1919–1930.

Bradstreet's, 1919–1930.

Brookmire Economic Service.

Cleveland Trust Company Bulletin, April 15, 1924.

Commercial and Financial Chronicle, 1919–1931.

Currie, L. B., "Bank Assets and Banking Theory" (MS. in Widener Library, Harvard University).

Ellsworth, P. T., "Some Aspects of Investment in the United States, 1907–1930" (MS. in Widener Library, Harvard University).

Facts and Figures Relating to the American Money Market (American Acceptance Council, New York, Boston, 1931).
Federal Reserve Bulletin, 1919–1930.
Harvard Economic Society.
Hearings before a Subcommittee of the Committee on Banking and Currency of the United States Senate, Seventy-First Congress, Third Session, Pursuant to Senate Resolution 71 (Washington, D. C., 1931).
Journal of Commerce, March 16, 1929.
Member Bank Call Reports, 1926–1931.
Moody's Investors Service.
National City Bank of New York Monthly Letter, 1919–1930.
New York Stock Exchange Year Book, 1928–1929, 1929–1930.
New York Times, July 13, 1931.
Review of Economic Statistics, 1919–1930.
Standard Statistics Company.
Statements of the Public Debt of the United States, 1920–1930.
Statistics of Income, 1919–1930.
Wall Street Journal, 1920–1930.

ADDITIONAL REFERENCES

Abbott, Charles C., "A Note on the Government Bond Market, 1919–1930," *Review of Economic Statistics,* XVII, 7–12 (January 1935).
"An Analysis of the Condition of the Central Banks of England, France, and the United States, 1911–19," *Review of Economic Statistics,* I, 13–25 (Monthly Supplement, September 1919).
Arens, H. F., and Bancroft, J. R., "Causes Affecting the Value of Bonds," *Annals of the American Academy of Political and Social Science,* LXXXVIII, 200–212 (March 1920).
Beckhart, B. H., *The New York Money Market,* 4 vols. (New York, 1931–1932).
Burgess, W. R., "The Money Market in 1929," *Review of Economic Statistics,* XII, 15–20 (February 1930).
—, *The Reserve Banks and the Money Market* (New York and London, 1927).
Carles, Frederick, *Essentials of Investment* (Philadelphia, 1919).
Chamberlain, Lawrence, *Principles of Bond Investment* (New York, 1911).
Chamberlain, Lawrence, and Edwards, G. W., *Principles of Bond Investment* (New York, 1927).
Childs, C. F., "United States Government Bonds," *Annals of the American Academy of Political and Social Science,* LXXXVIII, 43–50 (March 1920).
Crenshaw, R. P., "The Bond Market in Perspective," *Magazine of Wall Street,* XL, 844–845 (Sept. 10, 1927).
Currie, L. B., *The Supply and Control of Money in the United States* (Cambridge, Mass., 1934).
"Cycles of Business Activity, Stock Prices, Money Rates and Bond Yields, 1880–1929," *Annalist,* XXXV, 110–111 (Jan. 17, 1930).
Dewing, A. S., *The Financial Policy of Corporations* (New York, 1926).

"Economic Conditions Since the Armistice," *Review of Economic Statistics,* I, 9–28 (Monthly Supplement, December 1919).

Epstein, Ralph C., *Industrial Profits in the United States* (New York, 1934).

Fabricant, Solomon, *Recent Corporate Profits in the United States* (National Bureau of Economic Research, Bulletin 50, April 18, 1934).

Flynn, John T., *Security Speculation* (New York, 1934).

Hardy, C. O., *Credit Policies of the Federal Reserve System* (Washington, D. C., 1932).

Harris, Seymour, *Twenty Years of Federal Reserve Policy* (Cambridge, Mass., 1933).

Keynes, J. M., *A Treatise on Money* (New York and London, 1930).

King, W. I., *The National Income and Its Purchasing Power* (New York, 1930).

Kirshman, J. E., *Principles of Investment* (Chicago and New York, 1924).

Kuznets, Simon, *Gross Capital Formation,* 1919–1933 (National Bureau of Economic Research, Bulletin 52, November 15, 1934).

Lagerquist, W. E., *Investment Analysis* (New York, 1921).

Leven, Maurice, Moulton, H. G., and Warburton, Clark, *America's Capacity to Consume* (Washington, D. C., 1934).

Lownhaupt, Frederick, *Investment Bonds* (New York and London, 1908).

McCabe, E. F., "Fluctuations in Short-Time Bonds," *American Bankers Association Journal,* XXIII, 209–211 (September 1930).

Means, G. C., "The Growth in the Relative Importance of the Large Corporation in American Economic Life," *American Economic Review,* XXI, 10–37 (March 1931).

Meeker, J. Edward, *The Work of the Stock Exchange* (New York, 1922).

Mills, Frederick C., *Economic Tendencies in the United States* (New York, 1932).

Mitchell, Wesley C., "Rates of Interest and the Prices of Investment Securities: 1890–1909," *Journal of Political Economy,* XIX, 269–308 (April 1911).

—, "Security Prices and Interest Rates in 1910–12," *Journal of Political Economy,* XXI, 500–522 (June 1913).

Moody, John, "The Paradox of the Bond Levels," *Burrough's Clearing House,* XV, 12–13 (January 1931).

Motelle, A., "Bond Holdings of Insurance Companies," *Annalist,* XXVI, 701 (December 4, 1925).

Nerlove, S. H., *A Decade of Corporate Incomes* (Chicago, 1932).

Nourse, Edwin G. and others, *America's Capacity to Produce* (Washington, D. C., 1934).

Owens, R. N., and Hardy, C. O., *Interest Rates and Stock Speculation* (Washington, D. C., 1930).

Persons, Warren M., "The Basis for Credit Expansion under the Federal Reserve System," *Review of Economic Statistics,* II, 21–27 (January 1920).

—, "Money Rates, Bond Yields, and Security Prices," *Review of Economic Statistics,* IX, 93–102 (April 1927).

Persons, Warren M., and Edwin Frickey, "Money Rates and Security Prices," *Review of Economic Statistics*, VII, 29–46 (January 1926).

Recent Economic Changes in the United States — Report of the Committee on Recent Economic Changes of the President's Conference on Unemployment, 2 vols. (New York, 1929).

Reed, Harold L., *Federal Reserve Policy, 1921–1930* (New York, 1930).

Richter, F. E., and Standish, A., "Investments of Banks and Insurance Companies," *Harvard Business Review*, III, 414–423 (July 1925).

Riefler, Winfield W., *Money Rates and Money Markets in the United States* (New York and London, 1930).

Robbins, Lionel, *The Great Depression* (London, 1934).

Shaffner, F. I., *The Problem of Investment* (New York and London, 1936).

Snider, John L., "Security Issues in the United States, 1909–1920," *Review of Economic Statistics*, III, 98–102 (May 1921).

Spahr, W. E., *The Federal Reserve System and the Control of Credit* (New York, 1931).

Strong, Benjamin, *Interpretations of Federal Reserve Policy* (New York and London, 1930), ed. by W. Randolph Burgess.

"Ten Year Profile of Average Prices on New York Stock Exchange," *Annalist*, XIX, 72–73 (Jan. 9, 1922).

Warburg, P. M., *The Federal Reserve System* (New York, 1930).

Whitney, Caroline, *Experiments in Credit Control* (New York and London, 1934).

Whitney, W., "Bond Market a Victim of Circumstances," *Magazine of Wall Street*, XLIII, 642–643 (Feb. 9, 1929).

INDEX

INDEX

WALL STREET

AND THE

SECURITY MARKETS

An Arno Press Collection

Abbott, Charles Cortez. **The New York Bond Market, 1920-1930.**
  1937

Adams, Henry C. **Public Debts:** An Essay in the Science of
  Finance. 1898

Black, Hillel. **The Watchdogs of Wall Street.** 1962

Bond, Frederic Drew. **Stock Movements and Speculation.** 1930

The Boston Stock Exchange. 1975

Burr, Anna Robeson. **The Portrait of a Banker: James Stillman,
  1850-1918.** 1927

Carret, Philip L. **The Art of Speculation.** 1930

Chamberlain, Lawrence. **The Work of the Bond House.** 1912

The Chicago Securities Market. 1975

Finance and Industry: The New York Stock Exchange. 1886

Flynn, John T. **Investment Trusts Gone Wrong!** 1930

Forgan, James B. **Recollections of a Busy Life.** 1924

Fowler, John Francis, Jr. **American Investment Trusts.** 1928

Galston, Arthur. **Security Syndicate Operations.** [1928]

Glass, Carter. **An Adventure in Constructive Finance.** 1927

Grayson, Theodore J [ulius]. **Investment Trusts:** Their Origin,
  Development, and Operation. 1928

Greef, Albert O. **The Commercial Paper House in the United
  States.** 1938

Haney, Lewis H., Lyman S. Logan and Henry S. Gavens.
  Brokers' Loans. 1932

Hardy, Charles O[scar]. **Odd-Lot Trading on the New York Stock
  Exchange.** 1939

Hillhouse, A[lbert] M. **Municipal Bonds:** A Century of Experience. 1936

Hodgson, James Goodwin, comp. **Wall Street:** Asset or Liability? 1934

King, Jos[eph] L. **History of the San Francisco Stock and Exchange Board.** 1910

Lamont, Thomas W. **Henry P. Davison:** The Record of a Useful Life. 1933

Lefèvre, Edwin. **The Making of a Stockbroker.** 1925

McElroy, Robert [McNutt]. **Levi Parsons Morton:** Banker, Diplomat and Statesman. 1930

Medina, Harold R. **Corrected Opinion of Harold R. Medina, United States Circuit Judge in United States of America, Plaintiff, V. Henry S. Morgan, Harold Stanley, et al., Doing Business as Morgan Stanley & Co., et al., Defendants.** 1954

Meeker, J[ames] Edward. **Short Selling.** 1932

Meeker, J[ames] Edward. **The Work of the Stock Exchange.** [1930]

Moody, John. **The Long Road Home:** An Autobiography. 1933

Moody, John. **Profitable Investing.** [1925]

Moulton, Harold G. **Financial Organization and the Economic System.** 1938

Moulton, Harold G. **The Financial Organization of Society.** [1930]

Moulton, Harold G. **The Formation of Capital.** 1935

Moulton, Harold G., George W. Edwards, James D. Magee and Cleona Lewis. **Capital Expansion, Employment, and Economic Stability.** 1940

The New York Stock Market. 1975

Nicolson, Harold. **Dwight Morrow.** [1935]

Palyi, Melchior. **The Chicago Credit Market:** Organization and Institutional Structure. [1937]

Peach, W[illiam] Nelson. **The Security Affiliates of National Banks.** 1941

Pratt, Sereno S. **The Work of Wall Street.** 1921

Regulation of the Security Markets. 1975

Reis, Bernard J. **False Security:** The Betrayal of the American Investor. 1937

Rice, Samuel O., ed. **Fundamentals of Investment.** 1925

Sakolski, A[aron] M. **Principles of Investment.** [1925]

Satterlee, Herbert L. **J. Pierpont Morgan:** An Intimate Portrait. 1939

Scott, James Brown. **Robert Bacon:** Life and Letters. 1923

Herbert D. Seibert & Co. **The Business and Financial Record of World War Years.** |1939|

Steiner, William Howard. **Investment Trusts: American Experience.** [1929]

Sturgis, Henry S. **Investment:** A New Profession. 1924

Townsend, William W. **Bond Salesmanship.** 1924

Twentieth Century Fund. **The Security Markets.** 1935

Two Private Banking Partnerships. 1975

U.S. Congressional House Committee on Banking and Currency. **Report of the Committee Appointed Pursuant to House Resolutions 429 and 504 to Investigate the Concentration of Control of Money and Credit.** 1913

U.S. Senate Committee on Banking and Currency. **Stock Exchange Practices.** 1934

Van Antwerp, W[illiam] C[larkson]. **The Stock Exchange From Within.** 1913

Warburg, Paul M. **The Federal Reserve System:** Its Origin and Growth. 2 Volumes. 1930

Weissman, Rudolph L. **The New Wall Street.** 1939

Willis, Henry Parker. **The Federal Reserve System:** Legislation, Organization and Operation. 1923

Willis, H[enry] Parker and Jules I. Bogen. **Investment Banking.** 1936